EASTERN EUROPE IN THE POSTWAR WORLD

Also by Thomas W. Simons, Jr.

THE END OF THE COLD WAR?

EASTERN EUROPE IN THE POSTWAR WORLD

SECOND EDITION

Thomas W. Simons, Jr.

ST. MARTIN'S PRESS
NEW YORK

For information write:
Scholarly & Reference Division
St. Martin's Press, Inc.,
175 Fifth Avenue
New York, N.Y. 10010

First published in the United States of America in 1991

Printed in the United States of America
Second edition first published 1993

ISBN   0-312-06169-2

Library of Congress Cataloging-in-Publication Data
Simons, Thomas W.
     Eastern Europe in the postwar world / Thomas W. Simons, Jr. — 2nd
  ed.
        p.   cm.
     Includes bibliographical references and index.
     ISBN 0-312-09678-X (pbk.)
     1. Europe, Eastern—History—1945-   I. Title.
     DJK50.S58   1993
     947.085—dc20   93-10500
                                                            CIP

To the memory of my father and to my students in History 125 at Brown.

Contents

ACKNOWLEDGEMENTS

The Department of State made this book possible by assigning me as Diplomat-in-Residence at Brown for 1989-1990, although the views expressed in it do not necessarily reflect those of the Department. My debt to the Department and the Foreign Service of the United States is also both deeper and less direct. It extends back over the years and is entwined with my personal history. For I grew up in a Foreign Service family, and my father and mother were both educators before they became diplomats. Hence, whatever skills I have as a teacher and diplomat clearly owe a great deal to both of them, and I am grateful to them for it, as well as for lifelong support and affection.

But my father was also a trained historian, and if history has been my way of understanding and dealing with a difficult and changing world as I changed with it, it has been because it was his way too, and because I admired him. I would like him to have read and enjoyed this book of history, but he died too soon for that — it was one of the few things he left unaccomplished — in July 1990, at 87, just as I was being confirmed by the Senate as Ambassador to Poland and finishing the basic manuscript. So I dedicate it to his memory with a full heart.

We are a close Foreign Service family, so my daughter Suzanne and my son Benjamin know that this book would never have seen the light of day without the vigorous and at times despairing protective efforts of their mother, and my dearest friend, Peggy. Not only was she almost a co-teacher in the course, or at least an expert advisor on what younger people can stand and absorb, but against her deepest inclinations and best judgment she took on nearly the whole burden of our move from

Providence to Warsaw so that I could turn the course into this book. So she is much more than a co-author.

Both of us are affectionately grateful to our friends and colleagues in the Brown community — Mark and Betty Garrison of the Center for Foreign Policy Development, Howard (and Jan) Swearer of the Institute for International Studies, and especially Tom (and Sarah) Gleason of the Department of History, where this book is concerned — who took us in and offered us the splendid environment of scholarship and fellowship in which it grew.

Most of all, I would like to thank my students in History 125, to whom it is also dedicated. I expected a dozen, and there were more than eighty. They came in all shapes and sizes and with a range of backgrounds and interests and degrees of courage. Since we were together, some have stayed at Brown, others have scattered to the four corners of America and the world, including a number to Eastern Europe. While we were together, however, they taught me to teach, and helped me to learn again. Their intelligence, their enthusiasm, their willingness to work hard, their capacity for intellectual excitement gave me a sense of what it means to live in a community of scholars that I never had in my own student days, and that will be precious to me for the rest of my life.

I am thinking in particular of Tim Snyder, then a junior and now a senior at Brown, editor of its international affairs journal, but in the summer between co-editor of this book. He shares all the virtues described above in spades, but adds others peculiarly his own: exceptional quickness of mind, a gift for grasping and extending the essence of a thought and an argument, a writing style that is at once exceptionally spare and exceptionally rich, and modesty. This books owes him some of its good passages, and a great deal of its clarity and coherence. He has a bright future; I am grateful for our recent past together.

Finally, I would like to thank my editor at St. Martin's, Simon Winder, for a degree of tolerance and skill the more remarkable for having now been repeated through the production of two books.

PREFACE

This book is based on a course of the same title which I gave as an Adjunct Professor of History at Brown University in Providence, Rhode Island, during the second semester of the academic year 1989-1990. It is very much a history book, a record, and an attempt at explanation of events in Eastern Europe in the half-century that ended in 1989. History did not stop there, but the caesura of that year was so great that this history basically does.

I was trained as a historian, and while I have found the historical perspective marginally useful in a career as a working diplomat which is now more than a quarter century long, it has been absolutely essential to me personally, as a way to help me understand the world I was living and working in, and my place in it. The center of that world, since I left school and joined the U.S. Foreign Service in 1963, has been Eastern Europe and its neighbors to the east and west, the Soviet Union and the Western Europe which has emerged in the postwar period and is still going strong today. My service as a diplomat took me and my family to Geneva, to Warsaw, to Moscow, to Bucharest, and to London, with long spells in between working on East-West relations at the Department of State in Washington, D.C. The last spell, from 1981 to 1989, was particularly intense, for it included a tour of record length as Director for Soviet Union Affairs, until 1985, and then a tour as the Deputy Assistant State for European and Canadian Affairs responsible for the conduct of relations with the Soviet Union, the countries of Eastern Europe and Yugoslavia, during the last three years, when the area was moving toward and then into the revolutions of 1989. During those years I was not only current on information concerning the developments underway in the area and U.S. policy towards it, but I was there often, dozens of times, and had the chance, sometimes, to contribute to shaping the policy and the developments themselves.

Throughout the whole period I took what opportunities I had to do historical research, publish historical articles and in general to reflect historically on a part of the world I love and was learning more about, as well as on the United States' relationship to it and the U.S. role in it. And the Service gave me two wonderful opportunities to punctuate the quarter century with whole years of study and reflection, first as a Council on Foreign Relations International Affairs Fellow at the Hoover Institution in Stanford, in 1971-1972, and then as a Member of the Senior Seminar in Foreign Policy, in 1985-1986. But it was only when I was named Diplomat-in-Residence at Brown in the fall of 1989 and offered the chance to teach a real live credit course in the history of postwar Eastern Europe in the spring of 1990 that I was challenged to function once again as a full-time working historian.

I found the challenge daunting. This was partly because I had no idea of what kind of a teacher I would be. When I had last taught history, in the early 1960s, I was a distracted graduate student one reading ahead of my undergraduate charges: It had not been a job I wanted, nor a job I could do well, nor a job I did well. Since then I had learned a lot about the subject matter I was to teach, and I had done a great deal of public speaking, in the 1980s. But I had been speaking as an official on public policy issues, and that is essentially functional speech. At its best it resembles teaching history, but it bears no necessary relationship to it. And since one necessary element of teaching history is to consider and confront what others have said and written about a given field, there was a lot to read, a half decade's work on most topics, a decade's for some, a generation's for a few. The challenge was therefore multiple. At its core, however, was the challenge to leave functional speech behind me enough to fashion a coherent story of what happened over a turbulent and complex period in a way that did justice both to my own experiences and to the best scholarship available, and to make that story accessible to American undergraduates of the turn of the 1990s. It seemed overwhelming.

Whether or not it *was* overwhelming the reader will judge on the basis of this book. The beginnings were certainly difficult. The best that could be said for the first few lectures, over-full and over-complex, was that they aroused the fighting spirit and the hatred of injustice which characterizes American undergraduates at their best, to the point where they overcame their natural diffidence and began to tell me what I was doing wrong. For my part, I hated to give up the richness and the complexity. In the end, a balance was struck. It was a balance between the accuracy, the richness and complexity I insisted on giving them, and the limits to what intelligent and enthusiastic people who are taking three or four other courses need and can stand. If it is successful, it is a balance which is exemplary for the way democracy should work. As the weeks and months passed, I felt it was getting more successful and that, with proper editing, it was successful enough to offer to public judgment in book form.

I would also like to think that the story will be useful and accessible to the reading public beyond the university. Eastern Europe, the part of the continent outside the Soviet Union that was divided from the rest in the early postwar years, was important during the cold war. To use a phrase characteristic of Communist thinking and prose practice, "as is well known" the cold war started there; the area's peculiar life and status helped keep it going; and the nations and peoples of the area helped bring it to an end, to the extent it has ended. But Eastern Europe will continue to be important, and I think even more important, in the new era that is now taking shape. To the extent that the cold war is over, it is a large part of the Europe which must be brought back together in ways that support security and stability for the international community as a whole. But that process will be long and difficult, marked by both new opportunity and new danger, partly because Eastern Europe is different, in ways that need to be understood. To the extent that the cold war is not over, Eastern Europe's distinctiveness will be part of the reason. It is not what is was before World War II, and it is not so different that it cannot be understood. Its nations and peoples are simply emerging from a complex history of their own. But that history needs to be explained if we are to understand not just what is desirable, but also what is possible for all of us in the future. This book is an attempt to provide that explanation.

PREFACE TO THE SECOND EDITION

Rereading it two years later, I was pleased to see that overall my story had held up well. Still, new sources and new hindsight have required a general updating of the bibliography, more or less extensive revisions of the chapters covering the 1980s, and of course a whole new concluding essay. Calling this an "envoi", as I did in the first edition, with that word's sense of wishing a departing traveller well, would now be unbearably precious, since the East Europeans are now ploughing through very heavy seas indeed. So it has become simply an "afterword," albeit longer and more complex than the original.

Living far from Western libraries since 1990, I have also had to frequently disobey my self-imposed restriction to English-language sources, especially toward the end. I would only point out that the Polish, and to a lesser extent German, materials I have now cited are just as good, even though they require more work from those who really want to follow up. The dedication, however, remains the same: to my father's memory, and to my students at Brown.

Thomas W. Simons, Jr.
Warsaw, February 1993

EASTERN EUROPE IN THE POSTWAR WORLD

ONE

THE ROOTS

Eastern Europe is very diverse. The very question of whether it should be treated as a region — whether there is an Eastern Europe, as distinguished from Central Europe, or East-Central Europe, or Russia — is controversial. So is the question of which peoples, nations, or states should be included if there is a region to be defined. There are no perfect, objective answers to these questions, and I am not offering any in what follows. Whether they are asked, and what answer is offered, depends on whether the questions and answers are useful to specific people at specific times. At most times in history most people have found it useful to stress diversity, to focus on the separate experiences of the individual peoples and nations of this part of the world. I hope that my account will do justice to that diversity.

But in this book I am seeking in the first instance to fashion a coherent history of this part of the world during the four and a half decades from 1944 to 1989. This was a period when eight countries of this geographic area were governed by Communists and when six countries — Poland, the part of reunited Germany that was the German Democratic Republic, Czechoslovakia, Hungary, Romania, and Bulgaria — were governed by Communists of a particular kind, who were particularly close to the Communist rulers of the Soviet Union. For that purpose, I have found it useful to treat the area as a region, to focus on those six countries, and to deal as much with history and traits they had in common as with history and traits that distinguish and separate them from each other. Going back before the Communist period, I found three common traits in the histories of these people and nations that seemed to me particularly significant for their modern development: a peasant character, a legacy of dependence on outside powers, and a history of nationalism. It was not inevitable that these peoples and nations should share these characteristics — it took a long, contingent history to produce them, they have been defined for East Europeans by particular experiences, and their meanings have evolved over the period discussed here — but they are there, and important.

Geography had something to do with the area's peasant character, dependence, and nationalism, because geography facilitated and conditioned the foreign domination that in turn did so much to produce these three characteristics. The peoples of Eastern Europe are not well protected by any natural barrier.

Even with geography, however, there were degrees of defenselessness. The eastern part of the region in particular is open grassland, which has served again and again as an avenue for invasion. But the area divides into three geographical regions, running from north to south.[1] The northeast is defined by open plains, the continuation of Asia. It has been inhabited by Germans, Russians, Poles, and a few smaller groups of peoples they are related to and have dominated. To speak in contemporary terms, this region makes up most of Poland and eastern Germany. Arable land, interrupted at times by forests, is abundant, but the growing season is short. Eastern Europe is bordered on the north by the Baltic Sea, which has been controlled historically first by the Germans, then by the Swedes, and then in turn by the Germans and Russians.

The middle region is the basin of one of the world's great rivers, the Danube. The basin is surrounded by the Carpathian mountain chain in its familiar reverse-S curve, broken by the Danube where the river cuts through the mountains at the present-day border between Yugoslavia and Romania. The center of this region is the Pannonian Plain, which has been inhabited since the ninth century by Hungarians. Germans have lived to the west, Western Slavs (the Czechs and the people that became the Slovaks) in the mountains to the north, the South Slavs (Slovenes, Croats, and Serbs) in the mountains to the south, and non-Slavic Romanians in and over the mountains to the east. In this region lie the modern states of Czechoslovakia and Hungary and the northern parts of Yugoslavia and Romania. There is a limited amount of very good agricultural land, and the Carpathians afforded some measure of protection from invasion.

The region south of the Danube is predominantly mountains. It is conventionally called the Balkans, although the name refers to only one mountain chain among many. This part of Eastern Europe has been inhabited by a hodgepodge of peoples, mainly Slavs. It has also hosted Albanians, who trace their origins back to the Thracians; Vlachs, shepherds speaking Latin-based dialects that evolved into Romanian; and Muslims, either Slav converts or immigrants during the five centuries of Ottoman rule. Greeks inhabit the extreme south. Today the region contains the states of Albania, Bulgaria, Greece, Romania, and what was Yugoslavia. Little good agricultural land is available, and historically much of the land and the population has been given over to pastoral sheep-raising. The Balkans have been more culturally isolated than the north and middle regions. For half a millenium the north and middle were marchlands, frontiers of Europe against Asia, while the south was the European portion of the Ottoman Empire.

Compared to the western regions of Europe, Eastern Europe was sparsely settled. In particular, the cities were fewer and smaller, and they were settled in ways that created ethnic mixtures. Poland, the Czech lands, Hungary, and the Romanian principalities constituted the ethnic centers, but they were no more densely populated than the rest of the area. While France had perhaps 25 million people in the late eighteenth century, Poland, which was geographically larger, had perhaps half that many, and the Romanian lands held barely 2 million, if that. Even the ethnic centers were permeated by other peoples.

In this part of Europe political organization was much less stable and solid than in the more thickly settled, better-endowed West. By early modern times, in the fourteenth and fifteenth centuries, the western fringe of the area was already under Western rule: Venice ruled the Adriatic Coast, and the Holy Roman Empire under German leadership ruled Bohemia, Moravia, and large parts of what is now Poland. Local lords ruled kingdoms and even empires in the area during the Middle Ages, but the Great Moravian Empire, the Bulgarian and Serbian empires, the Polish kingdom, and then the Polish-Lithuanian Commonwealth were more impressive as state structures in the nationalistic retrospective view of the nineteenth and twentieth centuries than they were at the time. Beginning in the fourteenth and fifteenth centuries, these medieval structures were eaten away by the better organized dynastic empires around them, first the Ottoman (Turkey), then the Habsburg (Austria), and finally the Romanov (Russia).[2]

The Ottomans, the Habsburgs, and the Romanovs were not national empires in the modern sense. Though dominated by one nationality, they were in essence military empires serving dynasties. Their major purpose was collecting taxes to support the armies that served the sovereign. As these empires began to encroach upon Eastern Europe, the borderlands between them became a battleground and emptied of population, but the areas behind the front lines on the borderlands were then settled more thickly in order to provide soldiers and taxes. When the frontiers between the empires stabilized, this settlement was systematized in the form of military colonies of peasant soldiers and their families, to fight and farm.[3]

In many parts of the area conquerors destroyed the local elites and replaced them with foreigners. This happened throughout the Ottoman Balkans and in Bohemia and Moravia after the Battle of the White Mountain in 1620. Over time these new elites became more attached to the places where they ruled and more refractory to the commands of the faraway dynasties that had put them in place. Still, they kept their distance — social and often religious — from the peasant populations under their governance, and tended to invest in consumption even more wholeheartedly than the native elites who subsisted as subcontractors of empire in other regions. Ottoman rule was comparatively personalized, exercised without much legal inhibition by deputies of the ruler acting in his name, whereas the Habsburg and Romanov domains were organized more legalistically. Where the new elites of foreign origin shared their subjects' religion, it was because they had succeeded in imposing theirs, as in the Czech lands that the Habsburgs re-Catholicized after 1620. The Ottomans, by contrast, did not as a matter of policy seek the religious conversion of their subjects. Although many in Bosnia, Albania, and the Bulgarian lands did convert to Islam for reasons of self-interest, the Ottoman system called for self-rule by native religious communities, which were responsible for tax collection. Both the Ottoman and Romanov empires used communal responsibility for taxes to inhibit the departure of individuals and encourage stable peasant collectives.

Alien rule preserved subsistence peasantry in other, less subtle ways. It usually did not encourage commerce and industry, and thus undermined the cities. Most notably, the production of grain for export was encouraged: to Constantinople from the Ottoman south, to Western Europe from Poland in the north, and to Vienna and the German principalities from the middle region. As serfs in Western Europe were gaining freedom, landlords in the East were enforcing the peasants' ties to them and to the land in order to secure larger grain surpluses for export. This "second serfdom" began around 1500 in the non-Ottoman lands. To be sure, there were individual causes of this process in individual regions, but the result was the same throughout. Peasants were bound to the soil unless they could physically escape, over the mountains to Transylvania for Romanians, or into the steppes for Poles and those who became the Ukrainians, until Romanov rule caught up with them in the seventeenth and eighteenth centuries. The vast majority of peasants stayed where they were, bound to the land, forced into small peasant communities with no possibility of either leaving or developing new social forms.[4]

But what was the old social form? It is necessary to say a word here about peasant culture, because it is so important to the whole destiny and reality of the area. I once asked one of Poland's best rural sociologists, a man who knows the United States well, whether he had found any peasants in this country. His answer was that maybe he had found some in black communities in northern Louisiana, but that was the only place. As a French film of the 1960s on America put it, "Eight million farmers, and not a single peasant."[5]

In Eastern Europe, peasant life revolved around the family, the extended kinship line, whether or not this was formalized, as in the South Slav *zadruga*.[6] Blood ties were the basis for literally every aspect of life. The individual's only significant self-definition was as part of a collective. The purpose of economic activity was not profit but the family's maintenance and occasionally, with luck and hard work, its prosperity. In an area and era where control of land was the one reliable resource for family security, economic activity thus depended on family strategies for keeping and farming the land; when opportunities presented themselves outside farming, families also sent their sons and daughters into commerce or industry, in the cities or abroad. The Irish maid of American folklore exemplifies that kind of strategy; many if not most European emigrants came to the United States to earn money for their family at home to buy land. Individualism was learned upon arrival.

Politics were personal. Peasants divide the world into those who can be trusted, usually confined to those with blood ties, and those who cannot, usually everyone else. The latter were defined as enemies, to be manipulated if they could not be dispensed with. To peasant families and villages, self-sufficiency was the ideal, but because it was almost everywhere an impossible ideal, their relations with the outside world took the form of dispensing and seeking favors, in cash — for money was considered and used mainly in this framework — and in kind, in personal patron-and-client ties.

The degree and kind of such personalized relationships took a bewildering variety, and were defined and limited by custom, by tradition, by religion. Religion often played a major role in peasant life, but it too was made to fit the framework. Formal religion came to the village from outside and above, and it was integrated into village life to the extent it overlapped with peasant epistomology and ontology: What the peasants took from it, whether Catholic or Orthodox, or Protestant as in some parts of the Hungarian-ruled areas, was primarily its form and liturgy, rather than speculation, its collective rather than its individual aspect. Within the village the space Christian speculation might have filled was already inhabited by spooks and demons, and they remained. The ultimate questions — of death and other unexplainables that are essential to every culture — were often answered in terms of magic.[7] Religion shaped but did not fill the large framework of beliefs and habits that promoted conciliation, propitiation, and mutual advantage, which helped mediate between the peasant and the largely threatening environment.

Seen from the bottom up, then, despite all the variety of its aspects in various parts of the area, religion's framework and purpose were everywhere the same: It was designed to protect peasants from the outside world, and where possible to make it useful to them, through personal agency. Corruption thus came naturally to all of Eastern Europe, not just the lands under the Ottomans, where it was especially rife because the system did largely without rules and regulations, but everywhere. It provided a means of personal contact and influence with rulers on the model of village life.

By helping keep East European populations tied to the land, the multinational empires enforced peasant culture and therefore the identification of the individual with the family, a very small unit. By contrast, nationalism, the third starting point for understanding the area, implies that the individual identifies with a far larger unit, the nation. For the peasant, the unifying element is blood; for the nationalist, there must be other unifying elements — the common tongue, the national soul, some collective aspiration. By the dawn of the twentieth century, nationalism had captured the loyalty of a small but growing section of the Eastern European population. Just as peasant character had been sustained by foreign dominion, the slow decline of the multinational empires over the course of the nineteenth century awakened nationalism, but this relationship was quite complex.

In 1800, except for pockets in the mountains of Montenegro and Albania, Eastern Europe was entirely under the sovereignty or suzerainty of the surrounding empires. The last Polish partition of 1795, when the last remnants of the old Polish-Lithuanian commonwealth were absorbed into Russia, Austria, and Prussia, was followed nine years later, in 1804, by the first Serb revolt against the Ottomans. No sooner was foreign domination complete than the struggle for self-definition began.

The ruling empires had already begun to change in response to the challenge posed by the emergence of strong absolute monarchies farther west.[8] In the first quarter of the eighteenth century Peter the Great reformed Russia, and between 1780 and 1790 the Habsburg Emperor Joseph II began forcing his ramshackle dominions down the same path toward modern, centralized statehood. The French Revolution in 1789 and the Napoleonic period provided another potent stimulus for change, even in the Ottoman south. After Napoleon was defeated in 1815, the Habsburgs and Romanovs were able to restore some order in the middle and north, but the Ottoman Balkans remained restive. The 1820s brought the Greek revolt and then the liberation of part of Greece, the return of native princes in the Romanian principalities under Ottoman suzerainty, and then a major Ottoman-Romanov war, which in turn produced a new Russian-bestowed constitution for the Romanians and another spurt of Ottoman reform at home. Nor did the Western stimulus disappear in the 1830s. On the contrary: Even when Western governments ceased for a time to promote change in Eastern Europe in the hope of geopolitical advantage, there was now an ideology — liberal and sometimes democratic nationalism — that operated independently of them and sometimes against them. They were constantly tempted to co-opt it for their own purposes, either to defuse it or because they too were genuinely infected by it, as in the case of Napoleon III of France.

For the most part, however, Eastern Europe's direct foreign rulers — the Habsburgs, the Romanovs, the Hohenzollerns, and the Ottomans — did not try to reaffirm their rule on nationalist grounds. In the first half of the nineteenth century, nationalism was still largely associated with the decline of the old order and the rise of the middle class, and was thus considered subversive by all the Eastern monarchies. Romanov rule became truly Russian nationalist after 1825, under Nicholas I, but even then it identified nationalism as such as a threatening French product. It is worth emphasizing that the empires intended reform only to strengthen their rule. They still regarded the peasants as taxpayers and soldiers; they now wanted to make them better taxpayers and soldiers.

Despite this limited intent, however, the reforms implemented by the empires served to increase nationalism in the area. Precisely in order to produce more skilled and prosperous taxable subjects and soldiers, the empires began to sponsor educational and economic development. The intent was to strengthen the ruling dynasties, but the result provided opportunities for peasants to escape the land. Government grew in other directions, and became regularized and bureaucratized. As government became larger and more providing, it also became more invasive, demanding more money and soldiers. As peasant emancipation proceeded, behind the diminished local landowner there began to loom a larger governing entity, residing in a distant capital but represented by officials in the local county seat. These changes created a budding awareness of government as an institution in its own right — the state — rather than just as an extension of the monarch's will. For the peasant majorities, the traditional personal view of outside authority and the traditional distinction between the family or the village and the outside world both became somewhat more problematic.

Reform initiated by foreign empires also accidentally generated one of the main agents of their eventual destruction, for it was the midwife of the intelligentsia.[9] Peasant emancipation, when and as it occurred, was usually an act of state against recalcitrant nobilities. By diminishing their authority and their property, it created déclassé nobles, proud elites available for new social roles. The simultaneous extension of the machinery of state created new roles for them to fill. The modernization of government and economic development gave such men and women greater opportunities to work in the cities, and especially in the expanding bureaucracies, when they returned from their schooling and touring in the West. Nobles and boyars could afford education and knew how to take advantage of these opportunities.

These emerging elites and their families constituted a small, thin layer of their societies. They were most numerous in Poland and Hungary, where the landowning and governing nobilities had been relatively large; in some areas, such as Bulgaria and Slovakia, they scarcely existed. In such places, priests who were themselves sons of peasants took their place. Whatever their origins, however, these "modern" people were now stripped of their previous relationship to the peasantry and often of their traditional status, and they felt their separation from the masses intensely. That was part of what made them modern, and the sense of separation drove them toward Western experience and education, which in turn exacerbated it. For those who could afford it, this meant education in Western universities; even for those who could not, it meant tremendous receptivity to Western thought. And the remedy to social isolation that Western thought offered was for such people to lead the masses to new heights of coherent national power. Reform from above both paved the way for nationalism as an ideology and provided the officers' corps in search of an army to fight under its banners.

In this century we in the West are used to nationalism, but the Western mass nationalism we are used to is very different from what I am describing here, which is much more familiar to our contemporaries in the third and fourth worlds. Even before the word was invented and popularized in Russia later in the nineteenth century, the "intelligentsia" in Eastern

Europe denotes the group of educated people cut off from both the masses and the traditional structures of power, and tending to seek ways to lead the former against the latter. There were variations in degree of isolation, of self-consciousness, and of the intensity of the intelligentsia's claim to unique legitimacy. In Romania and Hungary, for instance, intellectuals have always been more integrated into the power structure of the day than in the Slavic countries. Compared to the West, however, the intelligentsia phenomenon was general. In the more fluid and prosperous societies of the West such people existed, were self-conscious, and played important social and political roles. But they generally defined and seized more legitimate roles in more consensual societies, were less cohesive as a group, and served more as yeast than as the hand that wielded the ax. In the East, the intelligentsia constituted a self-conscious social caste with some world-historical social purpose, and its members identified primarily with each other.

Like any other form of social self-awareness, nationalism does not exist in the abstract.[10] It emerges from concrete historical conditions, which it expresses and in turn seeks to transform. Western thought offered two concepts of nationality to East European intellectuals. The first was subjective; in other words, it held that individuals choose and define their nationality according to their conditions, needs, and ideals. This is the American definition, for a nation constituting itself out of a mixture of peoples in a new environment has no other choice; but it was also British and, even more, French. The second concept held that an individual's nationality is defined by objective characteristics, such as race, or language, or religion, and that each people has a natural genius. This notion was preeminently German, put forward in its most pregnant form at the turn of the nineteenth century by Johan-Gottfried Herder.[11]

The East European intelligentsias devoutly hoped that state-building would one day be a task for them, and they recognized that it would require compromises with people who might not share national characteristics. As a result the subjective concept of nationality had some influence. But by and large they accepted the objective version.[12] It had originated in conditions that were unmistakably like those of East European intellectuals. It was born of the dependency, the humiliation, and the isolation of late eighteenth- and nineteenth-century German intellectuals. Unlike Britain and France, which had been united for centuries, Germany did not become a state until 1871. The industrial revolution created new challenges from new masses in England and France, but in the end it also facilitated a general consensus among intellectuals and bourgeois in favor of liberalism. German intellectuals, by contrast, tended to identify German values with the peasant whom industrialization was destroying, and to believe that the impersonal norms of liberalism contradicted the natural German genius. Besides being less reconciled to the condition of their society, German intellectuals were less politically free than their French and British counterparts, and more than the latter they tended to posit a strong nation where German values provided community and where either the individual or class was less important. These were matters of degree, but it was that degree of emphasis on objectivist, communitarian, anti-urban nationalism that found most favor in Eastern Europe as the century rolled along.

The intelligentsia considered itself the proper alternative to the standing order, a "government of souls," as the phrase went, in opposition to the ruling governments of mere bodies and things. These new people in Eastern societies were resentful of the empires that had destroyed what they increasingly considered "their" nations. Still, they were attached to the state as such because it was their employer of first resort in these underdeveloped economies. Only a few anarchists wished to destroy the state; most of the intelligentsia wanted to run it. The barrier to such a revolution was of course the local empire, but the reason it seemed so high was because of the intelligentsia's real isolation from social power, from the peasant masses of their societies. The ruling monarchies proved time and again that they were adept at playing the anational peasantries against the emerging intelligentsias. Nationalism was weakest in the Ottoman domains. The elites that arose there, because they were a completely new class and not a transformed aristocracy, were more rooted in the peasantries, and did not need the spiritual synthesis of nationalism to unite them with the people. The Romanovs sponsored such local elites in order to weaken the Habsburgs, but of course neither they nor the Hohenzollerns nor the Habsburgs themselves had any interest in seeing a resurrection of the Polish state they had divided among them. As an ideology, nationalism was therefore strongest in the north, weakest in the south.

Paradoxically, this weakness of southern nationalism probably facilitated formal independence in the Balkans, for it implied that local elites were small and that the peasantries would probably not be arrayed with them in a united front against the empires. While this turned out to be not quite true, as by the end of the century nationalism had a broad social base in the south as well, it helped set and keep in train the century-long process by which Ottoman reform and wars were punctuated by the falling-away of its provinces into independent states: Serbia and Greece in the 1820s, Romania in the 1850s and 1870s, and Bulgaria in the 1880s.

These new states were of course very dependent on outside forces, politically, economically, and culturally. They had been freed with the help of foreigners and by international agreement, because after each eruption it seemed easier to see the states free than to deal with the in-house turbulence they caused, and three of the four had foreign monarchs. All of them were economically underdeveloped. Because they had tiny internal markets consisting mainly of subsistence peasants, they could not generate the savings needed for industrialization, and they therefore depended on foreign trade and foreign capital for economic growth. Because the native capital base was so small, the state played the preeminent role in whatever investment took place. Economically, the young Balkan states fell further behind the West as the century drew on, and it is perhaps fair to say this was one reason why nationalism spread from the elites to the impoverished masses.[13]

The Romanov and Habsburg empires were stronger and more durable than the Ottoman. They were more modern and had more efficient means of coercion and co-optation. The great Polish revolts of 1830 and 1863 would have freed any Balkan country from the Ottomans, but they were successfully put down. The agreement of the three northern monarchies that Poland should never again exist allowed a measure of cooperation among them. Their alliance broke down at the end of the nineteenth and beginning of the twentieth centuries as they competed for the southern lands the Ottomans left behind.[14] But even while their collusion continued, some national diversity emerged within their dominions, particularly in the Habsburg Empire.

Since the eighteenth century the Habsburgs had been reshaping their empire to remain competitive with the ominous new power in the north, Prussia, and this continued in the nineteenth. Led by King William I Hohenzollern and his chancellor, Otto von Bismarck, Prussia created a northern German confederation by defeating the Habsburgs in battle in 1866. That defeat in turn provoked another round of Habsburg reform at home. But the Compromise of 1867 was shaped by domestic as well as international pressures. The Austria-Hungary that emerged from it was more tolerant of minority nationalism than Russia or Prussia, but was still vulnerable to it, and the new structure lacked the power of the Russian and German states to repress it. In Prussia, emancipation had driven the peasants off the land into industry. In Russia, it had kept them tied to the land in communes. The end of serfdom in the Habsburg lands impoverished the peasants but did not give them many booming industrial cities to go to: When they did leave, it was often to American cities instead.

With significant exceptions — where great estates remained, and especially where they were run for absentee lords by managers, often Jews — emancipation in the Habsburg lands therefore turned peasant discontent away from the landlords toward the state. As a result, the peasant majorities within the empire who stayed on the land were more susceptible to the appeal of nationalism coming from the new intelligentsia. The Poles, Hungarians, and Czechs — the "historic nationalities" whose nobilities could hark back to states and empires they had once ruled — were developing nationalisms of their own. In the Compromise of 1867, the Habsburgs turned over much of the south to the nationally self-conscious Hungarian aristocracy and gave Galicia (their portion of partitioned Poland) to the local Polish nobility. They retained direct control over, roughly speaking, the modern Czech and Austrian regions of their empire, allowed the more traditional regions some autonomy under local elites, and then continued to play the nationalizing masses against their nationalizing junior partners. The result was the nationalities cauldron for which Austria-Hungary has remained famous.[15]

Despite rising nationalism in the area, however, and despite continuing international inspiration for it — the revolutions of 1848, Italian and German unification in 1870 and 1871 — two conditions continued to limit its dominance almost everywhere in the area. First, Eastern Europe's new states (in the south) and autonomous regions (in the middle) remained peasant countries with very small elites. They continued to be ruled by bureaucracies that were generally self-selected and most interested in personal power. Because Eastern Europe under multinational rule had so far missed the industrial revolution, the middle classes that were rising to challenge traditional elites were tiny by West European standards. Second, these tiny middle classes were often from minority ethnic groups, and in general ethnic groups were tremendously intermingled throughout the area. There were very few boundaries for ethnically homogeneous nation-states on the West European model, for every political entity of the area had ethnic minorities. Most of these minorities looked to their ethnic brothers and sisters on the other side of the frontier for salvation.

This stoked nationalism and anchored the appeal of the German, objectivist definition of nationality, but it also led the local elites to adopt the prevailing West European model of an ethnically homogeneous national state, whether it was to be liberal and constitutional, like the French and British, or authoritarian and constitutional, like the German. The existing ethnic conglomeration made the homogeneous national state a dream and, therefore, all the more attractive when dependence was the norm. But because dreams also call forth their own antidotes in politics, this part of the world, though ever more nationalist, produced or at least provided fertile ground for the great supranational ideologies that have marked our century: Marxism, to be sure, but also anti-Semitism, Zionism, and the forgotten ideology of Agrarianism. In this area nationalism and supranationalism may not have been born together, but they have been forced to live together, to reinforce each other, and often to die together in concrete terms throughout the twentieth century.

Notes

1. For a good, brief geographic survey, see Alan W. Palmer, *The Lands Between: A History of East Central Europe since the Congress of Vienna* (New York: Macmillan, 1970), 1-22.
2. On this whole formative period, see William H. McNeill, *Europe's Steppe Frontier, 1500-1800* (Chicago: University of Chicago Press, 1964), 2-14, 182-221, and passim.
3. On this point, see John R. Lampe and Marvin R. Jackson, *Balkan Economic History, 1550-1950. From Imperial Borderlands to Developing Nations* (Bloomington: Indiana University Press, 1982), 50-79. And Vojtech Mastny has now provocatively suggested that in the rubble of Yugoslav disintegration we can still see the outlines of what he calls "the enduring 'Military Frontier,'" because most of the fighting has taken place in this area, where the Habsburgs settled Catholic and Orthodox Slavs, now Croats and Serbs, to defend their empire against the Turks. See Mastny, "The Historical Eastern Europe after Communism," in Andrew A. Michta and Ilya Prizel, ed., *Postcommunist Eastern Europe: Crisis and Reform* (New York: St. Martin's Press, 1992), 4-6.
4. There is an increasingly rich literature in English on these developments. For a convenient synoptic view, see Kenneth Jowitt, "The Sociocultural Bases of National Dependency in Peasant Countries," in his edited volume, *Social Change in Romania, 1860-1940* (Berkeley: Institute of International Studies, University of California Press, 1978), 1-30. For more detailed coverage of both north and south, see four splendid essays in Daniel Chirot, ed., *The Origins of Backwardness in Eastern Europe. Economics and Politics from the Middle Ages until the Early Twentieth Century* (Berkeley: University of California Press, 1989): Péter Gunst, "Agrarian Systems in Central and Eastern Europe," 53-92, which sees a critical distinction between the lands from the Baltic to Bohemia and those farther east; Jacek Kochanowicz, "The Polish Economy and the Evolution of Dependency," 93-130; Fikret Adanir, "Tradition and Rural Change in Southeastern Europe," 131-176; and John R. Lampe, "Imperial Borderlands or Capitalist Periphery? Redefining Balkan Backwardness, 1520-1914," 177-209. Both Adanir and Lampe argue that Balkan backwardness was rooted in isolation rather than oppression. For a vivid description of what the grain trade meant to Polish society at the time, see Norman Davies, *God's Playground. A History of Poland.* vol. 1 (New York: Columbia University Press, 1982), 256-292. And for a stimulating treatment of what Russia's peasantry had become around 1900 — so different, and yet so similar — see Teodor Shanin, *The Awkward Class. Political Sociology of Peasantry in a Developing Society: Russia 1910-1925* (Oxford: Clarendon Press, 1972), 9-44.
5. The film was called *L'Amérique insolite*, and I saw it in the late 1960s but no longer remember the director or producer. The sociologist was Bogusław Gałeski, whose *Basic Concepts of Rural Sociology* (Manchester: Manchester University Press, 1972), draws on his own experience of living in Eastern Europe and remains the best short introduction for those interested in the area. I shall cite other works more directly relevant to specific elements of the postwar experience as we go along.
6. For further information on the sociology of rural life, see Irwin Taylor Sanders, Roger Whitaker, and Walter C. Bisselle, *East European Peasantries: Social Relations: An Annotated Bibliography*, vols. 1 and 2 (Boston: G.K. Hall, 1976, 1981).
7. For lively description of the related albeit different Russian peasantry's popular religion in this century, see Moshe Lewin, *The Making of the Soviet System: Essays in the Social History of Interwar Russia* (New York: Pantheon, 1985), 57-81.

8. For a recent survey applying the challenge-and-response paradigm on an all-European scale, see Andrew C. Janos, "The Politics of Backwardness in Continental Europe, 1780-1945," *World Politics* 41, no. 3 (April 1989): 325-358. The most recent exemplification of Theodore H. Von Laue's lifelong interest in this paradigm is in his *The World Revolution of Westernization. The Twentieth Century in Perspective* (New York: Oxford University Press, 1987), 11-113, 197-236.

9. There is an extensive literature, but it is mainly about the Russian intelligentsia. For an older but still useful collective work, see Richard Pipes, ed., *The Russian Intelligentsia* (New York: Columbia University Press, 1961). A good analytical introduction to the East European version is Zygmunt Bauman, "Intellectuals in East Central Europe: Continuity and Change," *Eastern European Politics and Societies* 1, no. 2 (Spring 1987): 162-186.

10. For a recent survey of the conceptual debate, see Anthony D. Smith, *Theories of Nationalism*, 2nd ed. (New York: Holmes & Meier, 1983).

11. On these origins, including the contrast between French and German concepts and their spread to Eastern Europe, Hans Kohn is still useful: *The Idea of Nationalism* (New York: Macmillan, 1944), 328-576. On the different histories that gave rise to the contrast, see his *Prelude to Nation-States. The French and German Experience, 1789-1815* (Princeton, N.J.: Van Nostrand, 1967). Sir Isaiah Berlin has returned again and again to the humiliated 18th century German origins of this objectivist nationalism, which then spread eastward and southward. See his *The Crooked Timber of Humanity. Chapters in the History of Ideas* (New York: Vintage, 1992), 35ff.(1978), 223ff.(1975), 243-247(1972).

12. For a fine short summary of the phenomenon, see Karl W. Deutsch, "Nationalism in Eastern Europe and the Communist World," in his *Nationalism and Its Alternatives* (New York: Knopf, 1969), 37-65. Readers who wish to go deeper may turn to the essays in Peter F. Sugar and Ivo J. Lederer, eds., *Nationalism in Eastern Europe* (Seattle: University of Washington Press, 1969).

13. This is the persuasively documented message of Lampe and Jackson, *Balkan Economic History.* The argument over the role of the state in East European and Russian economic development will of course be forever associated with the scholar who initiated it, Alexander Gerschenkron, *Economic Backwardness in Historical Perspective* (New York: Praeger, 1962), 5-30.

14. For a magisterial brief survey, see Sir Lewis Namier, "Basic Factors in Nineteenth Century European History," in *Personalities and Powers* (New York: Macmillan, n.d. [1955]), 105-117.

15. For a detailed examination of the emancipation process and its effects in the Polish northeast, see Stefan Kieniewicz, *The Emancipation of the Polish Peasantry* (Chicago: University of Chicago Press, 1969). For a good general survey based on core-periphery theory and focused on Austria-Hungary, see Iván T. Berend and György Ránki, *The European Periphery and Industrialization* (Cambridge: Eng., Cambridge University Press, 1982). And for a short course in comparative European nationalism that is as rich in detail as it is comprehensive in scope, see Hugh Seton-Watson, *Nations and States* (Boulder: Westview, 1977), 15-192.

TWO

INDEPENDENCE AND
DESTRUCTION, 1918-1941

W orld War I shattered the historic integument within which the peoples of Eastern Europe could develop national identities and states by fighting the multinational empires. Though the peoples of the area had a role, Germany, Austria, and Russia were removed from the area primarily by World War I. The Bolshevik Revolution of November 1917 forced Russia, which had been allied with Britain and France, out of the war. As its army dissolved, Russia conceded much of its western territory to Germany in March 1918 at Brest-Litovsk. Even then, the Germans continued to advance until June, controlling the Ukraine and moving the Russian frontier about six hundred miles to the east. After the victory of its erstwhile allies, Soviet Russia's borders again moved westward, but the full extent of Romanov dominion was not restored. Soviet Russia lost the Baltic regions and parts of its former Ukrainian, White Russian, Polish, and Romanian territories. After its defeat in 1918, Germany was reduced in size, forced to pay reparations, and substantially disarmed, the Rhineland became a demilitarized zone. Austria-Hungary disintegrated. Today there is a good deal of creative nostalgia for the old empire in the area itself; it is worth reading the informed account of a contemporary like Sir Lewis Namier on how the dissolution took place in order to be reminded of how final was the verdict on Austria-Hungary reached in 1918.[1] Out of the bodies of the empires emerged a whole series of independent East European states. Before the war, East European elites were leading embryonic movements for national independence; now they found themselves leading new states without mature national traditions. The main task of the new rulers was thus to build national states. Neither in the new states in the north and middle regions — Poland, Czechoslovakia, and Hungary — nor in the mix of new and old states in the south — Yugoslavia, Romania and Bulgaria — did it prove easy to use nationalism to build a modern state. Often the peasant populations still defined themselves largely by religion and kinship, rather than nationality.[2] Still, there were ways to make progress in integrating them into the new national societies. Land reform gave peasants reason to be grateful to the state, and the new states sided with peasant majorities in disputes with minorities, earning a measure of loyalty. But using ethnic issues to secure political majorities created dilemmas of its own. Although the postwar settlement had reduced the number of people in Eastern Europe who lived outside the borders of "their" nation by two-thirds, every East European state still included multiple peoples with traditions and histories different from those of the ruling nationalities. The impossibility of drawing state borders that corresponded exactly to nationality built an unavoidable dilemma into the postwar settlement. The states that gained territory and were therefore satisfied with the postwar settlement were filled with dissatisfied minorities. The states that were the least ethnically diverse were dissatisfied with the postwar settlement because they had lost the most territory.[3]

The most homogeneous new states were Hungary and, not counting its passive Turkish minority, Bulgaria. The postwar settlement had stripped both of territories and peoples they considered rightfully theirs, so both were resolutely revisionist. During the war Hungary was of course part of Austria-Hungary, and was therefore an ally of Germany. The Hungarian lands were invaded by Romania as the war ended, and the ensuing domestic crisis helped bring the Communist Bela Kun to power. The Western allies allowed Romania to overthrow the new Bolshevist regime and then pressured the Romanians to leave. Hungary was again ruled by its traditional aristocracy, now fortified by refugees from the lost territories. In June 1920, over its vociferous protests, Hungary was stripped of most of its prewar territory in the Treaty of Trianon. Bulgaria had also fought at Germany's side, and the Treaty of Neuilly, signed in November

1919, ignored its claims to southern Dobruja, which was given to Romania, and to Thrace, which went to Greece. Unlike Hungary's, the Bulgarian nobility was tiny, and in the immediate postwar period, Bulgaria was ruled by the only authentic peasant government the area has ever seen, under Aleksandar Stamboliskii. He was murdered in 1923, and thereafter Bulgaria was ruled by officers and bureaucrats under a clever ruler, Tsar Boris III.

The other states defined themselves as antirevisionist and supported the post-war settlement, organizing resistance to Hungary or Bulgaria. All of them, including Poland, were ethnically very mixed. Reconstituted Poland consisted of three areas with three different traditions of governance, and it contained large Ukrainian, White Russian, German, and Jewish minorities. The Czechs were barely a majority in the new Czechoslovakia. The largest minority there was the Slovaks, a mostly Catholic peasant people who were just emerging into national consciousness under the leadership of small-town priests and lawyers; they had been part of Hungary for centuries, and found the swarms of anticlerical Czech officials who descended on Slovakia to modernize them no more and sometimes less to their liking than the Magyars they replaced. But Czechoslovakia also included a million Germans in the industrialized mountain rim of Bohemia. Most of the Great Romania that emerged from the settlement was formerly Habsburg Transylvania, but it was ruled by boyar liberals from the less developed regions of the smaller, prewar Romanian state. Similarly, the new state of Yugoslavia included most of the formerly Habsburg South Slavs, but it was ruled by the more peasant and more warlike Serbs.

The task of building national economies was as daunting as the task of building new national states. Much of the area had been in war zones, and many fixed assets had been destroyed by the tramp of armies. More fundamentally, the East European economies had historically grown in order to serve foreign markets. Hungarian grain and Serbian pigs had been produced for Austrian markets; Romanian grain had gone to Western Europe; the Polish textile industry had worked for the Russian market. These markets were now cut off by new national borders, by the desire of former importers to build their own economies without imports, by politics as in Russia, and by poverty as in Austria. Because the peasants who produced agricultural goods for export were the vast majority of the populations, internal markets remained small.

Land reform gained support among elites throughout the area, for several reasons. It was expected to add to agricultural efficiency and to increase demand for manufactured goods. Land reform also had political goals. It hurt the foreign elites who had held the land, such as the Hungarian landowners in the new states of Romania and Yugoslavia. Also, it was intended to immunize peasants from the Bolshevik virus by giving them a stake in the new status quo. Romania introduced the most extensive reforms; Hungary, which needed reform badly, and Bulgaria, already a nation of small farmers, did least. Poland and Yugoslavia were somewhere in between. But whether they got land or not, nowhere were the peasants given the financial credit they needed to improve their efficiency significantly. Moreover, prices for manufactured goods rose faster than prices for agricultural products. Peasants reacted by becoming more self-sufficient, continuing to subdivide their land among their sons, and consuming more of their own production. After land reform, peasant living standards probably rose in the short run. But the amount of agricultural goods available for export tended to drop, and East European countries thereby became more incapable than ever of generating the investment necessary for industrialization. Governmental neglect of agriculture in countries where it formed most of the economy encouraged peasant self-sufficiency, and peasant self-sufficiency crippled efforts to industrialize and accelerated rural overpopulation and underemployment.[4]

The state has always had a larger role in the economy in Eastern Europe than in areas farther west. The debate among development economists, sparked by Alexander Gerschenkron's argument that in Eastern Europe and Russia the state was called on to replace the absent middle classes as the primary engine of economic development long before communism, continues to this day. However one sees that issue, it is certain that the state engine was unable to lift these economies out of underdevelopment during the interwar period. The dominant ideology of liberalism, borrowed from the West, delegitimized government intervention in the economy. Weakened by the inflation of the immediate postwar years and the vagaries of reconstruction, the state performed poorly even in the areas where its role was recognized, such as assuring the stability of currency exchange rates in order to attract or keep foreign investment. Deflation — ruthless in the 1920s, even more ruthless during the depression — was the main weapon, and because it brought layoffs in industry and kept agricultural prices low, it hit the small working classes and the peasant majorities hardest. In terms of its main purpose, it did indeed attract some Western investment in the 1920s, but the states typically spent hard currency either on defense or, again, to keep the currency stable; and the 1920s did not last.

Like liberalism in economics, democracy in politics was a Western import. Formally, Eastern democracy was sometimes more extensive than its Western model. For example, proportional representation, the practice of giving all parties gaining more than a minimum percentage of votes seats in parliament, was widespread. But the numerous parties that emerged were little more than interest groups or personal clienteles of major politicians. Their very multiplicity made it hard for governments to move in any direction at all. The worsening of the peasants' plight and the unwillingness and inability of the state to implement economic reform increased urban-rural social tension, which was already endemic. Peasants, who made up the vast majority of East European populations, were driven away from politics by their hostility to the cities and their attention to their own survival. Parliamentarism shriveled as the 1920s progressed: it was abolished in Bulgaria in 1923, in Poland in 1926, in Yugoslavia in 1929, and it never amounted to much in Hungary. Everywhere, the major function of government was to dole out enough economic and political favors to keep officeholders in office.[5]

This is not to say that representatives of peasant majorities were shut out completely from power. As noted earlier, Bulgaria had a real peasant government from 1919 to 1923. The Romanian National Peasant Government of 1928 to 1931 is perhaps the most honest that the country has ever had. The Czech Agrarian Party was the linchpin of the five-party system, the *petka*, which dominated Czechoslovak politics through most of the interwar period, and the Croat Peasant Party was usually the absent linchpin of Yugoslav national politics. These parties and others espoused a new ideology, agrarianism, which arose to express peasant aspirations. Agrarianism conceived a third way between capitalism and communism that would be appropriate to East European conditions and consonant with the "national genius" of these peasant countries. Specifically, it advocated agricultural self-management, industrialization to serve agriculture, and some measure of government oversight and control of the economy. The goal was to provide for the peasant majorities while escaping the area's historic dependence on outsiders for economic development. Agrarianism applied the peasant ideal of self-sufficiency to the whole national community. The Green International, an organization of the region's peasant parties headquartered in Prague, tried to sound an internationalist appeal for an Eastern Europe neither Red nor White.

In the end, agrarianism and the peasant parties never really took hold. The horizons of subsistence peasants were largely limited to their villages. The backbreaking work that consumed most of their year meant that they had little energy for politics. They had no resources to support broad and durable political movements, and leaders of the peasant parties quickly became professional politicians. In quiet times, they were rather easily bought or co-opted by the existing power structures, and in hard times they discovered that the funds required for the credits, the industrial supplies, the new food-processing industries, and the marketing networks that were needed to make agricultural self-management work simply did not exist. Yet because the one real asset the peasant parties had in the political struggle was the votes of their majority constituencies, they believed in democracy, most of the time in most places. The legacy of the interwar peasant parties was not concrete achievement, but rather an authentically democratic political value system.[6]

As the limits to agrarianism emerged, the elites of Eastern Europe were left with the ideology of nationalism as a means to build national states and justify their own power. Nationalism was particularly appealing during this period for three reasons.

First, by dismissing the importance of class distinctions and emphasizing ethnicity and language, nationalism symbolically abolished the isolation of the elite from the masses and its feeling of powerlessness regarding the problems of the peasantry. It glorified the peasant masses without requiring that anything much be done for them.

Second, the existence of national minorities provided an obvious focus for majority nationalism. Ruling elites, having just emerged from a national struggle for independence, understood conflicts between majority and minority populations in the same binary terms they had learned in the struggle against the foreign empires, and promoted the identity of state and (majority) nation with clear consciences. They tended to see discontented minorities as agents of outside enemies, and, ironically, they used the old strategies of denationalization developed by the multinational monarchies of yore. But of course such strategies provoked strong reactions from the remaining minorities. Under the supranational monarchies, every nationality could dream of independence. Nationalities that were minorities in the new states could not expect Eastern Europe's new borders to be redrawn again in their lifetimes. Desperation came naturally to them, therefore. It took a number of political forms: Some became willing tools of "their" states; others became extreme supranationalists of various stripes; Jews (who had no state anywhere) were impelled in both directions, toward Zionism, toward leftism — which was increasingly under the organizational and ideological spell of bolshevism — or both together. And the radicalization of the minorities locked the majorities into their own nationalisms that much more deeply.

Third, having provided specious but persuasive answers to the conflicts between city and country and majority and minority, nationalism also legitimized policies that appeared essential to building nation-states. Education, for instance, was a political issue par excellence in every country in the region. As Italian nationalist Giuseppe Mazzini had recommended, education was designed to turn anational peasants into conscious patriots. Also, education was used to assimilate recalcitrant minorities on the persuasive grounds of national security.[7]

The ideology of nationalism did not suffice to build nations. It did not address hard economic and political realities and provided superficial resolutions to real social divisions within East European populations. In fact, in regarding the consolidation of the state as synonymous with the well-being of their ethnic group, and by treating ethnic minorities as "objectively different," East European elites strengthened ethnic divisions and guaranteed that minority nationalism would be passionate and exclusionary. The Western model of the time provided no proper antidote. Despite some internationalism in the 1920s, the West generally viewed World War I as a successful national war. Importantly, West Europeans and Americans saw no contradiction between nationalism and making the world safe for democracy, because to them democracy meant self-determination under majority rule, albeit with protection for minorities. In the 1920s victor states joined successor states in a common fear of reviving supranationalism, whether it took the form of bolshevism or a Habsburg restoration in Central Europe.

Yet neither did the nationalism of the 1920s doom the new states of Eastern Europe. Trumpeted everywhere, national independence was nurtured with some modest success in some places. So long as the Western economies grew, and so long as Germany and Soviet Russia were not in a position to interfere, modest economic and political development was possible. The late 1920s in particular was a period of some political consolidation and moderate economic growth. The dependence and peasant character of the area were masked, and the region appeared to be on the path to becoming part of Europe.[8]

That path was blocked utterly by the Great Depression, though this was not immediately apparent. During much of the 1930s it seemed plausible to blame Eastern Europe itself for its troubles and to hope for solutions from within the area.[9] In reality, even the very qualified independence that Eastern Europe gained in the post-World War I settlement lasted not two decades, as we usually think, but one.

The depression virtually ended Western demand for Eastern agricultural goods. As a result, agricultural prices dropped dramatically, reducing the incentive for East European peasants to produce and sell a surplus. The peasant majorities were thrown back still further into self-sufficiency in order to preserve their families, and simply stopped buying outside the village, drying up what little demand there had been for manufactured goods. No longer able to sell in the region, Western suppliers stopped credit and called in the credits they had given. Every East European state responded by protecting its industry and exports. The area governments made some attempts to band together to increase their bargaining power with West European suppliers and purchasers, but their economies were doomed to compete for foreign sales across a narrow range of products, and political divisions between the states were too deep for them to overcome their competing economic interests. Czechoslovakia's more balanced economy made it a potential exception to this rule, but even it behaved roughly the same way as the rest of the regional governments: Reacting to pressures from its own agricultural sector, it too turned more protectionist and ended its traditional purchases of agricultural goods from farther east.

The Western political model, parliamentarism, had been weakened in the 1920s, and only Czechoslovakia and Romania were still even formally parliamentary democracies as the 1930s began. The Western economic model was weakened in the 1930s, not only by the wrenching experience of depression within Eastern Europe but also by the knowledge that the United States, Britain, Germany and then France were also suffering. Among the region's elites, the search for new ideologies began. The region's native ideology, agrarianism, had apparently failed in the 1920s, and its peasant troops, now withdrawn even more deeply into their families and villages, were harder and harder to coax out into the political arena.

As a radical alternative to Western liberalism, bolshevism had two black marks against it from the outset. First, it was the state ideology of Soviet Russia, and most countries in the area believed that Soviet Russia threatened their precious national independence. The Soviet Union was seen as the old imperial Russia in new clothes, hungry to regain the territories it had lost to neighboring Poland and Romania. Because Russia was a foreign threat, Soviet communism's appeal within fiercely nationalist Eastern Europe was limited largely to the national minorities: Ukrainians and White Russians in Poland, Slovaks in Czechoslovakia, and Jews everywhere. As economic depression worsened ethnic tension, minorities sympathetic to socialism looked increasingly like Soviet Russian fifth columns.[10] Second, the Soviet Union in this period was sinking into the horror of collectivization. What the peasant countries saw there was not the advance of industry under the First Five-Year Plan but the abolition of private land ownership and the physical destruction of millions of peasants by famine or by the police.

Social democracy was not really an alternative either. At this point, it had not achieved much success yet in the West. The British Labour Party got its first share of power in the Ramsay MacDonald government in the late 1920s, but his party split in 1931. Léon Blum's Popular Front government in France did not arrive until 1936. Roosevelt's New Deal in America was far away, and its economic results in the 1930s were mixed. Moreover, the urban working classes to which social democracy might appeal were still small in Eastern Europe, and it was easy for its political opponents to tar it with the brush of bolshevism.

So nationalism remained the ruling native ideology, and any improvement by import was likely to involve not less nationalism but more: the supranational nationalism called fascism. Since 1922 Fascist Italy had provided an alternative Western model to liberal democracy, one that embraced nationalism, that had brought the Italians new national pride and seemed to create new national strength. Radical politics were likely in the Eastern Europe of the 1930s because of the sheer weight of suffering brought to workers and peasants by the depression. But the weakness of the alternatives meant that radicalization would be to the right rather than the left. Fascism could co-opt the nationalism of East European majorities, while bolshevism's appeal was generally limited to national minorities.

The strength and then the surge of nationalism created special problems for the Jews in the 1930s and 1940s.[11] The Jewish minority was large in Poland, Hungary, Slovakia, and Romania. Jews were very prominent in trade, industry and banking, and the professions, and served as a surrogate for the urban middle class that was otherwise so small in these regions. Traditionally, Jews had been protected by the state, so that in the popular mind they were associated with the state. In the West the discontent created by economic depression was often directed against the state as such. In interwar Eastern Europe the new state was inordinately precious, so there such discontent tended to turn against Jews and other minorities, sometimes with state connivance. The association of Jews and power was eminently unfair to the majority of Jews, who were poor, but this poor majority lived in largely separate communities and was politically invisible.

In seventeenth- and eighteenth-century Europe, Jewish financiers funded the new absolute monarchs, only to be sacrificed by them in times of stress. This betrayal was repeated in the 1930s and 1940s by larger and more democratic polities.[12] Increasing opportunities for education expanded the claim of majority populations to middle-class status. In Poland, for instance, possession of a high-school diploma, the *matura*, practically defined membership in the intelligentsia. At the same time that the number of people seeking prestigious places in the government and economy increased, the availability of such positions was decreasing. In addition to shrinking the private economy, the depression forced governments to cut back the bureaucracy, the traditional employer of the intelligentsia. But politically it was far easier to blame the state's Jewish protégés for blocking access to the jobs in the economy and in government that new graduates felt they deserved than to blame the state itself.

In country after country, economic decline brought the rise of right radicalism, even before the Nazis came to power in Germany in 1933.[13] But it was right radicalism with a narrower social base and shorter political breadth than in Germany and Italy. It was good at fighting the only slightly less marginal left radicals, and it put real pressure on governments to co-opt it by stealing its clothes. But nowhere in Eastern Europe did right radicalism, and especially radical anti-Semitism, succeed in capturing power on its own. Popular anti-Semitism was endemic, but partly for that reason, it was incapable of providing a distinct ideological basis for mass parties. The regimes bent to the pressure for restrictions on Jews, but often limited or rescinded them. In the end, they rebuffed pressure for Nazi-style totalistic solutions. The main policy objectives of these ethnic nationalist regimes turned out to be more nationalist than ethnic, and they considered economic recovery to be the national imperative. In the early 1930s they sought recovery through tariffs, through centralization of investment, and especially through rearmament justified in terms of national security. It was this program of economy recovery rather than fascist ideology that led much of Eastern Europe into the orbit of Nazi Germany as the 1930s progressed.

The conquest of Eastern Europe by Germany in the 1930s was unique in the region's history, for Hitler was able to use a very modern understanding of power to his advantage. In the nineteenth century, Eastern Europe's primary international role had been as a potential addition to or subtraction from the power of others. This role was conceived primarily in territorial terms, and as the century progressed, it became clear that the allegiance of the increasingly self-conscious ethnic majorities was the key to control of territory. The Western democracies thus supported a democratic nationalism as a means to pry territories away from the empires, and the northern monarchies had earlier incited nationalism in the Balkans to weaken Ottoman rule. France had been the traditional standardbearer of the Poles in the struggle against the northern monarchies, and there is a statue of Tsar Alexander II in the capital of Bulgaria today, where there is none in Russia itself. Sometimes nationalism's foreign sponsors had believed in its virtue; always they had seen it as a way of depriving their competitors of militarily valuable territory. Territory continued to be very important, but World War I also taught Europe that military success depended on mobilizing all of society's economic resources for war and upon exhausting enemy societies as well as defeating enemy armies. Some understanding of the larger role of economic power in international political competition was reflected in the terms of the postwar settlement: After the Franco-Prussian War of 1870, Germany levied reparations on France largely as tribute, but in 1919 Germany was saddled with reparations not only to exact vengeance but to make recovery more difficult. Still, at the level of societies, thinking changes more slowly than political reality. Most people in post-Versailles Europe still understood the basis of power to be conventional military control of territory secured by ethnic majorities. In Eastern Europe majorities and minorities alike sought alliances and support from outside powers.

In the 1920s the United States, Britain, the Soviet Union, and Germany were not very susceptible to these appeals. The United States had contributed Wilsonian self-determination to the brew of East European nationalism, diluting but not replacing its Herderian attachment to "objective" national attributes. But the United States returned to political isolationism after the war, and while Americans made some investments in Eastern Europe and played a role in the management of the German reparations issue, they were too far away for much in the way of trade. Britain suffered almost continuous economic depression after the war, so it had fewer economic resources to spare for overseas ventures, and its main international concerns were managing its empire and countering French predominance on the continent.

Most of the significant diplomatic activity of the 1920s involved effecting a Franco-German reconciliation, the high point of which was the Locarno Agreement of 1925. At Locarno, France accepted German nonrecognition of the postwar adjustments to Germany's eastern borders. The Soviet Union and Germany reestablished ties at the Rapallo Conference in 1922 and covertly cooperated militarily throughout the interwar period. Soviet Russia did not recognize its borders with Poland and Romania, for it continued to claim Romania's Bessarabia and parts of the Polish Ukraine and Byelorussia. These were worrisome signs for Eastern European independence, but through the 1920s Germany was disarmed and internally divided, and Russia was isolated and internally preoccupied.

That left France and Italy in the arena as possible patrons and sponsors for the East Europeans in the 1920s. Both were World War I victor powers, but they had little else in common. France was the preeminent status quo power, dedicated to preventing the reemergence of a strong Germany. Its traditional ally for this purpose was Russia, on the theory that the enemy of my enemy is my friend, but Soviet Russia's internal weakness and immense self-regard in the 1920s removed it from the checkerboard. In Russia's place France turned to Eastern Europe, and built up an alliance system with the beneficiaries of the postwar settlement, Poland on the one hand and the Little Entente formed among Czechoslovakia, Yugoslavia, and Romania in 1920 and 1921 on the other.

The common denominator of antirevisionism was not enough to unite France's allies. The goals of the northern (Poland) and southern (Little Entente) parts of the alliance system were different. While France and Poland were primarily interested in containing Germany, France's Little Entente allies cared most about preventing a Habsburg restoration in Hungary and Austria and about containing revisionist Hungary and Bulgaria. Also, Czechoslovakia and Poland were at loggerheads throughout the interwar period over Těšín (also spelled Cieszyn or Teschen), a rich industrial border area with a Polish majority that the Czechoslovaks had seized by military force in 1918. Nor could Poland and Romania be expected to cooperate. Romania was unwilling to take on Poland's quarrels with the Soviet Union, Czechoslovakia, and Germany, and Poland was unwilling to take on Romania's quarrels with the Soviet Union and Hungary.

Nor would France compensate for the strategic weakness of its eastern alliance system by giving it a reliable economic underpinning. Faithful to the traditional territorial concept of power, it did not match its commitments of troops with commitments of credits, even when it had the means to do so. It did engineer some bank bailouts under League of Nations auspices, but as usual in Eastern Europe, the recipients spent most of these funds on nonproductive, often military, projects. The bulk of the money France allotted to stop revisionism had been used to prevent the customs union that Germany and Austria agreed on in 1931. When the collapse of the Vienna Creditanstalt in May of that year shriveled the sources of credit all over the area, France simply called in the debts owed it and refused further investments.[14]

Italy had been promised territories in the Mediterranean and in the Balkans in return for entering the war on the side of Britain in 1915, and looked forward to the fruits of victory as the crowning point of its long struggle to build an Italian nation. At Versailles Italy was denied the gains it had been promised (partly as a result of its own unwillingness to compromise), and the resulting disappointed nationalist appetite helped bring Mussolini's fascists to power in 1922. As a rightist island in Western Europe's democratic sea, Italy under Mussolini was ideologically inclined to compete with France, and this made it the natural patron of the revisionist East European states that were similarly dissatisfied with the postwar settlement.

During the 1920s France and its allies dominated the competition with Italy and its allies, but the depression moved both East European elites and populations to the right. Area governments co-opted the statist part of fascism, increasing state control of the national economies. Italy responded by redoubling its competitive efforts against France. It had few economic resources with which to compete, so the thrust of these efforts was political, including support for terrorism. The assassin who killed King Alexander of Yugoslavia and French Foreign Minister Barthou in Marseilles in 1934 was funded by the Italians. Italy's motives in the 1930s did not correspond entirely with those of its clients or with those of Germany. It supported Hungarian and Bulgarian revisionism against France's Little Entente allies, but it too opposed a Habsburg restoration, and it too worked to defend Austrian independence against an *Anschluss,* the unification of Austria with Germany.[15]

Most of what Italy could offer the region was not economic but political and ideological. If the international competition for Eastern Europe had been limited to Italy and France, its regimes would have looked forward the mid-1930s to more decline, further statism, and perhaps economic ...overy, as the Western economies improved and Western economic ..ources became available again. But the East European regimes believed ...at the most important national issue was economic recovery. As Nazi Germany recovered from the Depression and entered the area, this urgent desire for greater independence through economic recovery led them toward blighted dependence on the Germans. Unlike Italy and France, by the mid-1930s Germany had both political and economic resources with which to compete for influence within the region, and was ready to use them. Hitler surpassed his contemporaries in recognizing the importance of the ethnic base of territorial and military power. The Nazis bifurcated state-to-state relations and society-to-society relations, and willingly used Germans and rightists to influence other societies (just as the Soviets used national minorities and leftists), while keeping clean hands in diplomatic relations between governments.[16] But better than their competitors they also appreciated the economic bases of power, both at home, where the government used the state to rearm and remilitarize, and abroad, where Nazi Germany was soon engaged in intelligent and systematic economic penetration.[17]

For Poland and Czechoslovakia, the two countries whose borders Weimar Germany had never recognized and that Nazi Germany therefore threatened directly, the simple facts of German rearmament and active German nationalism exacerbated the desire of ruling majorities for national cohesion (for both countries had large German minorities) and gave a military cast to their own economic recovery plans. The basically free-market cast of their economies was preserved, but the economic role of the state was now extended to dominate the market in key areas such as investment.

Beginning already in 1934, Germany became a valuable trading partner for the countries it did not threaten directly, first Hungary and Bulgaria, then Romania and Yugoslavia. It provided stable markets for their agricultural products at above-world-market prices and sold industrial investment goods, as well as the more famous aspirins and cameras, in return. This exchange was not entirely to the advantage of the East European states; all trade was processed through blocked clearing accounts that forced all proceeds into bilateral channels with the Germans and thus prevented them from trading elsewhere, and tied them into German economic management. Still, the German bargain was irresistible, for it provided a measure of salvation for these prostrate agricultural economies, which lacked any other means of maintaining living standards and securing investment for industrialization. Hungary and Bulgaria, the two revisionist powers working to undermine the French-supported Little Entente, benefited especially. Germany succeeded in using economic policy to turn Italy's area friends Hungary and Bulgaria into favored clients. Meanwhile, Germany also served as a model of economic recovery under rightist auspices.

The political advance largely followed the economic. Hitler's first years in power were dedicated to internal *Gleichschaltung*, the fastening of the totalitarian system onto Germany itself, to economic recovery, and to throwing off the Versailles restraints on Germany's international freedom of action. The right to rearm was announced in 1935, and the Rhineland was remilitarized in 1936. France was in domestic political turmoil and would not resist the German advances without British help, which Britain refused to provide. The first fruit of Nazi diplomacy in Eastern Europe was the Polish-German Pact of 1934 on Non-Use of Force, signed by Polish leader Józef Piłsudski after France had turned aside his veiled suggestion of resolute action against the New Germany.[18] While maintaining a façade of diplomatic innocence, Germany turned to discreet but direct provocation of political instability. Using Germans and local rightists, it fomented domestic turmoil in Austria, Czechoslovakia, and Romania.

France tried to recoup by bringing in the Soviet Union as a counterweight in the Franco-Soviet Treaty of 1935, which was immediately followed by a complementary Czechoslovak-Soviet Treaty, and by reconciling with Italy to defend Austria against an *Anschluss*. Both these efforts had little effect. The Soviets were weak partners: Stalin's purges began in earnest in 1935 and destroyed the Red Army leadership along with many others in 1937 and 1938. Because Czechoslovakia had no border with the Soviet Union, the military mutual assistance clauses of these treaties could not be put into effect unless the Poles and/or the Romanians allowed Soviet troops to cross their territory into Czechoslovakia. Both were unwilling to do so, for fear that once Soviet troops entered their territory they would never leave. In a nutshell, the French alliance system depended on Soviet help that was unlikely to come, and in its absence on the strengths of Poland and the Little Entente, which were unlikely to be combined. Franco-Italian reconciliation was not to be. Italy had defended Austria's independence when a Nazi putsch threatened it in 1934. But it invaded Ethiopia in 1935 and helped the Spanish rightists under Franco in 1936. These actions caused French and British sanctions, and foreclosed the possibility of cooperation to defend Austria.[19]

German reentry into Eastern Europe was a massive success, and it found no Western ideological, economic, or political competition. The governments of the area saw the writing on the wall. They became more careful about their Western commitments and less willing to offend Germany and Italy, which allied in 1936. They openly displayed their hatred for and opposition to the Soviet Union and adopted more and more rightist trappings for themselves. Most tellingly, they began to pick up scraps from the German table. After destroying the Versailles settlement, Hitler turned to gathering Germans from the neighboring East into the Reich. When the West left Austria and Czechoslovakia to him in 1938 and 1939, East Europeans joined in falling on the spoils. Poland and Hungary took pieces of Czechoslovakia, which helped embolden Hitler in March 1939 to destroy the remaining non-German regions by declaring Bohemia and Moravia a German protectorate and by sponsoring a formally independent Slovakia.

The destruction of Czechoslovakia, which had retained the region's most democratic government under Tomáš Masaryk and then Eduard Beneš, changed the basic rules of international relations in Europe. It shattered the façade of respect for self-determination that Hitler had used up to then, for he was now exerting dominion over non-German peoples. In response, Britain and France gave unilateral guarantees to Poland and Romania. But in 1939 Britain and France seemed very far away, and Germany very near. After March, most East European governments truckled under to the Germans, trying to preserve their sovereignty in the face of overwhelming German power. They were generally successful in gaining Hitler's support, to the point that he was willing to sacrifice right radicals, such as Romania's Iron Guard, in order to maintain stability in the region. After unsuccessful alliance negotiations with Britain and

France, in August 1939 the Soviet Union also turned to Germany, agreeing to help destroy Poland in return for the Baltic Republics and parts of Poland and Romania with Ukrainian or White Russian populations. Poland was invaded by Germany on September 1, 1939, and by the Soviet Union on September 17. By March 1941 Germany dominated all of Eastern Europe save Yugoslavia. Austria and Czechoslovakia had been destroyed, Poland was occupied in six weeks, and Hungary, Romania, and Bulgaria formally allied with the Axis in the Tripartite Pact. Britain and France had honored their guarantees to Poland, but Germany demolished France's armies in the spring of 1940. Hitler ruled most of Europe, and Britain stood alone against him.

In World War I, the stakes were in southeastern Europe, as the balance wheel of great power rivalry, but the outcome was determined on the western front. Now the great stakes were in the north, but the outcome was determined in the south and east. This may have been true only in a narrow sense but it was still true. Germany needed all the forces it could muster to impose a rapid decision in the north while it still enjoyed overwhelming military preponderance, and it was obliged to divert part of them at a critical moment to the Balkans. Without telling the Germans beforehand, Mussolini invaded Greece in October 1940. There he got his nose bloodied, and the British reintervened on the continent from which they had been excluded at Dunkirk. By then organization of Operation Barbarossa, the German invasion of the Soviet Union, was well underway, but to save his foolish ally Hitler had to direct German armies through Yugoslavia and delay his eastern plans. The effort to force Yugoslavia into the Tripartite Pact in order to secure peaceful transit backfired in March 1941, when the government that had signed it was overthrown by a spontaneous national uprising. The Germans responded with invasion and full-scale dismemberment of the country. The occupation of Yugoslavia required troops, so the invasion of Russia that began on June 22 was not only later than planned but also used fewer men. Hitler's troops just failed to reach Moscow before winter and the Soviet army forced them to begin a retreat. On December 7 Japan attacked Pearl Harbor, and the United States joined Britain and the Soviet Union in the war against the Axis.[20]

Notes

1. L.B. Namier, "The Downfall of the Habsburg Monarchy," in Harold Temperley, ed., *A History of the Peace Conference of Paris*, vol. 4 (London: Henry Frowde and Hodder & Stoughton, 1921), 58-119. On Brest-Litovsk, see James Edmonds, *A Short History of World War I* (Oxford: Oxford University Press, 1951), 262.
2. See my "The Polish Peasant Revolt of 1846 in Galicia: Recent Polish Historiography," *Slavic Review*, 30, no. 4 (December 1971): 795-817.
3. For useful surveys on the "New Eastern Europe," see E.A. Radice, "General Characteristics of the Region Between the Wars," in Michael Kaser, ed., *The Economic History of Eastern Europe, 1919-1975*, vol. 1 (Oxford: Clarendon Press, 1975), 22-65, and C.A. Macartney and A.W. Palmer, *Independent Eastern Europe. A History* (New York: St. Martin's Press, 1966), 147-243.
4. See recent works by Radice, "General Characteristics of the Region between the Wars"; John R. Lampe and Marvin R. Jackson, *Balkan Economic History, 1550-1950. From Imperial Borderlands to Developing Nations* (Bloomington, Ind.: Indiana University Press, 1982); and Andrew Janos, *The Politics of Backwardness in Hungary, 1825-1945* (Princeton, N.J.: Princeton University Press, 1982). Some older general treatments are still useful: Hugh Seton-Watson, *Eastern Europe between the Wars, 1918-1941*, 3rd ed. (Hamden, Conn.: Anchor, 1951), 75-122; David T. Mitrany, *Marx against the Peasant* (London: Weidenfeld & Nicolson, 1951), 105-190; George D. Jackson, Jr., *Comintern and Peasant in East Europe, 1919-1930* (New York: Columbia University Press, 1966), 153-311; and Ghita Ionescu, "Eastern Europe," in Ernst Gellner, ed., *Populism* (London: Weidenfeld & Nicolson, 1969). And two older studies still make the problems vivid in specific contexts: David T. Mitrany, *The Land and the Peasant in Rumania. The War and Agrarian Reform* (London: Humphrey Milford, 1930), and Jozo Tomasevich, *Peasants, Politics, and Economic Change in Yugoslavia* (Stanford, Calif.: Stanford University Press, 1955), 233ff.
5. On interwar parties and parliamentarism, Hugh Seton-Watson's *The East European Revolution*, 3rd ed. (New York: Praeger, 1956), 23-48, is still valuable.
6. One contemporary view (and fear) was that the peasant majorities would sweep the political boards. In the early 1920s Sir Lewis Namier, whose dislike of peasants was perhaps the obverse of his personal combination of Jewishness and fondness for aristocracy, was writing that "Perfect theocracies may yet arise in Eastern Europe in the dark shadow of the 'conquering Cham'" (a Polish pejorative for the most benighted peasant): "Agrarian Revolution (1922)," in Namier's *Skyscrapers and Other Essays* (Freeport, N.Y.: Books for Libraries Press, 1968), 155. Namier was perhaps prescient, but not quite in the way he meant: As we shall see, to the extent that peasants conquered in Eastern Europe, they did so indirectly, and the theocracies they generated were not those Namier anticipated. For the actual record of direct peasant politics in one country, see Olga A. Narkiewicz, *The Green Flag. Polish Populist Politics 1867-1970* (London: Croom Helm, 1976).
7. "The leading universities in all countries maintained a fairly high standard, but in the village schools teaching all too often degenerated into the three R's plus a training in national hatred:" Hugh Seton-Watson, *East European Revolution*, 12, and at more length in his *Eastern Europe Between the Wars*, 138-146.
8. On the consolidation of the 1920s, see Macartney and Palmer, *Independent Eastern Europe*, 178-243.

9. For a bemused and intelligent meditation on what it means to be small with reference to this period, Henry L. Roberts, "Politics in a Small State: The Balkan Example," in his *Eastern Europe: Politics, Revolution, & Diplomacy* (New York: Knopf, 1970), 178-203.

10. On the minorities and minority issues in general, see Hugh Seton-Watson, *Eastern Europe between the Wars*, 268-319.

11. For a summary, see Ezra Mendelsohn, "Relations Between Jews and Non-Jews in Eastern Europe between the Two World Wars," in François Furet, *Unanswered Questions. Nazi Germany and the Genocide of the Jews* (New York: Schocken, 1989); for more extended treatment, see Mendelsohn's *The Jews of East Central Europe between the Two World Wars* (New York: Mouton, 1983). Of the individual country situations, Poland's has been best treated: for two recent histories, with extensive bibliographies, see Joseph Marcus, *Social and Political History of the Jews in Poland, 1919-1939* (Berlin: Mouton, 1983), and Celia S. Heller, *On the Edge of Destruction. Jews of Poland between the Two World Wars* (New York: Columbia University Press, 1977). The classic work on the appeal of communism to national minorities throughout the area is still R.V. Burks, *The Dynamics of Communism in Eastern Europe* (Princeton, N.J.: Princeton University Press, 1961).

12. This is of course Hannah Arendt's thesis in *The Origins of Totalitarianism*, new ed. (New York: Harcourt, Brace & World, 1966), 3-88 and passim.

13. The best treatment in English is still in the chapters by István Déak on Hungary and Eugen Weber on Romania in Hans Rogger and Eugen Weber, ed., *The European Right. A Historical Profile* (Berkeley: University of California Press, 1965), 364-407 and 501-574.

14. On the French role and then the German ascendancy, see György Ránki, *Economy and Foreign Policy. The Struggle of the Great Powers for Hegemony in the Danube Valley, 1919-1939* (New York: Columbia University Press, 1983), and Piotr S. Wandycz, *The Twilight of French Eastern Alliances, 1926-1936. French-Czechoslovak-Polish Relations from Locarno to the Remilitarization of the Rhineland* (Princeton, N.J.: Princeton University Press, 1988).

15. For a convenient survey on the Italian role in the 1930s, see Luigi Villari, *Italian Foreign Policy under Mussolini* (New York: Devon-Adair, 1956), 75-122.

16. Nazi use of area Germans is now thoroughly documented in Antony Komjathy and Rebecca Stockwell, *German Minorities and the Third Reich. Ethnic Germans of East Central Europe between the Wars* (New York: Holmes & Meier, 1980).

17. The locus classicus on German economic expansionism in the area, since qualified and disputed, is Antonín Basch, *The Danube Basin and the German Economic Sphere* (New York: Columbia University Press, 1943). The best recent work is David E. Kaiser, *Economic Diplomacy and the Origins of the Second World War. Germany, Britain, France, and Eastern Europe, 1930-1939* (Princeton, N.J.: Princeton University Press, 1980).

18. On the 1934 Non-Aggression Pact, see Wandycz, *Twilight of French Eastern Alliances*, 300-335.

19. On this whole process, see Esmonde M. Robertson, *Mussolini as Empire-Builder. Europe and Africa, 1932-1936* (New York: St. Martin's, 1972).

20. On Soviet-German relations and diplomacy under the Molotov-Ribbentrop Pact, see Anthony Read and David Fisher, *The Deadly Embrace. Hitler, Stalin and the Nazi-Soviet Pact 1939-1941* (New York: Norton, 1988). On the horrible dilemmas that

Munich and then Soviet-German rapprochement produced for the Soviet Union's Western neighbors, see Anna M. Cienciala, *Poland and the Western Powers 1938-1939* (London: Routledge & Kegan Paul, 1968) and Dov B. Lungu, *Romania and the Great Powers, 1933-1940* (Durham: Duke University Press, 1989). For a lively and immediate account of the period, see John Lukacs, *The Last European War. September 1939/December 1941* (New York: Anchor/Doubleday, 1976). And for a fine treatment of Mussolini's policy in the Balkans from the beginning of the war, see Macgregor Knox, *Mussolini Unleashed 1939-41. Politics and Strategy in Fascist Italy's Last War* (Cambridge: Cambridge University Press, 1982), 134-290.

THREE

THE WAR AND THE
VICTORS, 1939-1948:
TRIAL BY FIRE

By 1941, World War II had reproduced the geopolitics of the Eastern Europe of 1914, with minor variations. Most of the western and southern Slavs were again absorbed into German and Russian empires, and the independent states of the southeast, Hungary, Romania, and Bulgaria, were trying to play the great powers against each other for national gain. The variations included formally independent states in Croatia and Slovakia and an Italian role on the Adriatic and in the Balkans. Although the outcome of the conflict made these variations almost ephemeral, the heightened Croat and Slovak national self-consciousness that they left behind subsisted into the Communist era (and has now reemerged in independent statehood). In this as in so many other aspects of East European life, the experience of the war perpetuated and reinforced the experience of the past — the dependence, the strength of the peasantries and their traditions, the strength of nationalism — even as it altered their forms. Yet because this was effected by destruction from outside much more than by the peoples themselves, what contemporaries saw was the destruction and the immense confusion — economic, political, moral — that it brought in its wake.

Economic destruction was massive but uneven. Bulgaria and the Czech lands were geared into the German war machine and did not become war zones; for them the war actually meant increased production in some economic sectors. Though worn, their factories emerged intact and in greater number after the war. The same would have been true of Hungary and Slovakia had they not become war zones in 1944 and 1945, and of Romania and the eastern parts of Germany that became the German Democratic Republic and western Poland, had the Soviets not stripped them for reparations in the early years of their occupation. The most ravaged areas were Poland and Yugoslavia. A few examples should illuminate the scale of the economic destruction. In Poland, 30 percent of the buildings were destroyed; in Warsaw, only 13 or 14 percent, or 7 percent, of them remained standing: The figures vary but tell the same story. Agriculture was horse-powered in this part of the world, and cattle, pigs, and sheep provided much of the population's protein and animal fat. Poland lost 43 percent of its horses, 60 percent of its cattle, and 70 percent of its pigs; Hungary, 39 percent of its horses, 44 percent of its cattle, and 78 percent of its pigs; Yugoslavia, 60 percent of its horses, 54 percent of its cattle, and 50 percent of its sheep. At the end of the war a sixth of Poland's farms were not producing at all. Communications networks were also devastated: Hungary lost 90 percent of its large railway bridges, 63 percent of the medium bridges, 60 percent of its locomotives, and 86 percent of its freight cars; Yugoslavia lost half its railroad track and three-quarters of its railway bridges. In Poland losses to transport alone amounted to $3.5 billion, which would now be worth about $45 billion.

In Poland, Czechoslovakia, Hungary, Yugoslavia, Albania, Romania, and Bulgaria, there were 20 million fewer people at war's end, down from 89 to 69 million. The Soviet annexation of White Russian and Ukrainian territories from Poland, and Bessarabia and the northern Bukovina from Romania, accounts for some of those losses; the death or expulsion of 13 million Germans, including 3 million expelled from Czechoslovakia and 6 million from what became Poland, account for more. But millions of others were killed, dying horrible, violent deaths. Bulgaria and the Czech lands had relatively few war deaths, but Poland lost 6 million, 22 percent of its prewar population — divided fairly evenly between citizens of Jewish and Polish nationality. Between 1.2 and 1.7 million died in Yugoslavia. Romania lost half a million in the two wars it fought in succession, against the Soviet Union and then against Germany. Relative to population,

Romania's losses matched those of the American Civil War; yet compared to Poland, Romania was spared. But human beings and animals are resilient. Livestock herds replenished themselves quickly, and the East European baby boom began the moment the guns fell silent. Likewise, roads, bridges, and buildings can be rebuilt, and a good case can be made that it is more efficient to industrialize with new plant, as the postwar West German and Japanese experiences suggest. From that point of view, it can be argued that Czechoslovakia's intact industrial plant, which was such an advantage in the 1940s and 1950s, was a poisoned chalice in the long run. More important for the future of Eastern Europe even than the scale of the physical destruction was its structure, the sectors that were hardest hit and those that were most spared.

The human and material losses of the war fell disproportionately on the cities that held the bulk of the area's industry, workers, and traditional elites. The working class and especially the intelligentsia were decimated. A very high proportion of the 38,000 people killed by the German Gestapo in Czechoslovakia were intellectuals. Only a third of the 12,000 prewar members of the Yugoslav Communist Party survived; the leadership that emerged from the partisan struggle to rule the country was strongly peasant in origin, and this may help account for the salvationist left radicalism of the early postwar years. For the Polish intelligentsia the war was simply a hecatomb. About 200,000 people, a quarter of the prewar population of Warsaw, were killed in the 1944 uprising, and a very high proportion of these fatalities were young intellectuals. The Soviets helped: all of the nearly 15,000 Polish officers butchered in 1940 by the Soviet secret police, the NKVD, had the *matura* that marked the intellectual. At the most famous site, in Katyń Forest, 4,200 fell.[1]

In relative social terms the crippling of urban human and physical resources would have increased the weight of the peasantries by simple subtraction, but they were also given preferential treatment in the German war economy. The Germans used the region's peasant populations as food suppliers but left them substantially intact, and even protected them in some cases. Despite some attempts by the state to organize agriculture, such as the Bulgarian cereal export agency Hranoiznos,[2] the war generally reinforced the peasant proclivities for self-sufficiency and for selling their small surpluses on the black market, two practices that had marked the hungry 1930s. As strategies for survival, self-sufficiency and the black market were effective, and the peasantries emerged from the war strengthened rather than weakened. But they were also more than ever part of the national community in each country. The urban front ranks had been thinned, but there were many more rural troops now committed to the struggle. Although they may have suffered less, they too had suffered foreign subjugation, German or Soviet, because of their nationality. In many of these peasant countries, nationalism had been largely an urban phenomenon before the war. The peasants had defined themselves mainly by religion and kin, or, in the extreme case of 49,000 inhabitants of the Pripet Marshes of Podlesie in eastern Poland responding to the 1921 census, simply as *tutejsi,* "people from here." [3] After their emancipation from feudalism in the nineteenth century, they were forced to deal with the state, but the state belonged to others. By 1945 the lived experience of foreign control and persecution, distinguished by its harshness and invasiveness from the rule of the earlier governments and empires, had nationalized them to an unprecedented degree. The feeling of community was strongest in the countries that suffered the most and fought the hardest against foreign occupation, Poland and Yugoslavia. Not only were the Yugoslav Communists, leaders and troops alike, now of strongly peasant origin, but they constituted the first political movement in the history of the Yugoslav state that represented and promoted federalism across all its nationalities.

Finally, World War II promoted ethnic homogeneity in the national societies, again by destructive outside agency. The Molotov-Ribbentrop Pact of August 1939 and its subsequent protocols had famous consequences for East European borders. With Hitler's acquiescence, Stalin essentially restored the borders of the Romanov Empire. The Red Army imposed those borders in 1944 and 1945 wherever the local populations were unwilling to acquiesce, notably in the Baltic Republics and in Poland. Less famous is the formal adoption of the principle of matching populations and borders by moving people. The Molotov-Ribbentrop agreements provided for shifting Germans out of Poland, Russia, and the Danubian countries to Germany and for expelling the Poles of the expanded Reich into the German-run rump Poland called the General

Government. Stalin also transported 1.5 million Poles to Soviet Central Asia and Siberia. The principle of moving populations was carried over into the postwar settlement. Millions of Germans were expelled in the most appalling conditions, and hundreds of thousands died. The remnants of East European Jewry were also allowed to leave, those who were Zionists and those who were not but did not wish to live on in the scene of their desolation.

Poland became almost completely Polish Catholic. The population of Czechoslovakia was reduced by 3 million, but it was now almost entirely Czech and Slovak. Because the Slovaks and all the Yugoslav peoples now lived in federal states with some self-government, the 2 million or so Hungarians in Romania became Europe's largest "classic" minority west of the Soviet Union. The settlement following World War I had reduced the numbers of East Europeans living outside "their" national borders by two-thirds; World War II and its settlement reduced them even further. The stronger, more peasant nationalities within the national borders now had less minority tinder on which to light.[4]

The ethnic homogenization was perhaps an advantage for the long run. Yet, in the short run of the immediate postwar years, the violence by which it was effected had disastrous moral and political effects. Impersonal rules for political and economic life, respect and decency between all people regardless of status, are imperfectly learned and lived in the West, and in Eastern Europe they were never as widespread and as deeply rooted. But they existed nevertheless, as aspirations, even if only as attributes of superior status, especially in the cities. The war had damaged the cities most thoroughly, and those living in the rubble put a new premium on lying, stealing, and cunning, for survival and for the pleasure of seeing the tears in the enemy's eyes, rather than on civility and impersonal standards of conduct. All other things being equal, this was to be expected after four or six years of violence and destruction, but such attitudes could also be expected to fade as reconstruction proceeded. But other things were not equal because of the population transfers: They internalized and routinized the habit of violence, carrying ways of acting and thinking forgivable in war over into the peacetime world. The war had sanctioned the principle of population transfers; population transfers helped to insure that postwar politics would be soaked in blood.

The guns used against the Germans continued to fire in what amounted to civil wars. The Communist Polish government imposed by the Soviets later admitted that it lost 15,000 dead in postwar fighting, and more recent estimates have taken the figure to 30,000 Polish and 1,000 Soviet.[5] An exchange in Andrzej Wajda's 1957 film based on Jerzy Andrzejewski's novel *Ashes and Diamonds* is famous among Poles: A police officer accuses a young Home Army guerrilla of shooting at Poles, and he replies, · "And you shoot at sparrows." No one was shooting at sparrows: in a time of white-hot nationalism, they were shooting at conationals.

The destruction of inherited moorings was thus moral even more than physical. At the same time, it made East Europeans available for new enthusiasms and immense sacrifices.[6] These enthusiasms took two forms.

One was the widespread faith in a new war, liberation by the Anglo-Americans, the expulsion of the Russians, and the reestablishment of national independence within the old frontiers. East Europeans with such faith continued fighting for years, sometimes into the 1950s, in the Soviet borderlands, in the Tatras of southern Poland, and in the Făgaraş mountains of southern Transylvania. In the Tatras there was one commander nicknamed "Fire," Ogień, who had fought the Germans and continued fighting the Communists long after the war has ended, into the 1950s. He was supplied by the people in the valley villages, whence young men came to join him. A week after I went to Poland in 1968 five Warsaw Pact countries, including Poland, invaded Czechoslovakia. I heard that in those mountains they were digging up and oiling the weapons they had buried after Ogień was taken, to be ready for the great day when the war of good and evil would begin again. When my wife and I went to the Tatras the next year, "Long live Ogień" — "*Niech zyje Ogień*" — was still written on the huts where the shepherds spend the summer with their flocks. As it turned out, a friend of a friend, now a schoolteacher, had tried to join Ogień's band in 1951, but they were by then so embattled that they no longer took young boys. I asked him how Ogień had finally been taken. He said he had come down to the valley for a wedding; an informer had tipped off the police; when he was taken he asked to be left in his Polish Army uniform; and before he got to jail he was dead from the cyanide under the collar. In addition to the regular curriculum, this man was teaching secret classes in Polish history and literature. When I asked why he did it, in 1969, he said, "Poland lasted 125 years without a state, and it can last another 125 under the Russians."

Another hope was of a new world of social solidarity through social revolution, creating nations that were at last proud and free, exempt from minority and national problems, and superior to the exhausted capitalist nations of the West.[7] Either of these dreams could be achieved only at terrible cost, at the sacrifice of the lives and ethical values of the current generation. It was widely felt, on both sides, by the holders of both dreams that the cost had to be worth it, in order to make sure that what they had paid during the war, and were paying in the postwar period, would never have to be paid again.

And just as wartime destruction reinforced nationalism and expanded and deepened its social base in the peasantries, these dreams of escaping from dependence were themselves rooted in dependence, and required new and more forceful dependence to make them come true. For each corresponded to the ideology of a liberating power competing for influence over and control of the prostrate countries of the area. The radically different ideologies offered by the United States and the Soviet Union served not only as vessels for the moral desperation of East Europeans, but as models for the urgently needed reconstruction of the region's economies and polities. The more distant member of the wartime alliance, the United States, provided the more persuasive model for rebuilding. The U.S. economy was not only intact but more powerful than ever. After the war, its economic power was matched by ideological power: America's political ideology, in its then-current, New Deal form, was sweeping the world.[8]

Roosevelt's liberalism appeared to be more inclusive and democratic than the Western model of classical liberalism, which was associated with the failures of the interwar years. It also seemed to provide a more promising escape route from economic dependence and national weakness, for U.S. economic recovery and wartime victory had proven strength and democracy could be combined. The Soviet Union had broken Germany, but otherwise it appeared unsuccessful in domestic economics and politics. East Europeans saw these failures as the result of authoritarianism, which had also not worked for them. Moreover, East

Europeans had already had a taste of Soviet-style liberation during the war. Estimates on Red Army rapes in Berlin alone range from 20,000 to 100,000, and what is statistical for us was lived experience for the East and Central Europeans of the time.[9]

The appeal of New Deal liberalism was general, but East European states were pushed in different directions for a sponsor by their historical experience and by hard political reality. The Czechoslovaks believed they had been abandoned by the West in 1938 and again in 1939. Bulgaria and the Czech lands had not suffered much physical damage during the war, so many members of the elite in those areas could still see the Russians as brother Slavs. Poland hoped for salvation from the West; there, the urgency of the Soviet threat was unmistakable. Elements of the elite in Hungary, Romania, and even Bulgaria also tended to trust the Anglo-Americans to save them from the Soviet Union.[10]

Both the United States and the Soviet Union were conglomerates of many peoples, including East Europeans, and both were continental in scale, with universalist, messianic ideologies to match. The victory reaffirmed the conviction of the elites of both countries that their country was exceptional and destined to make history. Both understood their national security in terms of its systemic underpinning rather than merely in the classic terms of the balance of power. Of course, they had very different understandings of this relationship between economics and politics. Each was determined to use the lessons it discerned from the past to remedy the weaknesses it believed had caused the war. Of course, they drew different lessons.[11]

The U.S. government was convinced that the war had come about partly because America had withdrawn from Europe and from the League of Nations in the 1920s and partly because European statism in economics had inhibited economic recovery in the 1930s, and thereby allowed right radicalism to gain power. The United States was convinced that liberal democratic politics and market economics had been triumphantly vindicated as a system. Americans were anxious to return to the joys of living in that system and to bring the boys overseas home to it as soon as possible. The U.S. government therefore worried about the powerful pull of isolationism at home and the resumption of statism in Europe. On the positive side, it saw the antidotes to both American isolationism and European statism in liberal democracy and the market for Europe, and it had a modest confidence that another dose of Wilsonian self-determination would lead Europeans to adopt them.

The government and most Americans recognized that the Soviet Union had borne the brunt of the war effort and deserved security against a recurrence of the suffering it had endured. But Americans refused to recognize that in Eastern Europe, at least, self-determination was incompatible with Stalin's view of Soviet security requirements. Freely elected governments might well turn out to be socialist — Labour after all won a great victory in Britain in 1945 — but they were almost certain to be anti-Soviet.[12] Instead of squarely facing this contradiction between American values and Soviet interests, the United States fell back on universalist prescriptions for peace: the new United Nations and free trade.[13] The Truman administration that came to office on Roosevelt's death in April 1945 justified continued American direct involvement in the affairs of Europe to a skeptical Congress and electorate by promising that it would end when the world organization and the open world economy were in place and functioning.

The Soviet leaders were just as determined to prevent another devastating war. But they had a radically different conception of the causes of the World War II, and thus of how it was to be prevented from recurring. Like the Americans, they believed that victory had vindicated their system. Ten years before Germany invaded, Stalin had warned that the Soviet Union had a decade to develop and militarize before an attack came from the West. Stalin's plan for development, carried out in the 1930s, called for extreme centralization of all decisionmaking and aspired to control every significant aspect the lives of 170 million citizens. This system had industrialized the country and mobilized its resources and, with the help of Mussolini's invasion of the Balkans, German mistakes, and Allied assistance, had sufficed to hold back and then roll back the Germans. The horrible costs of the war — 20 million unnatural Soviet deaths is the usual estimate — on top of the devastation of the 1930s added a desperate cast to the Soviet attachment to their system: It had to be correct in order to justify and give meaning to such tremendous bloodshed.

Like the Americans, Stalin wanted to continue cooperation among the victors into the postwar world, both to help in the rebuilding — for the United States was the only major country with resources to spare — and to prevent the resurgence of Germany. But whereas the Americans believed that state intervention in European economies had allowed Hitler to come to power, Stalin believed that the reason Nazi Germany had risen and nearly conquered Europe was that the capitalist system was dangerously weak. Capitalism spawned fascism, and then did not resist it when it came. Whatever the accuracy of this assessment, it allowed him to recognize, as Americans refused to recognize, that the more capitalist the countries of Eastern Europe were, the more unfriendly they were likely to be to the Soviet Union.

Many believe today that Stalin had a grand plan to extend his system integrally throughout the territory conquered by the Red Army, as this was indeed what happened by the late 1940s and early 1950s. It seems, on the evidence, that he had a broad goal of maximizing Soviet influence on the continent of Europe, that in pursuit of that goal he had minimum requirements, but that beyond those he had preferences rather than fixed goals and improvised as he went along in pursuit of those preferences. He clearly preferred as much control as he could possibly get, but his goal was maximum influence for the Soviet state in Europe rather than control per se, and he was willing to accept less than total control to get and maintain influence.[14] Division of Europe on a systemic basis and imposition of full Stalinism on the Soviet side of the continent were not part of either his minimum requirements or his preferences. He would have settled for less, or more. What he got resulted from adjustment to circumstances.

The minimum requirements were of two kinds. First, Stalin insisted on the restored tsarist borders he had negotiated with Hitler in 1939 and 1940, which placed all of Lithuania, Latvia and Estonia, and parts of Finland, Poland, and Romania within the Soviet Union. Finland had been completely within the old empire, and he would probably have absorbed it as well had the Finns not demonstrated the high cost of doing so in the winter war of 1939-40. Sometime during the war Stalin decided not to annex territory beyond the old tsarist borders, probably because the course of the war itself demonstrated conclusively that not only the Finns but the other peoples of the borderlands would make very unruly direct subjects.

The only exceptions were the Northern Bukovina, originally taken from Romania in 1940, and the extreme eastern province of Czechoslovakia, Subcarpathian Ruthenia, which the coalition government in Prague ceded without fuss in June 1945. Both had Ukrainian populations that Stalin probably felt could not be left outside the Soviet Ukraine without peril, so the concept of restoration holds.

Second, Stalin required "friendly" governments in Poland and Romania. They were the neighbors from whom he had taken the most territory, but partly as a result they had the weakest Communist parties in the region, and at the same time there were no good alternatives to Communists to engineer reliable "friendliness." Thus, extreme force had to be used to impose Communist rule, to break the back of the feckless bourgeoisies and bureaucracies that had allowed their countries to serve first as a cordon sanitaire against Soviet Russia and then as springboards or auxiliaries in Germany's attempt to conquer it. Elsewhere, Stalin was more flexible, willing to adjust to shifts in the policy of Western governments and the consensus of Western opinion.

Because the American and Soviet conceptions of the causes of and the remedies for European insecurity were very different, major friction within the wartime alliance was inevitable. The division of Europe was not.[15] To understand why it came about, we must explore the concrete difficulties that separated the wartime allies. The character of disagreements between the United States and the Soviet Union was disguised for a long time because both tended to postpone discussion of future political arrangements pending assured military victory. The ultimate effect of this delay was to equate military occupation and political influence.

Stalin feared that the Anglo-Americans would sign a separate peace with Germany. Until the Normandy invasion of June 1944, he was very careful to avoid giving them excuses to do so. He kept the Red Army within the Soviet borders he and Hitler had agreed to in 1939 and 1940 and meanwhile angled for deals with East European conservatives. After the victories at Stalingrad and Kursk, in 1943, he tried to contact conservative German resisters. Only when this effort failed did he subscribe to the American goal of unconditional German surrender. He dealt civilly with the king and generals who engineered Romania's reversal of alliances and fronts in August 1944 and was following the same pattern with Hungary's regent Miklós Horthy until the Germans occupied Hungary in October.[16]

The opening of the Second Front in Normandy produced a basic change in Stalin's approach. It assured both military victory over Hitler and American and British engagement in the postwar political destiny of the continent. As the United States continued to delay political decisions and began to promote the United Nations as a way of bridging the gap between indecision and the approaching future, Stalin began to use local Communists to assert control in Poland, the country where the war began. Because the vast majority of Poles were anti-Soviet, Stalin could trust only Communists to govern in a way he could accept, though he had to haul many of them out of Siberian prison camps.[17]

The contradiction between American support of self-determination and the Soviet security interests surfaced first in Poland, in the sharpest possible form. Six weeks after Normandy, the Soviets set up a puppet Communist government in the newly liberated southeastern city of Lublin. When Warsaw rose in August under instructions from the London-based Polish government-in-exile in order to liberate itself before the Soviets arrived, the Red Army, camped just across the Vistula River, refused to help. As the Germans destroyed what was left of Warsaw, the Western allies were shocked by the spectacle of Soviets allowing Germans to slaughter Poles. Those members of the U.S. political elite who were most suspicious of Soviet purposes saw their credibility strengthened as a result.

The status of Poland was only one of the important issues on the table before Churchill, Roosevelt, and Stalin at Yalta in February 1945. Others were Germany, the UN, and Soviet entry into the war against Japan. Tradeoffs across issues produced a compromise. The Polish government would be expanded to include a few members of the London government-in-exile, and the three leaders issued a universalistic, American-inspired "Declaration on the Peoples of Liberated Europe" that promised free elections everywhere. The Soviets, however, were to have sole responsibility for administering and observing elections in Poland. Stalin saw the declaration as a Soviet concession to American public opinion; Roosevelt saw it as a triumph of principle that could be played to the American people as evidence of the end of the balance of power in international politics.

After Yalta, the Soviets moved quickly to assert their control of Romania. In March 1945 they threw out the increasingly restive generals they had been dealing with since the previous August and imposed a Communist-dominated government, which the West then refused to recognize. In April Harry Truman became the U.S. president upon Roosevelt's death. He and his administration were convinced that tougher talk was needed to secure American interests. The Soviets were shocked by this abrupt change in American rhetoric. When they were then excluded from the confused negotiations in Switzerland over the surrender of the German forces in Italy, the Soviets responded with a series of faits accomplis in Poland, including a state-to-state Friendship Treaty with the still-unexpanded puppet government. Throughout the first half of 1945, then, mutual Soviet-American suspicion ratcheted upward.

Conventional military power is the most traditional and most generally accepted means states have of exerting influence. Under pressure from the American public, Roosevelt had discarded this means when he told Stalin that American soldiers would return home within two years. In preparing for the Potsdam Conference scheduled for June 1945, the Truman administration decided that because direct means of influencing the Soviets had not worked, it should try the indirect means at its disposal, the atom bomb and economics. But the threats were never spelled out, and this indirect approach probably hurt rather than helped. Paranoid and conspiratorial as he was, Stalin may well have taken insinuation more seriously than he would have taken frank threats. In any case, he pretended not to notice, and was entirely unwilling to respond positively. The U.S. approach smacked of the blackmail and ultimata the Soviets believed the West had used against their insecure state since it was founded in 1917. Both the United States and the Soviet Union recognized that the use of military force between them was out of the question, and for that reason probably overestimated their economic leverage. The United States thought the Soviet economy was so badly damaged that Stalin needed its help. Following Lenin's theory of imperialism, the Soviets believed that the United States needed access to overseas markets in order to dump surplus production and avoid postwar depression. In fact, many Americans wanted into the Soviet market, and many Soviets wanted American help, but neither government was willing to sacrifice other interests to make economic cooperation possible. Both had alternatives. The United States had its immense domestic market and Western Europe; the Soviet Union had state coercion and a nascent empire in Eastern Europe. The focus of Allied attention was shifting from Poland to Germany. At Potsdam in July 1945, the West recognized provisional Polish administration of the formerly German western territories, and the Soviets agreed that reparations would be taken by the Allies only from their own zones of occupation. In principle, the Allies continued to agree on the goal of joint management of united Germany, but that goal began to fade in practice. With the inclusion of France on May 1, 1945, they organized four zones of occupation in midyear, and Soviet German policy was thereby focused on trying to keep the non-Soviet zones from being integrated into the capitalist system. More and more, Eastern European issues were coming to be dealt with almost entirely as a function of other, larger issues, systemic expansion or systemic defense. After Potsdam, they were not even the main symbols of those larger issues. They were dealt with predictably, and provoked self-righteous outrage, but they engaged little energy and attention.

The year 1946 was a year of hardening postures on both sides, as each side prepared to go it alone economically.[18] Americans were by now thoroughly disillusioned with the Soviets. The Soviets were also disappointed, and actively prepared to extend direct control over every area they occupied, in case cooperation failed. In turn, this preparation increased American suspicions. George Kennan's "Long Telegram" from Embassy Moscow hit Washington in February of 1946, and in March Winston Churchill delivered his Iron Curtain speech in Fulton, Missouri. The arguments of Kennan and Churchill provided the theory that Soviet expansionism could be contained only by outside resistance. Containment did not immediately become U.S. policy. In parallel fashion, the Soviet theory of the "two camps" of imperialism and socialism began to appear in speeches and writings around this time. The "two camps" theory was also no more than ideology: It did not yet guide Soviet policy.[19]

The worst East-West frictions during 1946 were in the Middle East, not Europe. The Soviets were demanding from Turkey a role in policing the Dardanelles and withdrew their troops from Iran in early 1946 only after

a major East-West confrontation. Many in the West, and most particularly in the American government, now became convinced that Kennan's and
Churchill's theories of internally driven Soviet expansion described the
reality unrolling before their eyes.[20]

The American response was to lift high the banner of principle —
self-determination, free elections, and democracy — in Eastern Europe,
but to concentrate in practical policy on consolidating Western Europe
against the Soviet threat. The Communist takeover of Eastern Europe
proceeded, so it seemed, apace, with rigged elections, show trials, and the
pervasive spread of police terror. The United States tried to exert
counterpressure, but economic leverage did not work with the Soviets, and
it had very mixed results with the East Europeans.[21] The United States had
too little economic leverage to make a difference, and the main effect of
trying to use it was to increase suspicion.

The British announced in early 1947 that they could no longer afford
to support the independence of Greece and Turkey. In order to convince
Congress that the United States should assume this responsibility, President Truman felt obliged to espouse worldwide containment (the "Truman
Doctrine"). He thereby connected the ideology of containment to foreign
policy, at least at the declarative level. Still, the ideology lacked the
practical policy issue it needed to gain shape and form. The issue, as it
turned out, was the fate of Western Europe. Grappling with the postwar
economic crisis made it apparent that West European recovery would not
be possible without German recovery. Yet, without an American commitment to continued engagement in Europe, German recovery was still
politically unacceptable to France. Any French government that tolerated
the strengthening of Germany without such an American commitment
would fall, and probably to Communists. Soviet haggling over German
reparations convinced Secretary of State George Marshall that the Soviets
wanted to cripple West European recovery in order to subvert Western
Europe. Deputy Secretary Dean Acheson had been promoting bold action
in Europe, partly because Soviet Middle East policy had convinced him
of Soviet aggressiveness everywhere; and now Marshall came on board.

Unlike the Truman Doctrine, the Marshall Plan announced in June
1947 was not sold to the Congress as an anti-Communist program.
Instead, it was defined as a program for European economic recovery open

to the Soviet Union and Eastern Europe as well. It should be recalled that Americans had learned from the period between the world wars that economic failure is the main cause of radicalism. The purpose of the Marshall Plan, clear to all, was therefore to save Western Europe from a wave of economically induced political instability that would bring Soviet-style communism to power. The centerpiece of the Marshall Plan was its inclusion of the three Western zones of occupation in Germany.[22]

The Marshall Plan came as a powerful shock to Stalin. It showed that his effort to accrue influence in capitalist Western Europe had provoked a counterreaction and that his influence in the area under his direct control was weak. Czechoslovakia, Poland, Hungary, and Bulgaria initially accepted Marshall Plan aid, despite three years of successful Communist political struggle. The Marshall Plan also guaranteed that most of Germany would slip away into the capitalist camp. Stalin cracked the whip, and the acceptances of East European states were withdrawn.[23] At the founding meeting of the Cominform in September 1947, Stalin's ideology minister, Andrei Zhdanov, announced the new ideological model of international politics, the struggle between imperialist and socialist camps. That winter Stalinism began to be imposed in earnest in every aspect of life all over Eastern Europe.

The Communist assumption of power in Prague in February 1948 had many local causes, but it confirmed the Western thesis that Soviet expansionism would be limited only by outside resistance. In June 1948 the Western Allies announced a currency reform for the three Western zones of Germany. This step was the obvious precursor to the establishment of a new West German state, just as uniting East and West German currencies in 1990 was a natural prerequisite to German unification. To prevent a West German alliance with the West, the Soviets resorted to the only leverage they still had available to them, and blockaded the Western zones in Berlin. While there was some talk that summer of delaying economic integration of the Western zones if the Soviets lifted the blockade, by autumn the running of the blockade was so obviously successful that the West rallied to the containment thesis and the policy based on it. The lines of the Cold War were drawn.

Notes

1. These assessments and data on the destruction are drawn from the following works: in general, Hugh Seton-Watson, *East European Revolution*, 3rd ed. (New York: Praeger, 1956), chap. 9, and E.A. Radice, "Economic Developments in Eastern Europe/German Hegemony," in Martin McCauley, ed., *Communist Power in Europe, 1944-49* (New York: Barnes & Noble, 1977), 3-21; on the Balkans, John R. Lampe and Marvin R. Jackson, *Balkan Economic History, 1550-1950. From Imperial Borderlands to Developing Nations* (Bloomington: Indiana University Press, 1987), 520-575; on Yugoslavia, Dennison Rusinow, *The Yugoslav Experiment, 1948-1974* (London: C. Hurst, 1977), 18; Bogdan Denitch, *The Legitimation of a Revolution. The Yugoslav Case* (New Haven: Yale University Press, 1976), 84; and Joseph Rothschild, *Return to Diversity. A Political History of East Central Europe Since World War II* (New York: Oxford University Press, 1989), 57-58; and on Hungary, Iván Berend and György Ránki, *The Hungarian Economy in the Twentieth Century* (New York: St. Martin's, 1985), 72-75. Rusinow estimates that the average age of Yugoslavia's 1.7 million war dead (11 percent of the population) was twenty-two and that they included 90,000 skilled workers and 40,000 intellectuals. On Warsaw's losses in the uprising, generally estimated at 200,000 but rising to 250,000 and especially heavy among the young, see Joanna K.M. Hanson, *The Civilian Population and the Warsaw Uprising of 1944* (Cambridge: Cambridge University Press, 1982), 202-203, and Richard C. Lukas, *The Forgotten Holocaust. The Poles under German Occupation* (Lexington: University of Kentucky Press, 1986), 219. To break my own rule and cite a foreign-language source, Krzysztof Dunin-Wąsowicz estimates Warsaw's wartime losses at 685,000 killed and murdered and 180,000 allowed to die, out of a prewar population of 1.3 million, and 80 percent of the physical plant destroyed: *Warszawa w latach 1939-1945* (Warsaw: Państowe Wydawnictwo Naukowe, 1984), 370-371. Lukas (38-39) puts Poland's total losses at 6,028,000, half Jewish and half non-Jewish, and 90 percent civilian. On the Soviet massacre at Katyń and other sites, the Russian government has now published the "smoking gun," a Politburo decision dated 5 March 1940 and signed by Stalin, which calls for shooting 14,736 Polish officers and other officials in prisoner-of-war camps and 10,685 Poles in other places of detention. See Celestine Bohlen, "Russian Files Show Stalin Ordered Massacre of 20,000 Poles in 1940," *The New York Times*, 15 October 1992, and Andrew Nagorski, "At Last, a Victory for Truth," *Newsweek*, 26 October 1992, 41. At the same time, Jacques Rupnik very properly recalls that 5,000 Polish intellectuals were killed by the Gestapo in German-occupied Poland that same spring: *The Other Europe* (New York: Pantheon, 1988/9), 81.

2. On the role of Hranoiznos, see Lampe and Jackson, *Balkan Economic History*, 541-544.

3. Antony Polonsky, *Politics in Independent Poland. The Crisis of Constitutional Government* (Oxford: Clarendon Press, 1972), 38. On the life of these peasants, see Joseph Obrebski, *The Changing Peasantry of Eastern Europe* (Cambridge, Mass.: Schenkman Publishing, 1976), with photographs taken by the author in the 1930s; Louise Boyd, *Polish Countrysides* (New York: American Geographical Society, 1937), 53-85, with photographs; and on the politics of this ethnically mixed area, Stephen M.

Horak, "Belorussian and Ukrainian Peasants in Poland, 1919-1939: A Case Study in Peasantry Under Foreign Rule," in Ivan Völgyes, ed., *The Peasantry of Eastern Europe. Vol. 1: The Roots of Rural Transformation* (New York: Pergamon, 1979), 133-156.

4. On the changes in the minority situation, see Leszek A. Kosiński, "Changes in the Ethnic Structure of East-Central Europe, 1930-1960," *The Geographical Review*, 59, no. 3 (1969): 388-402 and Nicolas Spulber, *The Economics of Communist Eastern Europe* (Cambridge, Mass.: MIT Press/John Wiley, 1957), 29-33. On Poland, see John F. Besemeres, *Socialist Population Politics. The Political Implications of Ethnic Trends in the USSR and Eastern Europe* (White Plains, N.Y.: M.E. Sharpe, 1980), 128-130 with citations. C.A. Macartney describes the Greek-Turkish exchange of the early 1920s and, writing in a more civil time, dismisses it as an option for the rest of Europe: *National States and National Minorities* (London: Humphrey Milford/Oxford University Press, 1934), 430-450. Noting how Hitler's espousal of population exchange was turned against the Germans at war's end, Sir Lewis Namier concludes sardonically, "Hence their wrath:" "Basic Factors," in *Personalities and Powers* (New York: Macmillan, n.d. [1955]), 117. The Federal German Government has published massive documentation on the process in English as *Documents on the Expulsion of the Germans from Eastern-Central Europe* (Bonn: Federal Ministry for Expellees, Refugees and War Victims, n.d.), in several volumes. For specific figures on Poland, see Zbigniew Pelczynski in R.F. Leslie, ed., *The History of Poland Since 1863* (Cambridge: Cambridge University Press, 1980), 444-445.

5. Flora Lewis, *A Case History of Hope* (New York: Doubleday, 1958), 7, and Pelczynski in Leslie, *History of Poland*, 295, with citations.

6. As it does so often, contemporary literature conveys the confused moral urgency of the time better than most analysis. Examples: Adolf Rudnicki, "The Crystal Stream," in Maria Kuncewicz, ed., *The Modern Polish Mind* (London: Secker & Warburg, 1962), 123-144; Czesław Miłosz, *The Captive Mind* (New York: Vintage, 1981); C. Virgil Gheorghiu, *The Twenty-fifth Hour* (New York: Knopf, 1950); and one of my favorites, Eric Ambler, *Judgment on Deltchev* (New York: Knopf, 1951), the book that led to his break with the British Communist Party.

7. The strength of this dream can still be felt in retrospective personal accounts ranging from the tender to the bitter: Teresa Toránska, *Them: Stalin's Polish Puppets* (New York: Harper & Row, 1987); Sandor Kopacsi, *In the Name of the Working Class* (New York: Grove, 1987); Zdeněk Mlynář, *Nightfrost in Prague: The End of Humane Socialism* (New York: Karz, 1980); and, both tenderly and bitterly, part 2 of Milan Kundera's *The Joke* (New York: Harper & Row, 1982).

8. See Franz Schurmann, "Selections from the Logic of World Power," in Charles S. Maier, ed., *The Origins of the Cold War and Contemporary Europe* (New York: New Viewpoints, 1978), 60-61 and passim, for intriguing political analysis of American ideological dynamics in this period.

9. For the flavor of this particular aspect of the new postwar world, see Cornelius Ryan, *The Last Battle* (New York: Simon and Schuster, 1966), 484-493 and 520, and Erich Kuby, *The Russians and Berlin, 1945* (New York: Hill and Wang, 1968), 260-288.

10. For examples of such hopes among the Romanian elite, see Geir Lundestad, *The American Non-Policy Toward Eastern Europe, 1943-1947: Universalism in an Area Not of Essential Interest to the United States* (Tromso: Universitetsforlaget, 1978), 225-256.

11. I have found the following the most helpful accounts of the origins of the Cold War, and have drawn heavily on them in the summary that follows: Wilfried Loth, *The Division of the World, 1941-1955* (New York: St. Martin's, 1988); Vojtech Mastny, *Russia's Road to the Cold War* (New York: Columbia University Press, 1979); Lynn Etheridge Davis, *The Cold War Begins: Soviet-American Conflict over Eastern Europe* (Princeton, N.J.: Princeton University Press, 1974); Lawrence Aronsen and Martin Kitchen, *The Origins of the Cold War in Comparative Perspective* (New York: St. Martin's, 1988); Geir Lundestad's *The American Non-Policy Towards Eastern Europe*, the collection of essays edited by Charles S. Maier, *Origins of the Cold War and Contemporary Europe*, and Thomas Paterson, ed., *The Origins of the Cold War* (New York: Heath, 1991). Melvyn P. Leffler, *A Preponderance of Power. National Security, The Truman Administration, and the Cold War* (Stanford, Calif.: Stanford University Press, 1992), now gives us a massive and detailed study of the U.S. side of the emerging equation. In addition, William Hyland, *The Cold War is Over* (New York: Times Books, 1990) is idiosyncratic, like this work, but (it is hoped like this work) studded with insights.

12. In a September 1943 memo, Polish party ideologist Alfred Lampe asked "What kind of Poland would not be anti-Soviet?" and his answer was bleak indeed: Rupnik, *The Other Europe*, 85. Or, as Stalin asked Czechslovak President Beneš in December 1943, "Where can one find any Poles one could talk to?": Mastny, *Russia's Road to the Cold War*, 138; see 167ff. on his efforts to find some.

13. This is the main point of Lundestad's work, *American Non-Policy Toward Eastern Europe*.

14. This is Mastny's main point in *Russia's Road to the Cold War*, closely argued on the basis of the maximum/minimum distinction.

15. This is Loth's main point in *Division of the World*.

16. On Soviet contacts with the Germans in the summer of 1943, see Mastny, *Russia's Road to the Cold War*, 73-85; on their dealings with the Romanians and Hungarians in the fall of 1944, *ibid.*, 195-207.

17. Roman Werfel in Torańska, *Them: Stalin's Polish Puppets*, 107.

18. For a sense of what it meant to be a participant, see W.W. Rostow, *The Division of Europe after World War II: 1946* (Austin: University of Texas Press, 1981).

19. An intriguing if still necessarily speculative argument in the scholarly literature is that in this period Stalin felt obliged to reconstitute the party — which he had effectively destroyed in the purges — in order to overcome the independence of the military and the population he had had to tolerate to win the war. Reconstituting the party meant allowing a new surge of revolutionary fervor and a modicum of tolerance for promotion of separate roads to socialism by the East European parties. This suggestion was first put forward systematically by William D. McCagg, *Stalin Embattled 1943-1948* (Detroit: Wayne State University Press, 1978), and it is of course controversial: see Werner G. Hahn, Jr., *Postwar Soviet Policy: The Fall of Zhdanov and the Defeat of Moderation, 1946-53* (Ithaca, N.Y.: Cornell University Press, 1982) versus Gavriel D. Ra'anen, *International Policy Formation in the USSR. Factional "Debates" during the Zhdanovschina* (Hamden, Conn.: Anchor Books, 1983), and in relation to the Tito-Stalin split, Ivo Banac, *With Stalin Against Tito: Cominformist Splits in Yugoslav Communism* (Ithaca, N.Y.: Cornell University Press, 1988), 24-28. For a summary, see Jerry F. Hough, "Debates about the Postwar World," in Susan J. Linz, ed., *The Impact of World War II on the Soviet Union* (Totowa, N.J.: Rowman and Allanheld, 1985), 253-281.

20. On the significance of the Middle East, see Loth, *Division of the World*, 105-134, and Hyland, *Cold War is Over*, 25-56.

21. See "Attempts to Use Economic Leverage and Their Limits," in Lundestad, *American Non-Policy*, 379-408.

22. On these developments, see John Gimbel's fine *The Origins of the Marshall Plan* (Stanford: Stanford University Press, 1976). In the end, the Marshall Plan injected $12 billion, or about 2 percent of the recipient countries' Gross Domestic Products, over four years. The equivalent in today's dollars would be perhaps $180 billion, but the equivalent four-year G.D.P. contribution for Eastern Europe would be only $20 billion: Lawrence Summers, "The Next Decade in Central and Eastern Europe," in Christopher Clague and Gordon C. Rausser, eds., *The Emergence of Market Economies in Eastern Europe* (Cambridge, Mass. and Oxford: Blackwell, 1992), 31.

23. In his long retirement, then Soviet Foreign Minister Vyacheslav Mikhailovich Molotov once gave a vivid account of calling the East Europeans off the Marshall Plan after initial hesitation: see Woodford McClellan, "Molotov Remembers," *Cold War International History Project Bulletin* (Washington, D.C.: Woodrow Wilson International Center for Scholars), no. 1 (Spring 1992), 20.

FOUR

HIGH STALINISM: TRIAL BY ICE

W hen they looked out at the world the war left behind, in 1944 and 1945, some East Europeans dreamed of escaping their ruinous historic dependence through American-sponsored liberal democracy and the market, others through Soviet-sponsored social revolution; but most were more practical, and threw themselves into the task of reconstruction through state-led industrialization. There was intense political struggle over which ideology and which people should direct the process, but very little over the basic goal of creating industry rapidly.[1]

Yet this consensus brought with it its own acute dilemma. Every state in Eastern Europe was short of the capital that industrialization required. Much of what little industrial plant there had been was destroyed by the war, or was being carried away by the Soviets, and the Soviet Union was intent on tapping into the region's resources for its own reconstruction and development. Because the Soviets clearly had neither any interest in providing capital nor the capacity to do so, Eastern Europe was forced to choose between two alternatives.[2] Either the region's countries could draw from their own resources, using the state to direct saving and investment, or they could borrow from the West, which meant the Americans, who were the only westerners with resources to spare.

If they chose bootstrap industrialization — rapid industrialization without access to outside resources — Soviet Stalinism was the one working model. It had actually been tried next door and was still going strong. Between 1944 and 1948 Stalinism was in most places (Bulgaria and

Yugoslavia were the exceptions) no more than an option. Stalin continued to hope for Western cooperation and aid, and knew that Eastern European countries were going to be difficult to control. Moreover, these countries were used to capitalist economics and already had higher living standards than the Soviet Union. Soviet central planning already had its hands full running the Soviet economy; it had no mechanisms for directing and adjusting the economic development of economies at different levels.[3]

So in this period Stalin permitted a variety of interim economic approaches. Both in the states dominated by Communists during this period — Poland, Yugoslavia, Romania, and Bulgaria — and in those where Communists had only considerable influence — Hungary and Czechoslovakia — there was substantial freedom to set economic policy, within the consensus calling for state-directed reconstruction through industrialization.

Nowhere except Yugoslavia was full Stalinization the objective of economic policy. Everywhere all parties in the early postwar coalitions, Communists and non-Communists, supported land reform, nationalization of large industry, and planning for reconstruction that would recoup war losses and lay the groundwork for further industrial expansion.[4] Compared to what came later, these were modest goals. East European Communists who wanted more believed that they could afford to wait. Raging inflation continued to punish the middle classes that were already so damaged by the war, and meanwhile they expected the growth of industry through reconstruction and development to enlarge their pool of political support by expanding the working class. While some sectarian Communists fully expected to go beyond these minimum goals to full Stalinization, other Communists sincerely believed that beyond these minima the economic future was open.

Both land reform and nationalization were directed not only toward consensus economic goals, but in the first instance and wherever possible toward ethnic national goals. It is true that many believed that distributing land above a certain acreage to the peasants and bringing industry under central government control without compensation would produce more economic efficiency. This appeal to efficiency was uncertain; what was not uncertain for new coalition governments needing support was the desire of the peasant majorities for land and the desire of majority populations to see minorities punished. Much of the distributed land and many of the nationalized businesses had previously belonged to Germans and Hungarians. Immediately after the war, Czechoslovakia, Poland, and Romania took over ex-German properties, and Yugoslavia those of both Germans and collaborators, in order to avoid paying compensation. Where remnants of landed nobility still existed as a political force, as in Hungary and to some extent in Poland, land reform was also designed to end their influence.

Whether they dominated the governments or shared power with others, Communists could take some credit for policies that were popular on national grounds. This helped them to diminish the aura of aliens, of stooges arriving from Moscow in the baggage of the Red Army. Beyond that, however, both land reform and nationalization had mixed political results. Because land reform was a consensus policy in these coalition governments, peasant gratitude was spread around. Where the Communists directly administered land reform, as in the new Polish western territories divvied up by Party General Secretary Władislaw Gomułka (as vice premier), they gained some support from the beneficiaries. But the peasant parties in the coalitions were generally even more radical on land reform than the Communists, and also profited politically.[5]

When the first reconstruction plans were put into effect in most countries in 1946 (the Romanian plan was not introduced until 1948, because the Romanians were not very skilled managers, and the Soviets were wreaking havoc with their economy), all had Stalinist elements, such as strengthened central planning, extensive nationalization, and restricted consumption. Investment as a percentage of national income reached new heights: 20 percent in Poland, 16 percent in Czechoslovakia, 9 percent in Hungary, and 7 percent in Bulgaria. Britain, with twice the per-capita income of the average East European country, invested 22 percent in 1948.[6] But the reconstruction plans still assumed private small manufacturing, private services, and (except for Bulgaria, a land of small farms and fanatical Communists where collectivization of agriculture started early) private agriculture. Like the political results, therefore, the economic recipes were mixed.

And in these first postwar years the second alternative — industrialization using Western help — did not seem chimerical. Poland and Czechoslovakia, which were wartime allies, succeeded in tapping considerable Western resources. They received the bulk of the relief aid channeled through the United Nations Relief and Rehabilitation Agency (UNRRA), largely funded by the United States, to the tune of $1 billion (about $15 billion in 1992 dollars) before the program lapsed in 1947. They were also in a position to trade effectively with the West: Poland's coal supplied 15 percent of Western Europe's needs in 1946, and Czechoslovakia could sell industrial products.[7]

Nevertheless, the Americans did favor the free market, and as East-West struggle gradually replaced wartime cooperation, the pattern of their actual behavior slowly showed that they would not aid states that ostentatiously preferred statism to the free market. In southeastern Europe, Bulgaria, Hungary, and Romania, as former enemies, could hardly expect American largesse whatever they did, but Yugoslavia had been a wartime ally, and like Poland and Czechoslovakia it received a great deal of UNRRA aid. So it was a kind of test case. But it was governed by the most radical Communist regime in the area, and it embarked on a radical course in politics and economics that began to alienate the West and to shrink aid levels already in 1945. So when Poland and Czechoslovakia fell into disfavor too, the second option — industrialization using Western capital — teetered on the brink of oblivion.

It was the nationalization of industry, or rather its emergence as a political issue in the East-West struggle, that pushed the Western option for industrialization over the brink. Nationalization was no more politically controversial at home in Eastern Europe than land reform, but unlike land reform, it was not approved by the West. This reproval was not simply ideological, or a result of Western identification with the East European middle classes. After all, France and Britain nationalized extensively in this period without ceasing to be close American allies. The crux of the matter was that nationalization in Eastern Europe struck at existing Western investment, and especially at those Western-owned enterprises the Germans had taken over. For instance, in prewar Poland Western companies had owned 52 percent of the mining and metallurgical industries, 87.5 percent of oil extraction, 60 percent of the chemical industry and 81.3% of electricity production. Even in 1946, 51 percent of the Romanian oil industry was owned by Anglo-Dutch firms, 11 percent by

Americans, and 28 percent by Soviet-Romanian joint companies whose Soviet share was confiscated German capital. In 1946, 1947, and 1948 the nationalizing governments delayed compensation, just as the Western countries delayed economic assistance. In the deteriorating political atmosphere of the time, the issues of compensation for nationalized property and the provision of Western economic assistance inevitably became linked and politicized.[8] This linkage reinforced those on both sides who were convinced that the other side was engaged in systemic expansion. The polarization of opinion eroded away any political basis for U.S. aid, and this in turn made the East European governments more willing and even eager to nationalize. And it was through this process that their options for development shrank from two to one: They would have to industrialize from their own resources.

The upshot was to relink practical development to the struggle of desperate dreams. If Stalinism was the one working economic model for bootstrap industrialization, it was also much larger than economics. It was part of a coherent, if terrifying, larger system, and adopting its economics would clearly have drastic general consequences throughout society in each country. Stalinism meant revolution.

This was because Stalinism destroyed underdeveloped economies from above, by design and by force, in order to save them. Rapid, heavy industrialization was the first goal of economic Stalinism, to which everything else was geared. This sort of industrialization requires massive influxes of capital, which in Eastern Europe seemed to be in permanent short supply. To generate this capital, Stalinism would starve consumption and collectivize agriculture. Also, the Soviets at this time believed that planned industrialization should be managed not by traditional elites but by new elites drawn from the working class. As the East European working class was even weaker than the middle class, it would have to be created from the peasant majority. Political, social and cultural revolution were therefore necessary preconditions for success of the Soviet economic approach. East Europeans did not have to imagine this sequence of causes: they had observed it in the Soviet Union of the 1930s.

Stalinism was sure to hit the newly empowered, newly nationalized peasantries especially hard. The peasant way of life was the primary obstacle to Communist economic development, so under Stalinism peasants would lose their freedom and their land. But the oppressive implications of Stalinist economics extended to all Eastern Europeans, not only the peasants. Stalinism necessitated a closed economy in which human resources, like all others, are completely subject to central control. For example, consumer goods would not (to say the least) be available upon demand. Prices would reflect the preferences of planners, not the market. All sources of wealth, including foreign trade, would be controlled by the state. Total control of all economic resources meant that there would be no more private sector, no more private manufacturers, service people, or farmers. The private sphere, as such, would be abolished at worst, illegitimate but tolerated at best. Such a degree of control could be achieved only by a coercive dictatorship backed by a strong and ubiquitous internal security apparatus.

Most East European countries agreed that democratizing social changes and substantial industrialization under state auspices were the keys to escaping from backwardness and weakness. Stalinism divided democracy and industrialization and forced East Europeans to choose between them. The Stalinist recipe for industrialization required that politics be subsumed by economics, that significant private economic decision makers be eliminated. It required the substitution of the state for society, the reality of minority rule for the hope of democratic majority rule. East Europeans were long accustomed to authoritarian rule by self-selecting bureaucracies, but their previous experience with authoritarianism had been with what an Austrian Social Democrat once called "despotism tempered by anarchy," [9] which left most people to strive and suffer alone. Stalinism would end anarchy and require very real despotism. On the other hand, New Deal liberalism, though very appealing ideologically, began to recede to the category of mere dream. The appropriate dictum was Chou En Lai's "Distant water does not put out fires," the appropriate analogy Porfirio Diaz's "Poor Mexico: so far from God, so close to the United States of America."

Left to their own devices, East Europeans mounted a fierce native resistance, and it naturally centered on the newly empowered and newly nationalized peasant majorities. In the early postwar coalitions it was the peasant parties, armed with a refurbished agrarian ideology, that provided the most coherent political alternatives to the (even more coherent)

Stalinist Communists.[10] They were included in the postwar coalitions everywhere in the region except Yugoslavia and the Czech lands. They were naturally the strongest element in the consensus for land reform. In Poland, Hungary, Romania, and Bulgaria, the historic peasant parties gained power in alliance with the Communists and the Social Democrats. The powerful Democratic Party in Slovakia was essentially a peasant party, drawing its support from the Catholic countryside. By agreement among the Allies, the Czech Agrarians and the most strongly nationalist parties in the other countries were excluded from politics on the ground that they had collaborated with the Germans or the authoritarian pro-German regimes. This outside intervention into regional politics inadvertently helped to fuse agrarianism and nationalism. Though some of the newly unaffiliated conservatives and nationalists joined the Communists, believing that they would gain power, most moved into the peasant parties. Centrist and democratic before the war, the peasant parties now formed the right wing of each postwar coalition.

The agrarian concept of development treated the East European countries as if they were peasant villages, writ large. Like peasants, the countries of Eastern Europe were excruciatingly dependent on outside forces. The peasant parties applied the principle of self-sufficiency, learned in the village, to the nation. The agrarians supported a third way between capitalism and communism, which would give the land to those who tilled it; introduce a degree and kind of industrialization that would process agricultural products, provide farming machinery, and give jobs to their underemployed sons and daughters; and establish a democratic political system that would maximize their voting leverage and open up education and administration to peasants. The peasant parties were also very attached to private property, and therefore hostile to the public ownership and public direction of economic development that were essential to the brand of industrialization that most others favored.

This agrarian vision of gradual development under private auspices for the advantage of the peasant majority was very potent in the immediate postwar years for three reasons. It had the new support of conservatives and nationalists, it seemed to combine the two goals of industrialization and democracy, and it suggested a way out for exhausted populations increasingly frightened as the East-West ideological struggle heated up and economic options narrowed to the stark choice between the unreality of the free market and the perfect reality of Stalinist terror.

Such were the Communists' main competitors. Though the peasant program for development is fairly clear, it is difficult, even in retrospect, to define the goals of local Communists. At the height of the Cold War, after they had achieved political dominance in each government and tight centralized government control of each economy, and after all the East European countries had become imitations of the Soviet Union, it seemed that these accomplishments had been planned from the outset and that the decision to carry out full Stalinization had been tempered only by their hope for Western aid and their desire to reduce domestic resistance as much as possible by clever tactics. But this was not at all clear at the time, and perhaps not even to the Communists.

Hugh Seton-Watson has identified three stages of varying lengths in the assertion of Communist rule: real coalitions, with real power-sharing; bogus coalitions, dominated in fact by Communists even though other parties were still formally in government; and total control. In the first stage, the Communists co-opted as many Social Democrats as they could into an alliance of urban forces based on a program of state-directed nationalization and reconstruction. They directed the alliance against the peasant parties by identifying them with the reactionary, nationalist past and with the region's historic dependence on foreign capital and foreign economic and political models. They insisted that the agrarians were front men for bankrupt nationalist reaction and by the end of 1947 had broken them everywhere. Then, in the second stage, the Communists turned on their Social Democratic allies, drove those they could convert into unified socialist parties and those they could not out of politics, and often into prison. This stage was completed by the end of 1949. In the third stage, the Communist purged themselves and became full Stalinist parties unconditionally devoted to the Soviet model and Soviet orders. In this schema Poland and Yugoslavia skipped the first stage, because their coalitions were never real, and Czechoslovakia skipped the second, for it passed abruptly from a true coalition to total Communist control in February 1948. Seton-Watson's model is quite descriptive and is likely to have a long scholarly life.[11]

While the model describes what happened in retrospect, it does not explain the actual sequence of events except by implicit reference to a common plan. The record has been difficult to uncover, for the archives, long closed or incomplete, are just beginning to open up in the post-Communist period and many of the most important players are in any case dead or dying. Nevertheless, enough has surfaced over the years to satisfy me that there was in fact no single blueprint for the area. A theory with real explanatory power must therefore account for variation as it searches for the verifiable common denominators of Communist intentions and strategies in Eastern Europe. And the two most important variables appear to me to have been direct Soviet strategic interests and the strength and trustworthiness of the local Communist parties, as the Soviets judged them.

Stalin was determined to dominate the two countries with the weakest Communist parties in the region, Poland and Romania. The Romanian Communist party had fewer than one thousand members, and the Polish Communist party was only slightly larger in proportion to total population. Both parties drew heavily from the countries' Jewish minorities; both had been severely weakened by the purges of the 1930s (the Polish Party had even been abolished, and was reconstituted under another name only during the war); and yet their defense of Soviet policy under the Molotov-Ribbentrop Pact had reinforced the conviction of almost all their compatriots that they were mere coteries of Soviet agents. Because Stalin regarded Poland and Romania as strategically important, he had to impose their rule for lack of alternatives, to impose it by force because they were so weak, and then to find ways to strengthen them in their domestic political battles. In March of 1945, as the Soviets replaced the uneasy coalition that had ruled Romania since the coup of August 23, 1944, with an unambiguously Communist-dominated one under Petru Groza, they also resolved the Hungarian-Romanian struggle over who deserved Transylvania more in favor of the Romanians. And at Potsdam in June, the negotiations among the wartime allies were paralleled by invisible but equally urgent negotiations between Stalin and his Polish Communist clients over which Neisse River branch to claim for Poland's new western border, with Stalin sticking (successfully) to the Western Neisse in response to their desperate pleas on internal political grounds.[12]

The Polish Communists used their new western territories as a patronage plum to gain some support among the repatriates from now-Soviet eastern Poland whom they settled there. The Romanian Communists wasted their chance by going out of their way to favor the Hungarian minority in Transylvania. While the Poles embarked on the path of extending their support where they could, the Romanians remained the sectarian and extremist minority they had always been. Though the Romanian and Polish Communists were treated similarly by the Soviets, the differences in their character pushed them in different directions as the Soviets helped them to power. Much has happened since then, but the seeds of the contrast of 1989 — Polish willingness to negotiate, albeit with Soviet support, and Romanian monolithic unity under Ceaușescu to the bitter end, albeit against the Soviets — had already been planted.[13]

Hungary is a different case, for strategically it was not very important to the Soviets, and its Communists achieved power with less Soviet help. Hungary had doubled in size between 1938 and 1941, absorbing territory in Ruthenia, Slovakia, and Transylvania, and it was something of a reluctant German ally until March 1944, when Germany occupied the country and replaced its government. Even then the Horthy regime continued to dicker for a separate peace, until the Germans closed it down in October and ran the country through local fascists. Hungary's energies were then placed fully at the service of Germany, and this went on well into 1945, when Stalin offered a coalition of generals and all major political parties called the National Independence Front as a provisional government. The Soviets protected their interests in Hungary by annexing Ruthenia from Czechoslovakia in October 1944 (compensating Czechoslovakia by ordering the Polish army out of Teschen at the same time) in order to create a common border and by keeping troops in Hungary, ostensibly to safeguard the lines of communication to their occupation zone in neighboring Austria. At least initially, these measures were enough to satisfy Stalin. He was willing to give Transylvania to the Romanians and willing to watch the Hungarian Communists be thrashed by a peasant party, the Smallholders, in free elections in October and November 1945.

The Hungarian party was very small, with fewer than 2,500 members in 1944. It was also overwhelmingly Jewish in a country where politics had traditionally revolved around the tension between modern, capitalist,

Jewish Budapest and the depressed Christian countryside, represented in Hungary's intelligentsia-dominated politics by a particularly strong, self-conscious agrarian populism, and it was politically burdened by its association with the Bela Kun Communist dictatorship of 1919, in which several of its current luminaries had held minor posts. But even after Hungarian Communist leader Mátyás Rákosi was summoned to Moscow following his electoral defeat, his party moved only slowly and carefully over the next two years to assume full control. Throughout this period the Soviets told the Hungarian Communists that Hungarian freedom was necessary compensation for Polish slavery, and that Hungary could expect to reach socialism in ten or fifteen years' time.

Aware of its weaknesses, the Hungarian party was extremely subtle in its tactics to destroy the Smallholders between 1945 and 1947. Here too the Soviets provided some tactical assistance. To avoid stiff reparations, Smallholder president Zoltán Tildy accepted purges of his party and Communist control of the police. In May 1947 the Soviets seized the Smallholder leader Béla Kovács and claimed that his crimes implicated Prime Minister Ferenc Nagy, who then resigned. In 1948 all major non-Communist parties were dissolved or merged into the Communist party, and in May 1949 thoroughly rigged elections produced an announced 95.6 percent approval rate for a single-candidate list. Despite this tactical dexterity, however, the Hungarian Communists were extremely sectarian. This sectarianism showed when full Stalinism descended on the country at the end of the 1940s, for Hungary then became the most brutally repressive country in the bloc. In late 1949, for example, the party's ranking "home Communist," László Rajk, and 2,000 other Communists were executed, 150,000 were imprisoned, and 350,000 were expelled from the party. The reaction came in October 1956, when the original party simply disintegrated.[14]

Bulgaria and Czechoslovakia were also of only moderate strategic importance to the Soviets. The Red Army left Czechoslovakia in December 1945 and Bulgaria in late 1947. In Czechoslovakia, moreover, Stalin had in President Eduard Beneš a model non-Communist Soviet ally, a man determined to make his country work in harmony with the USSR. Czechoslovakia was the most, and Bulgaria the least, industrialized of the countries in the region. But they were similar to each other, and different from Hungary, in that they had the area's strongest Communist parties.

The Czechoslovak party operated legally before the war and had over a million members in 1946. The Bulgarian party had over half as many members as the Polish in a country a quarter Poland's size, and had managed to keep about 10,000 partisans under arms against the Bulgarian government during the war.

In these two countries, the Soviets could afford to allow the local Communists to compete for political power with their own resources. The differences between the two parties surfaced during this competition. Bulgaria has a particularly brutal tradition of politics, in which the Communists fully share. Ruthless purging of the opposition began in the fall of 1944 and continued well into 1945. Tens of thousands were killed. Led by Georgi Dimitrov, the Bulgarian Communists were especially savage in breaking the Agrarian Union, a peasant party that emerged as their strongest competition. The process finished with the judicial murder of the Agrarian leader Nikola Petkov in late 1947. Petkov had been encouraged by the United States to compete with the Communist-led government and had much popular support. While they were still waiting for a peace treaty and diplomatic recognition from the Americans, the Bulgarian Communists had left Petkov relatively in peace. When the U.S. Senate ratified the peace treaty in June 1947, he was arrested on the floor of the parliament and hanged on September 23. The United States extended diplomatic recognition scarcely a week later.[15]

The Soviets were practically invisible in the Bulgarian takeover. The same was true in Czechoslovakia, but otherwise the Communist accession to power was very different. The Czech Communists were the largest party in the country, and received a plurality of 38 percent of the vote in the 1946 free elections. As the main party in government, they were naturally blamed for the government's perceived mistakes or inadequacies, and began to lose support in 1946 and 1947. Between the summer of 1947 and February 1948, the Czech Communists were driven left by rising East-West tensions and domestic difficulties. By the time Cominform was founded in September 1947, the French and Italian Communist parties had been dropped from their governments, Marshall Plan aid had been offered to Europe, and the prospects for U.S.-Soviet cooperation in Europe were dim. At the first Cominform meeting, the Czechs were fiercely criticized by Stalin's ideological chief Andrei Zhdanov for not answering the question of power, and this helped radicalize them. But they radicalized not only to please the Soviets but also to keep ahead of their accelerating loss of popularity.

In late 1947 they authorized the Communist minister of the interior to remove non-Communists from the the police apparatus. He continued the purges after being instructed to stop by the majority of the non-Communist ministers on February 18, 1948. On February 20 the Slovak Democrats, Czech Populists, and National Socialists resigned from their ministries, believing that the Social Democrats would join them and force Beneš to form a new government. In the worst case, they believed, Beneš would simply not accept their resignations. The Social Democrats did not join in, and Beneš accepted the resignations of the other ministers, leaving the Communists solidly in control. Communist Prime Minister Klement Gottwald, who during the interwar period told fellow members of the Czechoslovak parliament that "we go to Moscow to learn from the Russian Bolsheviks how to wring your necks," proved to be an apt student.[16] But it was Beneš's failure of nerve that decided the issue. The president who had watched his nation abandoned at Munich allowed his country to fall once again into foreign oppression ten years later.[17]

With the singular exception of Romania, Bulgaria and Czechoslovakia were the last East European states to reform in 1989. Just as domestic political support had helped them to power, it probably helped them resist, for a time, the rising demand for political change. Lacking similar domestic support in the postwar years, other local Communists were forced to rely more on the Soviets in their struggle for power. The working classes of which they considered themselves the revolutionary vanguard were small and Social Democratic. That was why, after allying with Social Democrats to crush the agrarians, the Communists proceeded in 1948 and 1949 to force the Social Democrats into unified workers' parties. The absence of a major peasant party in the Soviet zone of occupied Germany was not the major reason why this merger was completed there in 1946, but it was one reason.[18] Generally, the Communists picked up as much support as they could by splitting the other parties in their coalitions and by spearheading land reform and nationalization of industry, nationally popular programs directed against the Germans. The effort of East European Communists to appeal to nationalism was perhaps one reason among many why Stalin felt these parties needed purging.

None of these efforts were convincing to very many people. Stalin once said that introducing communism in Poland was like putting a saddle on a cow[19]; nationalist slogans and Soviet-backed governments fit together about as gracefully. Still, East Europeans knew by this time that communism was a very likely part of their future, and the Communists gained some mass support. But everyone knew that the Communists were minorities imposed by an outside power and that their imposition was the cause of civil war.

The Communists knew that to end the civil wars and begin development, to shift from violence to persuasion, they would have to appeal to the traditional definers of national goals, the intelligentsia. They did not refrain from using violence against members of the intelligentsia, but they had other forms of persuasion as well. Many Communists were themselves intellectuals, able to sell their politics as high culture: Communism claimed to be the historic last term of the Western rationalist tradition, yet it also presented a tempting metaphysic. It had tamed history and reduced destiny to a science, and this had strong appeal to dependent intellectuals in these dependent societies. Intellectuals here had often defined themselves as caretakers of the national soul on behalf of the masses, and the Communists could put unprecedented state power at the disposal of those willing to cooperate; under communism, moreover, that power could be used to provide justice and social development, and thereby build new national strength and independence over time. Communists could transmute the lead of the intelligentsia's traditional isolation from the masses into the gold of triumphant governance with the masses, if intellectuals were radical and faithful enough.[21]

The intensity of the struggle for the minds of intellectuals extended to all of politics and carried the realm of politics into the realm of faith. The destruction and confusion of the war years cut many traditional links to the outside world and to inner values, and made them all the more precious for that reason. And now the postwar world brought East Europeans not the restoration of those links, not the relief of normality, but continuation of destruction and confusion. It brought wild, daily oscillations among ideals, low cunning and high heroism, compromise and sacrifice, national independence and national subservience, all for high, often deadly stakes. The Communist brand of political competition drove postwar politics toward a choice between chaos and order, and the starkness of this choice produced both exhilaration and despair.[22] The memory of that confusion and sacrifice — the desire to reverse it, to justify it, to preserve it, or to eliminate its results — is stamped on all those who lived through it. As the family is the East European institution that has best survived the ravages of this century, this memory has been impressed upon their children, and their children's children.

Stalinism's economics, politics, and intentions were imposed so violently and so thoroughly that they have permeated the whole area ever since.[23] These origins were fitting, for political dictatorship was required to make economic Stalinism work. The coercion and strict limitation of private life feared by those who had opposed communism now became a reality. In theory, Stalinism gave all power to the people, who exercised it through their elected councils, called soviets. This imported theoretical system, which did not describe the reality of power in the Soviet Union, corresponded to the reality of East European practice far less even than Western democracy had between the wars. Most East Europeans opposed communism, and the working classes that the Communists expected to provide support were small. By Communist reasoning, governing bodies elected by populations that were not dominated by the working class were bound to make incorrect decisions. They would vote against history. In practice, therefore, they substituted the party for the working class that they hoped would emerge from industrialization.

Thus, political power was monopolized by the party, and its leadership was chosen not by election but by the Soviets and itself for its superior knowledge and understanding of the direction of history. Power was centralized within the party, devolving into the hands of three or four or a dozen men in each country, led by the famous "Little Stalins." Communists tried to close the wide gap between theory (rule by a working-class population) and reality (rule by self-selecting elites) by propagating the myth of the monolithic, all-wise, and all-powerful Party.[24] Just as nationalism had served to lessen the alienation of the nineteenth-century intelligentsia, the myth of the party served to convince party members that they were parts of the peoples they ruled.

But party rule necessitated political dependence on the Soviet Union. The opposition of most of the populations was intense, and even the parties were in danger of infection, given the extravagant hypocrisy of their role in society.

These dangers were met by police violence, which sought to create an atomized society in which every subject, alone, faced the overwhelming power of the socialist state. Such police rule depended, first, on experienced Soviet advisors, who set up and ran the internal security forces and, second, on the presence of the Red Army and/or the threat of its intervention. Direct political dependence on the Soviets was reinforced by the economic dependence created by Stalinist industrialization within closed economies cut off from the West. Until 1956 the Soviet Union took many more resources out of Eastern Europe than it put in, but that was not the essential point. The key to Eastern Europe's economic dependence was that Stalinist industrialization concentrated on building steel industries, the sinews of power in the late nineteenth and early twentieth centuries. Steel is made from iron ore and hard coal; none of the East European countries had much iron, and none except Poland and to a lesser extent Czechoslovakia had hard coal. With the area cut off from Western resources by the Cold War, the Soviets were the only available source of these raw materials.

The ties between the countries of the area were almost entirely bilateral, and they were mainly between each and the Soviet Union. Just as the East European regimes wanted their subjects to face the power of the state alone, so Stalin preferred to deal with each of them one by one. The East European leaders had very few ties with each other to begin with, and the purging that followed the 1948 Tito-Stalin split further reduced contact between them by warning of the danger of guilt by association. The so-called Soviet bloc that formed was, as one economic analyst has put it, like a wheel with very thick spokes to the Soviet axle, but practically no rim.[25] This system of relations, consisting of East European states separated from each other but politically and economically dependent on the Soviet Union, found its ideological expression not in internationalist socialism but in the idealization of everything Soviet, and indeed of everything Russian. This ideology culminated in the adulation of Stalin himself, as if all history had funneled up into this single man.[26]

Speaking of Stalinism in terms of structure may give the misleading impression that the purpose of Stalinism was order. Stalinism was no more conservative than Nazism had been. It was directed toward a better future rather than a better past, and as it conceived that future as the end of history, it was thus entirely oriented toward dynamism. Hitler and Stalin both believed that progressive change required conflict. Stalin used a language of fronts, of storming, of war against the remnants of the feudal and bourgeois pasts. To Marx's analysis of class conflict, he added the theory that the class struggle becomes more desperate as the proletariat approaches victory, as the losers become frantic in their effort to hold off the inevitable. The theory justified the pervasive violence not just against the visible class enemy outside but against the insidious and cunning class enemy threatening the Stalinist parties themselves from within.[27] This psychology of warfare fed on growing fears that the Cold War would turn hot, and those fears turned to near panic after the Korean War began in June 1950. Thereafter, the industrialization campaign in Eastern Europe was geared on Stalin's orders to military production. Accelerating requirements for economic production in these already desperately stretched economies coincided with the worst of the party purges.

Stalinism was not simply a defensive war against the past and the subversive outside world. It was mainly a war of transformation within each country. The Stalinists were determined to bring Eastern Europe up to the forefront of history, by persuasion when they could, by force when they had to. Their particular understanding of the workings of history was the philosophical basis of their plan to master it through economic development. Generally, historical determinism and prescriptive philosophy do not mix well. If the course of history is fixed, so are the actions and choices of individuals. Freedom becomes an illusion. Marx argued that the course of history was determined by objective economic laws, which would eventually generate socialism. But if victory in the class struggle is foreordained, what is the need for individual revolutionaries? Precisely because his revolution was carried out in a precapitalist society, Lenin had a plausible answer: to act as a surrogate for a working class that does not yet exist. Thus, the Soviet Communist party and the Communist parties of Eastern Europe considered themselves to be the vanguard of proletariat, generals with a strategy (socialism) but without an army (the working class). Industrialization would produce such a working class.

Industrialization absorbed rural overpopulation, as collectivization pumped surplus labor into the cities. Both also served other, related purposes: to break the back of the hostile classes, the feudal remnants and the peasants who were petty-bourgeois capitalists in embryo; to feed the new workers who would produce more weapons for defense against imperialism; to increase wealth and welfare over the long term. Mass education — the educational revolutions effected in every country — was part of the same war of transformation. It was partly intended to raise the cultural level, to make education available to those who had always been deprived of it. But its two main goals were, first, to transform the peasants flooding the factories into socialist city workers and, second, to overwhelm the retrograde humanistic intelligentsia (already decimated by the war in many places) with waves of peasant and worker children who would be loyal to the party that had given them this historic opportunity for social advancement.

Despite their faith in their version of determinism, Stalinists recognized that a huge gap separated the hard present and the radiant future. To be sure, there were tremendous achievements, very quickly achieved. It has been calculated that in the Soviet Union the first spurt of Stalinist industrialization transferred 27 million people from the country to the city, and it forced rural exodus on the same scale in Eastern Europe.[28] With annual growth rates of 10 and 12 and 15 percent for industry, factories sprang out of the ground, as it seemed, overnight. Systems of mass education and mass health care beyond the wildest dreams of prewar East Europeans were created in half a decade.

The human and material cost was extremely high. The Stalinists knew that the current generations would have to sacrifice to build the future, and that they would have to be forced to do so. This forced sacrifice, the dark side of industrialization, took various forms: class warfare in the countryside, workers' barracks floating in alcohol, consumption levels ruthlessly squeezed to provide the capital for industrial construction, incessant and pervasive propaganda, and the police state. These were the years of the knock on the door in the night. Hundreds of thousands disappeared into prisons and labor camps; tens of thousands never came back. In these years the Romanian police simply shot people and left their bodies in doorways to be discovered in the morning, "to encourage the others," as Voltaire commented after the British executed an unsuccessful admiral.[29]

The Stalinists were dealing with populations that were among the most wary and clear-eyed in the world. Despite the party monopoly on information, which blamed every evil that could not be denied on class enemies and Western intelligence agencies, most East Europeans knew very well what was taking place in their countries. The difference between the lived experience of the people and the statements of their rulers resulted in terrible moral confusion. Living with unreality, East Europeans fell back even more firmly onto their traditional understanding of politics as moral drama, rather than as effective action to achieve limited goals. And compromise with a lie remains a lie.

Because the regimes enforced control of expression in order to control opinion, it was impossible to express opposition. Even attempts to propose alternative ways of seeking approved objectives were impermissible. Thus, lying became a necessary part of life for the great majority of people, both rulers and ruled.[30] The rule of the lie permeated society down to its foundations, down to the single institution that the authorities could never completely control, that East Europeans had always cherished, and that they now clung to as to the ark of the covenant: the family. The family remained a group, united by blood, that could be trusted. Outside the family and a small circle of friends, there was only collusion, hypocrisy, and force.[31]

A society that was forced into daily hypocrisy was a necessary, but not a sufficient, condition for the success of the Stalinist program. Communists still wanted to resolve, not just suppress, the gap between the radiant future and the terrible present. Thus, the East European governments sought to organize this society of the lie around one official deception. Because the future had to be utopian, the Stalinists insisted that the present was triumphant. Triumphalism was the essence of the spirit of Stalinism. It celebrated the triumph of the Soviet Union. As we have seen, the crushing postwar dependence of Eastern Europe upon the Soviet Union reduced socialist internationalism to the worship of Stalin. The political and economic dependence that had always afflicted Eastern Europe was now glorified in the name of future independence, when the countries would be strong and modern and inhabited by rational, modern people. In other words, if they sacrificed enough East Europeans could hope to reach the state of development that Stalin's Soviet Union had attained. They of course already considered themselves more advanced than Russians, and in glorifying dependence on the Soviet Union, Stalinism rooted nationalism even deeper into the East European national psyches. Triumphalism, the official lie, proved impossible to manage. With hindsight, however, it is possible to identify some of the actual changes in society that Stalinism did bring, five "triumphs" that took root.

First, Stalinism represented the triumph of ideas over every other social reality. As a criterion for social advancement, Stalinism replaced property and skill with loyalty to ideas — to the ideas of the moment, those that the rulers proclaimed were correct, but ideas nonetheless. In principle, the working class was the bearer of correct ideas, but in practice the tickets to social advancement were education, access to which was determined by the party, and party approval, achieved through loyalty to the party. The party insisted it embodied the best interests of the working class, but in truth it consisted of an amalgam of individuals of diverse social origins. The ideas that it enforced were its own. The system embodied intellect in power, the ideal of East European intelligentsias over the century of their existence.[32]

Second, Stalinism enforced the triumph of the state over society. The predominance of the state was masked by the myth and power of the party, but the party ruled through government apparati that were far more powerful than any Eastern Europe had ever had. We have seen how the role of the state in the economy was greater in Eastern Europe than in the West, and how adopting the Western model of parliamentary democracy and economic liberalism in these countries with sparse industry and small middle classes had simply reinforced the state as the locus of both political and economic power and as the dispenser of both political and economic favors. Stalinism replaced one syncretic clique at the top of this interlocking pyramid with another, and it immensely reinforced the pyramid. It was the apotheosis of the East European tradition of the state as the single repository of political and economic power and the single engine of political and economic change.

Third, while Stalinism was in fact a triumph of politics, it enforced a linguistic claim that politics had been replaced by triumphant economics. Politics as the interplay of group interests within agreed rules for indeterminate outcomes no longer had any official value. Because the party had access to objective truth, dispute was unnecessary. Politics subsisted under Stalinism only on international issues, as the struggle of the two camps. Political disagreement was defined as illegitimate hostility and, under High Stalinism, most often as treason. It was literally impossible to debate the genuine political issues: dictatorship, the power of the police, relations with the Soviet Union. The most pressing political question, national paths to communism, was similarly off limits. If Stalinist economic principles were objectively true, they were also universal, applicable everywhere. The very question of national paths implied relevant national differences and the need for subjective choice between alternatives, which by Stalinist definition meant that the questioner had left socialism.

So the only remaining legitimate issues were economic. Newspapers of the time were filled with production figures and heroic tractor drivers and lathe operators. Naturally, economics became politicized. When all economic decisions are centralized, all criticism is necessarily directed at the leaderships, for there are no businessmen left to blame. Despite this politicization, economic issues were somewhat easier to discuss than politics. For that reason, much of the political debate took the form of discussion of economics.

Fourth, Stalinism insisted on the primacy — the triumph — of industry over agriculture, of the city over the countryside. Not only did it break the peasant parties and thereby end the agrarian dream of a third way between communism and capitalism, but it reduced agriculture and the countryside to dependent variables in the equation of industrial development. They were objects of urban control, used as sources of food, raw materials, and labor for the cities and their factories. Except to control them and extract these resources, the regimes generally left them to wither on the vine of history. The Stalinists carried their hatred and contempt for the peasantry — and a residual fear of the peasant parties — with them through the years. Decades later, after Stalinist economic policies had bled the village dry of surplus labor and reduced agriculture to a monster of inefficiency, they found it hard to recognize that agriculture was a necessary component of successful industrialization. Centuries before, the West had learned that industrial revolutions must be accompanied by agricultural revolutions. When Stalinist industrialization reached its natural limits of development in the 1960s and 1970s, Communists had not yet learned that lesson.[33]

In East European conditions the Stalinist triumph of the city over the countryside had a fateful corollary: It kept anti-Semitism alive in public consciousness and made it a potential political football.[34]

The Germans had killed the great majority of Eastern Europe's Jews, and most of those who remained were allowed to leave in the late 1940s, first by the coalition regimes and then, at the beginning, by the Stalinists themselves. Jews of Polish and Romanian origin constitute nearly half of

Israel's population today. In principle, the Stalinists were dedicated to creating new, modern communities, perhaps national in form, but certainly socialist in content, where ethnic differences would become irrelevant where they persisted at all. In practice, too, they were usually anti-anti-Semitic. But because the cities and middle classes had historically been heavily populated by national minorities, the peasant majorities had always associated modernization and industrialization with Jews and Germans. East European conservatives and racists had capitalized on this association, and had added the link between Jews and bolshevism. They were aided by five years of Nazi propaganda about the Judeo-Bolshevik plot to control the world. Because the men and women who had chosen to become Communists before the war had very often come from the national minorities, those who emerged to take up larger roles in postwar political life were often of minority origin, and the national minority most heavily represented among the Communists were the Jews. This was particularly true in the two states the Soviets were most determined to control, Poland and Romania, and in Hungary. The Stalinist regimes that arrived in the baggage of the Red Army drew disproportionately on Communists of Jewish origin to staff themselves. Jews were visible, in the economic ministries, in culture, in the police, and at the highest levels of Communist rule. A Hungarian joke of the early 1950s asked why there was one non-Jew on the Hungarian Politburo, and answered that they needed someone to sign decrees on the Sabbath. And as the years went by, as the educational system began to produce the native Communists the regimes needed to continue party rule without the violence that was required at first to fasten it into place, these origins created a weapon that could strike at their heels, or at its foundations.

For fifth, and most paradoxically, Stalinism was the triumph of the old status society over the new class society it was so determined to introduce and then drive forward to classlessness. The Stalinists saw themselves as modernizers — in Russian terms as Westernizers — forcing rational behavior and rational thinking and rational, impersonal rules and values upon black retrograde masses still mired in the Middle Ages. They believed they were replacing the personalized parish politics and the politicized economics of the past with scientifically determined, objectively verifiable rules of development. The Stalinists believed they were creating a more bounteous, juster, and freer world where the government of men would be replaced by the administration of things.

But, in order to make this grand transition, Stalinists had to enforce binary, military politics. The just in their fortress (us) battled against the unjust in their cellars (them). Because the just were so few, the Stalinists were determined to increase their numbers by creating conditions that would produce new recruits. To do so, they were obliged to recruit the backward masses into the fortresses of power and reason, the factories and the party. They had to do so quickly, in a space of years rather than decades. The time allowed for the cultural change between a status society and a class society was inadequate. Because the government used moral terminology in its recruitment, and because the process of industrialization was so rushed, peasants and former peasants could easily understand what was happening to them in terms of the paradigm of status. Moreover, the peasants had no cause to regard the new states, which centralized power in the hands of a few men selected by political skill, as more objective than their past rulers. Instead, they were seen as dispensers of favors, with a newfound bounty of status positions to offer. History avenged itself on the East European Stalinists, not just because they were so different but also because they were so much the same.[35]

Notes

1. For a bittersweet retrospective on this consensus, see Włodzimierz Brus and Kazimierz Łaski, "The Objective of Catching Up," in *From Marx to the Market. Socialism in Search of an Economic System* (Oxford: Clarendon Press, 1989), 22-35. For a convenient brief description of what the economic system actually meant in practice, see Alan A. Brown and Egon Neuberger, "Basic Features of a Centrally Planned Economy," in their edited volume, *International Trade and Central Planning* (Berkeley: University of California Press, 1968), 405-415.
2. That these were the alternatives was the thesis put forward already during the war by Paul Rodenstein-Rodan: "Problems of Industrialization of Eastern and South-Eastern Europe," in A.N. Agarwala and S.P. Singh, eds., *The Economics of Underdevelopment* (New York: Oxford University Press, 1963), 245-255.
3. On this problem, see Vselevod Holubnychy, "Some Aspects of Relations Among the Soviet Republics," in Erich Goldhagen, ed., *Ethnic Minorities in the Soviet Union* (New York: Praeger, 1968), 86-93, and Michael Kaser, *Comecon. Integration Problems of the Planned Economies,* 2nd ed. (London: Oxford University Press, 1967), 17-21,

30-31. The most stimulating thoughts on the longer-term effects of keeping national borders intact and exporting the Soviet model across them are still in Jerzy F. Karcz, "Reflections on the Economics of Communism and Nationalism in Eastern Europe," *East European Quarterly*, 5, no. 2 (June 1971), 232-259.

4. On nationalization, land reform, and initial collectivization, Nicolas Spulber, *The Economics of Communist Eastern Europe* (Cambridge, Mass.: MIT Press/John Wiley, 1957), 43-270, is still excellent.

5. For a convenient summary of early land reform, see "The Early Postwar Period," in Karl-Eugen Wädekin, *Agrarian Policies in Communist Europe. A Critical Introduction* (The Hague: Allenheld/Osmun/Martinus Nijhoff, 1982), 31-43, and the country-by-country chart in Ivan Völgyes, "Economic Aspects of Rural Transformation in Eastern Europe," in Ivan Völgyes, Richard E. Lonsdale, and William P. Avery, eds., *The Process of Rural Transformation. Eastern Europe, Latin America and Australia* (New York: Pergamon, 1980), 104. For useful accounts of land reform and collectivization, see Nicolas Spulber, "Uneasy Symbiosis in Land Tenancy," in his *Socialist Management and Planning* (Bloomington: Indiana University Press, 1971), through the 1960s, and George W. Hoffman, "Rural Transformation in Eastern Europe Since World War II," in Völgyes, Lonsdale and Avery, *Process of Rural Transformation*, 21-41, which takes the story to the mid-1970s and includes its urbanization aspect.

6. These figures are taken from Hugh Seton-Watson, *The East European Revolution*, 3rd ed. (New York: Praeger, 1956), 245.

7. The UNRRA figure is from ibid., 233-234; the figure on Polish coal is from Geir Lundestad, *The American Non-Policy Toward Eastern Europe, 1943-1947: Universalism in an Area Not of Essential Interest to the United States* (Tromso: Universitets forlaget, 1978) 216-217.

8. Data on foreign ownership are scattered through Spulber, *Economics of Communist Eastern Europe* and Seton-Watson, *East European Revolution* as well as John R. Lampe and Marvin R. Jackson, *Balkan Economic History, 1550-1950. From Imperial Borderlands to Developing Nations* (Bloomington: Indiana University Press, 1982), for the Balkans in particular, and there is now a good case study of Romania: Maurice Pearton, *Oil and the Romanian State, 1895-1948* (Oxford: Clarendon Press, 1971), esp. 185-326.

9. I am sure it was Viktor Adler, but I can no longer cite where I read it.

10. For a specific example, see Olga A. Narkiewicz, *The Green Flag. Polish Populist Politics 1867-1970* (London: Croom Helm, 1976). For some general thoughts, see my "A Century of Peasant Politics in East Central Europe," *Peasant Studies Newsletter*, 4, no. 2 (April 1975): 26-29.

11. Seton-Watson, "The Seizure of Power," *East European Revolution*. See also Thomas Hammond, ed., *The Anatomy of Communist Takeovers* (New Haven, Yale University Press, 1975).

12. On these Polish Communist negotiations with Stalin, see Vojtech Mastny, *Russia's Road to the Cold War* (New York: Columbia University Press, 1979), 299-300, with citations.

13. On the Polish party, see M.K. Dziewanowski, *The Communist Party of Poland. An Outline of History* (Cambridge, Mass.: Harvard University Press, 1959) (the estimate of 20,000 members in July 1944 is at 187 and 346), and Jan B. de Weydenthal, *The Communists of Poland: An Historical Outline*, rev. ed. (Stanford: Hoover Institution Press, 1986) (cites the same estimate at 46 and 228). There is now a very detailed account of the takeover in Poland between December 1943 and July 1945, based in part on new

party documents that became available only in the 1970s: Antony Polonsky and Bolesław Drukier, *The Beginnings of Communist Rule in Poland* (London: Routledge/Kegan Paul, 1980), gives vivid examples of the problems arising from the party's heavily Jewish composition at 51. In post-Communist Poland, archives, memoirs, and testimony on this period are appearing in volume and may change the picture, but already in the 1980s enough were available to permit a fine new synthesis by a skilled historian, Krystyna Kersten, now available as *The Establishment of Communist Rule in Poland, 1943-1948* (Berkeley, Calif.: University of California Press, 1991). On the Romanian party, see Kenneth Jowitt, *Revolutionary Breakthroughs and National Development. The Case of Romania, 1944-1965* (Berkeley: University of California Press, 1971), 78 and passim, and Robert R. King, *A History of the Romanian Communist Party* (Stanford: Hoover Institution Press, 1980), which cites the figure of 1,000 at 59 and touches on the importance of recruitment among minorities at 33-38. During my time in Bucharest in the mid-1970s the informal estimate for party numbers in August 1944 was even lower.

14. On the Hungarian party, Bennett Kovrig, *Communism in Hungary. From Kun to Kádár* (Stanford: Hoover Institution Press, 1979), 448, cites an estimate of 30,000 Party members in February 1945, but this may reflect recruiting behind Soviet lines in the liberated portions of Hungary since Budapest had been encircled the previous December; Miklós Molnar, *A Short History of the Hungarian Communist Party* (Boulder: Westview, 1978), 58, considers the 3,000 members cited in the Party's official history for the end of 1944 to be an unreliable maximum estimate. The best treatment of this period is "Communists in Coalition, 1944-1948" in Charles Gati, *Hungary and the Soviet Bloc* (Durham: Duke University Press, 1986), 13-126. The figures on the 1949 purges are from Joseph Rothschild, *Return to Diversity. A Political History of East Central Europe Since World War II* (New York: Oxford University Press, 1989), 137, in a chapter that is good on the area purges in general. As Hungarian politics moved toward roundtable talks in the spring of 1989, memories of the party's postwar divide-and-conquer "salami tactics" were still vivid enough to be a factor in the opposition's insistence on negotiating together, or not at all: see László Bruszt and David Stark, "Remaking the Political Field in Hungary: From the Politics of Confrontation to the Politics of Competition," in Ivo Banac, ed., *Eastern Europe in Revolution* (Ithaca, N.Y. and London: Cornell University Press, 1992), 33.

15. On the Bulgarian party's whole history, see John D. Bell, *The Bulgarian Communist Party from Blagoev to Zhivkov* (Stanford, Calif.: The Hoover Institution Press, 1986). For estimates on partisan numbers and party membership at the time of the 9 September 1944 coup, see Nissan Oren, *Bulgarian Communism: The Road to Power, 1934-1944* (New York: Columbia University Press, 1971), 216-218 and 257, and John R. Lampe, *The Bulgarian Economy in the Twentieth Century* (London and Sydney: Croom Helm, 1986), 121. For a touching recollection of the effect of Petkov's execution on the morale of embattled liberals in the U.S. government, see H. Stuart Hughes, "The Second Year of the Cold War: A Memoir and an Anticipation," in *Commentary*, 48, no. 2 (August 1969), 27-32.

16. Cited in Hugh Thomas, *Armed Truce: The Beginning of the Cold War 1945-46* (New York: Atheneum, 1987), 268.

17. On the Czechoslovak party, see Paul E. Zinner, *Communist Strategy and Tactics in Czechoslovakia, 1918-48* (New York: Praeger, 1963) (1945-46 membership figures on 124) and the first part of Edward Taborsky's *Communism in Czechoslovakia 1948-1960*

(Princeton, N.J.: Princeton University Press, 1961). On the "elegant revolution," see Victor S. Mamatey and Radomír Luža, eds., *A History of the Czechoslovak Republic, 1918-1948* (Princeton, N.J.: Princeton University Press, 1973); Martin R. Myant, *Socialism and Democracy in Czechoslovakia, 1945-1948* (Cambridge: Cambridge University Press, 1981); and Karel Kaplan, *The Short March: The Communist Takeover in Czechoslovakia* (New York: St. Martin's, 1987).

18. On the merger of April 1946 in the Soviet zone, see Henry Krisch, *German Politics Under Soviet Occupation* (New York: Columbia University Press, 1974), which ends with it, and Ann L. Phillips, *Soviet Policy Toward East Germany Reconsidered. The Postwar Decade* (New York: Greenwood, 1986), 32-41.

19. A recent citation is Michael T. Kaufman, "40 Years of Communism in Poland: Stalin's House on a Soft Foundation," *New York Times*, 18 August 1989; but note that William Hyland makes Germany the cow: *The Cold War is Over* (New York: Times Books, 1990), 52.

21. Czesław Miłosz's *The Captive Mind* (New York: Vintage, 1981), remains the best and most moving evocation of the intellectuals' dilemmas under Stalinism, but Zygmunt Bauman, "Intellectuals in East-Central Europe," *East European Politics and Societies*, 1, no. 2 (Spring, 1987): 162-186, adds good analytical and historical perspective. On the initial enthusiasm of young Communist believers against the background of postwar collapse, see Jan T. Gross, "Consequences of War: Preliminaries to the Study of Imposition of Communist Regimes in East Central Europe," *ibid.*, 3, no. 2 (Spring, 1989), 213-214.

22. See Zbigniew Brzezinski, *The Soviet Bloc: Unity and Conflict*, rev. ed. (New York: Praeger, 1961), 167, on the Stalinist "dilemma of the one alternative."

23. The literature is vast; some has been cited earlier, and more will be cited later; but there is a recent vignette that conveys some of the flavor of the period in Jacques Rupnik, *The Other Europe* (New York: Pantheon, 1988/89) 109-128 ("Stalinism: The Ice Age"). For a summing-up by a veteran, see Włodzimierz Brus, "Stalinism and the 'Peoples' Democracies,'" in Robert C. Tucker, ed., *Stalinism. Essays in Historical Interpretation* (New York: Norton, 1977), 239-256. On purposeful atomization as the first step on a very twisted path, see Elemér Hankiss, "Demobilization, Self-Mobilization, and Quasi-Mobilization in Hungary, 1948-1987," *East European Politics and Societies*, 3, no. 1 (Winter, 1989), 105-51.

24. On the Party as Hero, see Paul Neuberg, *The Hero's Children. The Post-War Generation in Eastern Europe* (New York: William Morrow, 1973), 11-42, and more analytically (and I think fundamentally), Kenneth Jowitt, *The Leninist Response to National Dependency* (Berkeley: Institute of International Studies, University of California Press, 1978), 34-62.

25. Peter J.D. Wiles, *Communist International Economics* (Oxford: Blackwell, 1968), 3ll.

26. In an interview with Milovan Djilas, George Urban quotes back a marvelous Stalinist passage Djilas wrote in November 1942: George Urban, ed., *Stalinism. Its Impact on Russia and the World* (New York: St. Martin's, 1982), 214. The full text of Urban's exchanges with Djilas and Leszek Kołakowski, another Stalinist who became a relentless and effective anti-Stalinist, is well worth reading (180-278).

27. And hence the purges. On the theory, see Leszek Kołakowski, *Main Currents of Marxism. Vol. 3: The Breakdown* (Oxford: Oxford University Press, 1978), 38. On the East European purges themselves, the best testimony comes from Czechoslovakia, which was most traumatized by them: Jiří Pelikán, ed., *The Czechoslovak Political*

Trials 1950-1954 (Stanford: Stanford University Press, 1971); Eugen Loebl, *Stalinism in Prague*. *The Loebl Story* (New York: Grove, 1970); and Karel Kaplan, *Report on the Murder of the General Secretary* (Columbus: Ohio State University Press, 1990), a chilling account of the Czechoslovak witchhunt and the Slánský trial, preceded by a convenient areawide summary: 1-37.

28. In addition to 27 million in the 1930s, another 24 million moved from country to city between 1939 and 1959, another 8.4 million between 1959 and 1964, and another 16 million between 1964 and 1970: Moshe Lewin, *The Gorbachev Phenomenon. A Historical Interpretation* (Berkeley: University of California Press, 1988), 34. On Eastern Europe, see Huey Louis Kostanick, "Characteristics and Trends in Southeastern Europe: Romania, Yugoslavia, Bulgaria, Albania, Greece, and Turkey," and Leszek Kosiński, "Demographic Characteristics and Trends in Northeastern Europe: the German Democratic Republic, Poland, Czechoslovakia and Hungary," both in Kostanick, ed., *Population and Migration Trends in Eastern Europe* (Boulder: Westview, 1977), 11-48.

29. Or so it was remembered when I was in Bucharest in the mid-1970s.

30. See Kołakowski's comments on the organic role of the lie under Stalinism in his interview with Urban, ed., *Stalinism*, 257-263, and his eloquent pages on the famous Short Course in party history, in *Main Currents*, 93-97.

31. The basic work is Kenneth Jowitt, *Leninist Response*, but Moshe Lewin should also be consulted: "From Village to Megacity," in Lewin, *Gorbachev Phenomenon*, 13-42, and his earlier "The Social Background of Stalinism," in his *The Making of the Soviet System: Essays in the Social History of Interwar Russia* (New York: Pantheon, 1985), 258-285.

32. This is the thesis of György Konrád and Ivan Szélényi in *The Intellectuals on the Road to Class Power* (New York: Harcourt Brace Jovanovich, 1979). It is ably argued but still requires tempering, which I have sought to provide.

33. In addition, it industrialized without building adequate urban infrastructure. For consideration of the consequences, see György Konrád and Ivan Szélényi, "Social Conflicts of Urbanization: The Hungarian Case," in Mark G. Field, ed., *Social Consequences of Modernization in Communist Societies* (Baltimore: Johns Hopkns University Press, 1976), 162-190.

34. I shall cite works concerning anti-Semitism under communism as it relates to individual countries, but the best summary is still Paul Lendvai, "Communism and the Jews," in his *Anti-Semitism Without Jews* (Garden City, N.Y.: Doubleday, 1971), 3-88. See also Charles Gati, "A Note on Communists and the Jewish Question," in his *Hungary and the Soviet Bloc*, 100-107, and now Krystyna Kersten's moving and reflective *Polacy. Zydzi. Komunizm. Anatomia półprawd. 1939-1968 (Poles. Jews. Communism. The Anatomy of Half-Truths, 1939-1968)* (Warsaw: Niezalena Oficyna Wydawnicza, 1992), which deserves translation into English.

35. For a convenient short summary of the whole Communist period after it was over, see J.F. Brown, *Surge to Freedom: The End of Communist Rule in Eastern Europe* (Durham, N.C. and London: Duke University Press, 1991), Ch. I, "Millennium becomes Memento Mori," 7-44.

FIVE

DE-STALINIZATION,
1953-1956

We have seen how the overall East-West dynamic and similar internal dynamics in each country flowed together toward Stalinism, but there was one other dynamic that contributed to the making of the Stalinist system in Eastern Europe and that became even more important when Stalin's death in March 1953 removed the system's linchpin. This was the dynamic of relations among parties and countries within the system, and it centered in these first years on Yugoslavia.

Yugoslavia and Albania were unique among the Stalinist countries of Europe for having liberated themselves largely by their own efforts under Communist leaderships that accordingly enjoyed real domestic political support. Albania had and has had a complex history of its own that will figure only very occasionally in this general survey. Yugoslavia's history is also nothing if not complex, but it was also critical to the history of all the rest in these early years. Under Tito (a *nom de guerre* of Josip Broz), in 1945 Yugoslavia embarked already on the area's most Stalinist program of political *Gleichschaltung*, rapid industrialization and pugnaciousness vis-à-vis the West (over Trieste). But the Yugoslavs' loyalty to Stalin and the Soviet Union was freely given, and Stalin gradually came to worry about the insistence on Communist freedom of choice that underlay it, for it implied that local Communists had the right to differ from the Soviet Union: It raised the specter, in other words, of national paths to communism. So with East-West tensions mounting toward an unforeseeable culmination, in June 1948 Stalin broke with Tito in the confidence that the latter's own party would replace him with a more faithful leadership. When this did not happen he embarked on a dogged campaign of excommunication, vilification, and intimidation which lasted till his own death.[1] He expected the other area parties to rally round, and he made sure they did. The Soviet-Yugoslav split thereby triggered the final fastening of full Stalinism onto the area, and defined nationalism as the issue with which it would have to wrestle after he was gone. Given the nature of the system, the stakes were very genuine. Because ferocious nationalism was endemic to Eastern Europe and had been reinforced by the war and postwar experience, the Tito-Stalin split made it imperative for the Soviets and their clients to deny that there was anything national about the Stalinist model. If the Soviet path to socialism was distinctively Russian, communism would be even more vulnerable to nationalist criticism. Stalinism was therefore defined as pure socialism, obligatory to all socialists. Every East European leadership embarked on uniform introduction of the full Stalinist model, built around the person of Stalin.

Driven by Stalin's need to assert Soviet infallibility after the Yugoslav defection, Stalinization turned every society into a battlefield. Regimes destroyed enemies, putative enemies, and then merely potential enemies of socialism. They began with the destruction of the private property that had supported the feudal and bourgeois classes; proceeded to the collectivization of agriculture, taking control of the land and the peasants who could become bourgeois; and finished by thoroughly purging their own ranks. The most enthusiastic and fanatical revolutionists, men like Rudolf Slánský in Czechoslovakia and László Rajk in Hungary, the people most likely to support the authority of the party against any rival, were first publicly pilloried in hallucinative show trials and then hanged. The effect was to transform the parties into pyramids of bureaucrats and to replicate Stalin's return to rule by the state in the Soviet Union. For the time being, Stalin was reassured that no leader after Tito would put construction of a national base for communism ahead of Soviet dictates. And beginning in June 1950 the Korean War pushed Stalinization to fresh extremes.

Of course, the area's Communist parties also had practical reasons to purge themselves. All of them had swelled with opportunists and enthusiasts during the struggle for power, so some streamlining was in order, and the pace of revolutionary transformation guaranteed severe tension in every aspect of national life, requiring the parties to maintain a strict inner discipline. But, as a 1968 Czechoslovak party report on its own purges argued,[2] the extreme centralization of power in these systems allowed the purges to gain a momentum of their own. They degenerated into vicious struggles for power among a few men.

As East European Communists turned against each other, a Western bloc was consolidating. This process was driven not only by the bizarre spectacle of revolution run amok in Eastern Europe but also by the persistence of real difficulties with economic recovery even after the Marshall Plan was in place and operating. In the fall of 1949 Britain was forced to devaluate the pound radically, and economic concern was transformed into a sense of general crisis by the advent of the Korean War in 1950. This sense of impending doom catalyzed the formation of a united West.

The main potential alternative to the crystallization of a Western bloc along liberal, democratic, capitalist lines was the possibility of a socialist Western Europe, blazing a trail between capitalism and communism. The Schumann Plan marked the beginning of the end for this option.[3] In May of 1950 French Foreign Minister Robert Schumann proposed a coal and steel community based on free-market principles. Britain's international preoccupations under Labour governments were decolonization and the special relationship with the United States, so it had stood aside from previous attempts to lay the foundations for West European union. Now Britain was offered membership in the coal and steel community too, but it was made clear that the plan would go into effect with or without its participation. When Britain stayed aloof again, the plan went forward. It proved the first anchor for Franco-West German reconciliation and the embryo for greater economic unification, but without socialism.

Another obstacle to formation of a Western bloc was the problem of arming West Germany. The United States, Canada, and ten countries of Western Europe had created the North Atlantic Treaty Organization (NATO) in 1949, but its commitments were very vague. Though a European Defense Force (EDF) coordinated by NATO was under discussion, agreement on the role West German troops should play seemed impossible. The Korean War convinced the United States that a West German contingent in the EDF was absolutely necessary for European defense. The French, who had strongly opposed such a role from the beginning, responded in September 1950 with the Pleven Plan. Named for their current prime minister, this proposal was designed to burden West German troop participation with so many preconditions that it would never occur. The stratagem backfired, for the principle of West German rearmament was thereby accepted, and West German Chancellor Konrad Adenauer then bargained the American desire for West German troops against his desire for West German sovereignty. Negotiations continued for two years, culminating in two treaties signed in May 1952. One ended West Germany's occupation status, and the other created an EDF with a West German contingent. Meanwhile, Adenauer had sold the West on the principle of German reunification in freedom, meaning by "free" electoral choice. As free elections were unacceptable to East Germany, reunification was delayed for the forseeable future. West Germany thereby achieved the status of a more or less permanent, and armed, member of the Western alliance.

Stalin responded that same year, 1952, with what appears in retrospect to have been a desperate, last ditch attempt to stave off West Germany's final absorption into a resurgent capitalist camp. In a series of diplomatic notes, he offered a neutral, unified Germany. This offer was rejected by the West, and by most West Germans, whose institutions were already too strong and attractive to sacrifice for a fresh start toward national reunification.[4]

Joseph Stalin died in March 1953. In the midst of the leadership infighting that broke out immediately thereafter, Lavrenti Beria, head of the secret police, attempted to use Germany to bolster his political position. He tried to make Stalin's offer more agreeable to West Germans by having his East German allies introduce some liberalization. In order to appeal to the West Germans, these reforms favored the intelligentsia. At the same time, those elements in the East German Communist leadership that were not allied with Beria were pressing for still more rapid and consistent pressure to raise production, even at the cost of alienating workers still further. Production norms were raised again in May. Speculation that they were trying to provoke an uprising that would force Soviet intervention, cancel Beria's appeal to the West, and preserve their own power has never been confirmed but is very plausible. A national uprising broke out June 16; Soviet troops intervened on June 17; Beria was arrested in Moscow on June 26; and his East German allies followed him into prison within two weeks. Order reigned in the shambles of East Berlin reconquered by the Red Army, and the work of creating a separate East German state began in earnest.[5]

The Western response to revolt in the German Democratic Republic (GDR) was indignation. Mobilizing public and international opinion is of course a political act that puts pressure on the perpetrator of an outrage, but if that is the extent of response and the offending government has the means to insulate its population(s), it can still deal with the consequences largely on its own terms. So it was in 1953: The truth was that the West was so preoccupied with putting in place a stable defensive system at home that it viewed Eastern events mainly in that context. East Berlin confirmed the worst Western views of the opponent and the threat, but seemed to require (or permit) no further significant action across the East-West divide. And this gave the Soviets and their East European clients not precisely a breathing space but rather a margin for maneuver that they had not felt they enjoyed before. From their point of view it came just in the nick of time. The dependence of the Stalinist leaderships on the Soviets and on Stalin personally meant that his death created immediate political problems. The fact that the Soviet Union plunged immediately into sharp political struggle for his succession had two contradictory effects in Eastern Europe.

First, the Soviets were preoccupied with their own affairs, and they were no longer able to exert the minute, day-to-day control that classic Stalinism required.[6] The East European countries thereby gained a new margin of freedom. Second, however, the political future and even the lives of the individual East European leaders still depended on their ability to adjust to the smallest changes in a now erratic and indeterminate Soviet official line. The ideology that legitimized their rule required them to imitate Moscow. As they did not know which leader would prevail, they could not be sure which one(s) they should imitate. The 1953 revolt in the GDR was an early case study of this new situation, which continued until 1956.

At home the Soviets began to "de-Stalinize" fitfully, erratically, in certain areas. And they expected their clients to follow suit: Soviet de-Stalinization did not represent a move away from their authority over the region. On the contrary, they wanted to secure their hegemony over the region, just as they wished to strengthen Communist rule at home. To do so, they moved slowly to substitute party rule by assent for police force and the cult of Stalin. Under Stalin the party too had been ruled by the police, an organ of the state; now the Soviet party wished to resume charge. The first manifestations of de-Stalinization in the Soviet Union and then in Eastern Europe were thus the curbing of the police, the freeing and rehabilitation of political prisoners, and the expulsion from the leaderships of those who were blamed for police excesses.

The Soviet Union could afford such an experiment. Communism had arisen indigenously there, had been in power for nearly forty years, and had won the war. Relying on assent was a far more dangerous proposition for Eastern Europe's Communists. They had been in power less than ten years. Most of their populations had grown up under the old regimes, and remembered them ever more fondly as the trauma of Stalinist industrialization proceeded. Policy changes in Eastern Europe did not mean just gains or losses for one or another faction, as they did in the Soviet Union: At least potentially, they threatened the very existence of the Communist regimes. When Mátyás Rákosi was finally forced to retire in Hungary in July 1956, he did so on grounds of hypertension.[7] That was perfectly credible, for every East European leader was suffering from political stress.

Reining in the police removed some of the restraints upon party members and citizens. Changes in foreign policy ideology facilitated a further loosening of state control and allowed local political forces more freedom. The basic theory of the confrontation of the two camps, the imperialist camp led by the United States and the peace camp led by the Soviet Union, was firmly in place. The militaristic development and siege mentality of High Stalinism had been justified within this theory by the assessment that the imperialists were driving the world toward war in ever more frantic efforts to resist the advance of socialism. Now, with Stalin gone, the Soviets helped engineer the Korean Armistice of mid-1953. Reassured by Western passivity during the East German uprising and the turmoil that flared briefly about the same time in Czechoslovakia, Romania, and Bulgaria, and by the successful Soviet test of a hydrogen bomb in August 1953, Soviet analysis moved now in new directions. It discerned increasing contradictions within the imperialist camp (as we have seen, there were such contradictions) and postulated hopefully that they would make the imperialists less aggressive. It prescribed moves by the socialist camp to accelerate those contradictions by removing excuses for imperialist consolidation. Even after the French killed the EDF and accepted West German membership into NATO, the Soviets stayed the course and continued to try to improve East-West relations: hence the Austrian State Treaty in May 1955 and the "spirit of Geneva" that followed the 1955 Summit Meeting there.

Because the Soviets saw a diminishing Western threat and wished to reduce it still further by conciliatory moves, the military push for heavy industrialization, and the need for a siege mentality to support it, gradually abated. In order to correct what were chastely called disproportions resulting from overemphasis on heavy industry, a "New Course" in economics was proclaimed and implemented: It increased the purchasing power of workers and peasants, reduced production norms in industry and compulsory delivery quotas in agriculture, and shifted investment from heavy industry to light industry, consumer goods, and agriculture.

All of the contenders for power in the Soviet Union supported some movement in these directions, so questions of pace and degree became the essential issues in the struggle to succeed Stalin. After Beria's ouster in June 1953, the man who had taken the top government post, Georgiy Malenkov, became associated with a stress on light and consumer goods industries as well as reduction of East-West tension. The party leader, Nikita Khrushchev, also favored improved East-West relations, but in addition he associated himself with a whole new stress on agriculture and most especially with a wholly traditional high priority for heavy industry. The traditional Stalinists also remained attached to heavy industry, but they were wary of underestimating the imperialist threat. Put briefly, Khrushchev gained power by allying first with the Stalinists on the issue of heavy industry, which led to the ouster of Malenkov from the premiership in early 1955, and then with the defeated consumerists against the Stalinists, first in the secret speech attacking Stalin at the 20th Party Congress in early 1956 and then with the ouster of the so-called anti-party group in mid-1957.[8] Despite this short and simplified account, the struggle was long and intricate, and it went back and forth, month by month, and year by year, for four long years. During those four years the East Europeans had to hang figuratively on every twist and turn, for they were convinced — and their experience gave them reason to be convinced — that the penalty for a mistake was to hang literally.

Most Soviet policy developments had urgent but indirect consequences for East European leaders, as symbols of the ascent of leaders and the emergence of a new line. By contrast, when Khrushchev began an effort at reconciliation with Yugoslavia, the consequences were both urgent and direct.[9] The Soviets wanted to reestablish their unquestioned primacy in the world Communist movement, but they also wanted to make that primacy consensual, and for that they needed explicit Yugoslav assent. To get it, they sought a direct modus vivendi with the Yugoslavs. Tito was not unwilling to bargain, as long as the bargain included Soviet recognition of the right of every Communist party to choose a path to communism that accounted for national conditions, as long as the Soviets admitted their guilt for the split and agreed to treat Yugoslavia as a sovereign equal in the future, and as long as Khrushchev was willing to oust the East European leaders who had joined most rabidly in the anti-Tito campaign. When it came to the "bloc," Tito was willing to help the Soviets solidify the other East European regimes by giving them his blessing, but only at the price of major changes in the regimes themselves. Because every one of them had consolidated the control of their parties by purging real and potential opponents on grounds of pro-Titoism, this price was stiff indeed.

Khrushchev made reconciliation with Yugoslavia one of the main planks in his competitive political platform at home. This complicated Soviet negotiations with Yugoslavia, stretched them out for years, and left their outcome in doubt pending definitive resolution of the Soviet leadership struggle. Even after Khrushchev's victory in 1957, relations with the Yugoslavs remained volatile. East European Stalinists were already threatened by the prospect of de-Stalinization as no Soviet leader could be. The additional possibility of Tito's vengeance left them more inclined to delay changes in the hope that someone besides Khrushchev would win in the end.

The post-Stalin years were a period of tremendous political tension in every East European country. Much of the tension was subterranean. As a Polish friend once said to me, every time you read an editorial in the party daily that began "The unity of the socialist camp has never been firmer," you knew something terrible had happened. But it was nevertheless real, and the stakes were deadly. Populations more nationalistic than ever had been wrenched from their fixed societal moorings first by the war and then by Stalinist industrializations; millions of cynical and surly ex-peasants were crowded into new cities with inadequate infrastructure, where even policemen went out only in groups, when they went out at all, and they were considered the first resort for frightened local leaders; the last resort, the Soviet fixed pole, was no longer so fixed. In order to relieve that tension, every regime felt obliged to look more to its own resources and less to the unpredictable Soviets. Zbigniew Brzezinski calls this trend "domesticism." [10] The regimes were not asserting a right to a national path to communism — that smacked too much of the Titoist heresy, and gave too much legitimacy to domestic nationalist feeling — but the practice of taking local factors and conditions into account spread.

In most countries taking local conditions into account paradoxically led the leaderships to cleave even more closely to the Soviets, either because they were too frightened or because they were not frightened enough to differentiate themselves.

The Soviets continued to intervene directly, as of right, in East European domestic politics. When the Polish leader Bolesław Bierut died in March 1956, right after Khrushchev's attack on Stalin, the Soviets vetoed his replacement by Roman Zambrowski, on the grounds that Zambrowski's Jewish backround would undermine his support among Poles. But more important than Soviet perceptions about a leader's acceptibility to his people were his personal loyalty and connections with Moscow factions. The fact that Imre Nagy in Hungary was not a Jew probably had something to do with his taking the premiership in 1953 from the Jewish Rákosi, who remained party first secretary,[11] but even more important was his record of unconditional loyalty to the Soviet Union through his long years as a Comintern agricultural expert in Moscow. Politics within the Communist family remained highly personalized. Rákosi recovered sole power in Hungary by expelling Nagy shortly after Khrushchev had forced Malenkov to give up the Soviet premiership in early 1955, and Rákosi was forced out only after Khrushchev's secret speech against Stalin had made his Stalinism finally intolerable.

The famous tension between "home Communists" and "Muscovites," those who had spent the war at home and those who had spent it in Moscow, was now less important. Even while Stalin lived it had not entirely determined the course of the purges, for while the Muscovites had triumphed in Poland, Czechoslovakia, Hungary, and Bulgaria, they had been purged by the home Communist Gheorghe Gheorghiu-Dej in Romania. The tension between Jews and non-Jews had an even more mixed outcome. It had not been an issue in Bulgaria. The victors in the purges had been non-Jewish in Czechoslovakia and Romania but Jewish in Poland and Hungary.

As de-Stalinization continued on its volatile course, a new cause of leadership change emerged. In 1956 East European leaders were brought down by their subjects, instead of by Soviet intervention or political defeat by a Communist rival. The keys to understanding which leaders survived de-Stalinization and which did not are to be found in the effects of the de-Stalinization process on East European populations, which varied from country to country. In general, the most and least industrially developed countries weathered de-Stalinization most smoothly. They made adjustments in personnel and policies along Soviet lines: They relaxed economic pressure on both workers and peasants, provided something more for consumers, reduced police pressure, and announced amnesties for many and rehabilitation for some of the party purge victims. These measures sufficed in East Germany, Czechoslovakia, Bulgaria, and Romania.

The most industrialized countries were Czechoslovakia and the GDR. Stalinist industrialization had caused great strain to their economies, and its relaxation allowed them to function more efficiently. In the GDR, moreover, both the party and the population were still under tight control following the June 1953 revolt. In Czechoslovakia, the purges had been a national trauma, but they had also removed potential troublemakers from the party, and the fact that Gottwald died in Moscow just after Stalin meant that there was no Little Stalin left in place to struggle against. De-Stalinization was taken up by younger functionaries who had been formed by the purges and who largely stuck together.

Both Romania and Bulgaria remained largely peasant countries in 1953, and Stalinist methods of industrialization were still producing impressive new results. In Bulgaria there was little anti-Soviet sentiment because there was little anti-Russian sentiment, and the Bulgarian party was still disciplined. It managed to oust the local Little Stalin, Vulko Chervenkov, in April 1956, just before unrest broke out to the north. Chervenkov had already yielded his party post to Todor Zhivkov in 1954. Romania was very anti-Russian, and its party was still very weak. Romania was the last to produce a reconstruction plan, it had the heaviest rate of investment for industrialization — 34 percent of "produced national income" in 1953, a terrifying figure — but also the slowest rate of agricultural collectivization. By way of compensation, perhaps, it had a cunning Communist leader: Gheorghe Gheorghiu-Dej had managed to purge out his most Stalinist rivals already in 1952, and he managed in 1954, a full year after Stalin's death, to execute the leadership rival most likely to represent liberalism and nationalism, Lucreţiu Patraşcanu.[12]

In the most and least industrialized countries, therefore, the leaders kept afloat by extending their bases of support within their parties on a less demanding but still neo-Stalinist program.[13] Except when they had to eat crow for Tito at Khrushchev's behest, the question of relations with the Soviets was resolved in a way that satisfied both, and did not become a public issue. The leaders of the GDR, Czechoslovakia, Romania, and Bulgaria were not forced to seek new support beyond the Soviets and their parties. In most of Eastern Europe, the old dichotomy of us versus them, and the myth of the party as the heroic and scientific substitute for the working class, survived de-Stalinization intact.

Not so in Poland and Hungary. In these two countries, Stalin's death set in train political processes that raised the national issue in terms of relations with the Soviet Union and the legitimacy of (non-Soviet) national paths to communism. Both had started about half to two-thirds peasant, with pockets of industry, extremely weak Communist parties, and populations that were very anti-Russian. In both, Stalinist industrialization had compounded social stresses. In particular, it had both repressed and expanded the intelligentsias. This was true in all the East European countries, but in Poland and Hungary, more than in any of the others, the intelligentsias had a traditional ethos of national leadership, which had remained very much alive under communism.

Always weak, and now thrown into confusion by Stalin's death and spurred by broad popular discontent, groups in the Polish and Hungarian leaderships seeking to broaden their appeal began to look for support beyond the Communist apparatus, to the Communist intelligentsia.[14] Much of the political debate was therefore couched in Communist terms, and given the Stalinist insistence that the only political question was how best to fight the imperialist enemy, much of it was therefore formally "about" the economy. This was especially true in Hungary. In June 1953 Nagy as premier advanced a New Course for the economy that closely resembled what Malenkov was promoting in the Soviet Union. Under Rákosi, who remained the party chief, Hungary had been a particularly brutal police state, and the pace of industrialization and collectivization had also been particularly rabid there, so the New Course was very controversial. Ostensibly an economic plan, the New Course in Hungary declared Nagy's links to Malenkov and implicitly attacked the legitimacy of the political apparatus needed to support High Stalinist industrialization. In both Poland and Hungary, economic debate led straight into politics, because behind it lay the question of who was responsible for the errors and disproportions in the economy and why the leaderships had run so roughshod over local circumstances. The answers to these questions pointed to Moscow and raised the issue of national paths to communism.

For Communist leaders, "national paths" was by no means a code for ending socialism. Nagy in particular had total faith in the party, and his interpretation of what had gone wrong was spectacularly narrow, limited to the mistakes of individual personalities, to what he called the Bonapartist traits of Stalin and the Rákosi Stalinist clique.[15] This narrowness was striking, because a personalist and moralistic definition of politics was very characteristic of political thinking in general in peasant and postpeasant Eastern Europe. We have seen how Stalinism reinforced the peasant understanding of politics as a binary, moral struggle. Still, Nagy's personalism was not only a sign of the times and the place but also a natural first step away from Stalinism. If a leader can make errors, even if these errors are conceived only as a misapplication of universal principles, it follows that he has to make choices among better and worse alternatives. Thus, the application of the principles of socialism requires knowledge of concrete circumstances, and each party has a legitimate Communist right to choose its country's path, because it knows its country best. That conclusion, as Rákosi saw and charged, and as Nagy and his supporters denied, was potentially Titoist, and potentially anti-Soviet. Whether that potential became real or not was a matter for politics, as it always is. When it came to politics, however, there was a critical difference between Poland and Hungary, and it lay in the situation of their parties. The Polish party had not purged itself as savagely as the Hungarian, and it had a Communist leader in reserve.[16] This was Władysław Gomułka, the party general secretary during the struggle for power. Although he had been removed from the party in 1949 and had been under house arrest since 1951, he had not been killed or forced to recant. Gomułka was politically astute enough to keep his thoughts to himself as the political crisis built. Moreover, Edward Ochab, the successor to Bierut whom the Soviets imposed on the Polish party in March 1956, was a loyal centrist who lacked the personal ambition that might have spawned a new series of purges. The Polish party leadership was able to avoid the crystallization of factions around concrete programs associated with Soviet factions. In Hungary, by contrast, Nagy had created a program that was clearly linked to one Soviet faction, Malenkov's, and the arch-Stalinist, Rákosi, was still in power. The disorder that resulted, as Nagy was ousted after Malenkov in 1955 and as Rákosi was forced from power after Khrushchev's secret speech a year later, split the Hungarian party.

Khrushchev's secret speech of February 1956 was a shock everywhere in Eastern Europe's post-Stalin landscape, but in Poland and Hungary it produced disillusionment bordering on religious conversion among the Communist intelligentsia to whom the embattled leaderships were just then seeking to appeal. Their extreme feelings of guilt became a moral commitment never again to collude in such crimes and a dedication to a new Communist purity and idealism. This wave of defensive moralism engulfed the young Communist intellectuals who had joined in order to create a new world in the early postwar period and to whom the leadership had been appealing for support since Stalin's death.[17] Nagy surrounded himself with such people. Gomułka did not, but they worshipped him from afar as a savior in exile.

In June 1956 the workers in the western Polish city of Poznań revolted. Although the rising was put down in blood, all the groups in the leadership now turned to Gomułka to implement shifts in policy that would save the situation by taking Polish national characteristics into account. Once the others had agreed, however, Gomułka became the leader of a united Polish party — he attended his first regular Politburo meeting on October 13 — and the idol of a united Polish nation. The trouble was that the Soviets had not yet agreed and were not sure they would agree. On October 17 the Soviet ambassador delivered a formal invitation to the Poles to visit Moscow. When the Polish Politburo begged off on the grounds that its Central Committee had not yet ratified the deal, on October 19 a top Soviet leadership delegation headed by Khrushchev arrived uninvited in Warsaw, determined to be consulted, as Soviet tanks moved toward the capital. Faced with Polish party and national unity around Gomułka, the Soviets decided over two days of strenuous negotiation to take a gamble that the man and his limited brand of national communism under firm party leadership would not eat into the essentials of the system. Soviet troop movements ceased on October 20, and on October 21 the Polish Politburo elected its new slate.

In Hungary the intelligentsia then rose in solidarity with the victorious Poles. The situation then developed in a way that convinced the Soviets they could not afford another such gamble. For in Hungary the students were joined by the whole population, workers and lumpen elements from the Budapest streets combined, angry and eager to correct all the evils Stalinism had wrought. In face of that uprising the heavily factionalized and demoralized Hungarian party simply disintegrated. During the night of October 23 Nagy was finally brought back as premier, and on October 25 he was joined by János Kádár, who had also suffered under Rákosi, as party leader; but in the meantime the Soviets also brought in tanks to control the streets. They were first welcomed, then fired on by mysterious assailants, then, as fighting spread, withdrawn. The excited Hungarians took this to mean that the Soviet political will had been broken — a mistake the Poles never made — and they proceeded to take over both the economy and the political system from below, with workers' councils in the factories and proliferating political parties, all operating almost without reference to the Communists.

Nagy was constantly behind this wave. At some point the Soviets decided that he could not get control of it and began to move their tanks back toward Budapest. Even as they did so, they formally recognized the legitimacy of national paths to communism, in a Soviet government declaration of October 30, 1956. Nagy and his colleagues were more impressed with the tanks than with the declaration. Appalled at Soviet betrayal of him, for the first time in his life Nagy went outside the party to become leader of the Hungarian nation. In the three days between October 30 and November 1 he proclaimed a full multiparty system, then negotiations to withdraw Hungary from the Warsaw Pact, then Hungary's neutrality. There is some evidence that Soviet counsels on what to do were divided (the October 30 declaration is part of it), but Nagy's betrayal certainly swung the balance in favor of full-scale repression. In four days of heavy fighting the Soviets retook Budapest and installed Kádár, who had just fled to join them, and a regime of repression that simply flattened Hungarian political and social life for four long years.[18] The personal politics the Communists claimed they were replacing now avenged itself on them, and in blood.

Where were the people in all this? Their discontent forced the relaxation of economic and police pressure, giving the Stalinists their argument that such relaxation threatened the regime and giving the party liberals their argument that only relaxation that turned into reform could save the regime. Popular discontent had also forced the leaderships to consolidate support from the party and in Poland and Hungary to reach out to party intellectuals. As party bureaucrats and intellectuals debated policy in both countries, both groups tried to reach out to the broader masses. Also, the people — students and workers together, and especially young students and young workers — provided the crowds supporting the Polish and Hungarian leaderships against the Soviets. In Budapest young workers and the lumpen elements provided the street fighters. After the fighting was over, Hungarian workers continued to resist Soviet occupation in a total general strike throughout the country that lasted almost a month.[19]

Before 1956, Stalinists had feared a revolt of the lumpen elements, led by the remnants of the feudalists and the bourgeoisie. The risings of 1956 confirmed these fears, to some small extent. The rabble — Pegleg Janko and his Budapest street fighters straight out of *Threepenny Opera* — did enter the fray. The old parties promptly reappeared and squabbled over how to divide the ministerial posts after the Communists were gone. In the aftermath, the remaining Stalinists insisted that reactionaries and lumpen elements had controlled the uprisings.[20] Despite this claim, the real lesson of Poland and Hungary in 1956 was completely different, and, although it was never admitted, it sank in. The events of 1956 showed that the new working class, the pride and hope of the insecure Communist regimes all over Eastern Europe, and the new working intelligentsia, children of peasants and workers who were supposed to swamp the old bourgeois humanists, were at least potentially disloyal. The proletarian army that the party as the proletariat's revolutionary vanguard had tried to create by establishing industry was now there, but in Hungary at least, it had rejected the generalship of its creators.

Neither admitted nor perceived was the transposition of peasant values and peasant habits into the heart of the new revolutionary working class. Imre Nagy — his personalism, his moralism, his stubbornness — symbolized it, but it went much further and deeper. In both Poland and Hungary the workers spontaneously organized themselves during 1956 into factory councils. These councils formed national networks that became real forces in politics, completely outside the trade unions led by Stalinist bureaucrats. The councils ran the general strike in Hungary and then what was left of resistance to the Kádár regime well into 1957. The Gomułka government in Poland needed two years to wrestle them into insignificance.[21]

In 1950 the Yugoslav party had formally turned the economy over to worker self-management, as an act of creative communism that validated its claim to national coequality with the Soviet party.[22] The fact that the new Polish and Hungarian factory councils resembled Yugoslav self-management was one reason why the regimes saw them as a threat. In neither case did the workers attack socialism as such, or support a return to capitalism or private ownership. Communism in Eastern Europe had made that much progress by 1956. By the same token, however, because socialism as such was not at issue, workers very quickly added political demands to their concrete economic demands.

Perhaps most suggestively, these workers' councils stood for worker control of the factories, for self-government on a local basis without regard for the requirements of outside authorities or the national economy. This meant that the new working class resembled the peasantry from which it had just emerged. The factory councils reproduced the ideal of peasant self-sufficiency, which had historically been the region's greatest obstacle to economic development, in the very heart of the industrializing cities. The peasantry had not gone away: It had transformed and imbedded itself in the new, ostensibly more modern Communist Eastern Europe.

All the protagonists drew conclusions from the crises of 1956. The populations discovered that pressure brings concessions, but that too much pressure brings repression. The intelligentsias had been confirmed in their role of captains of the national soul, but everywhere except Poland and Hungary they were also confirmed in their isolation. They knew that they could not play their role alone and that they needed to seek support among the workers rather than among the peasants.

The Soviets and the East European regimes had been forced to appreciate the importance of national issues. East European Communists therefore had both a limited license from the Soviets and a challenge from their peoples to try to capture national issues for themselves. Also, the old shape of the national issue — for or against Titoism — was transformed. Tito's endorsement of the second Soviet intervention in Hungary, however carefully qualified, meant that the Yugoslavs recognized that Soviet use of force to save socialism was justified in some circumstances. The Yugoslavs thereby sacrificed the credibility of their support for national paths of communism, and Yugoslavia began the long, slow road to irrelevance for developments in the rest of "socialist Europe." [23] For the time being, the Soviet Government Declaration of October 30 recognizing national roads to communism remained a dead letter. But below the surface, the challenge of the national issue was clearer than ever before.

The regimes that felt too weak to take on that challenge had the option of trying to defuse the national issue by welfare economics, of stealing the new working classes away from the new intelligentsia by raising living standards. Every regime worried less about peasants and the bourgeois and more about workers and intellectuals, and focused its political energies on preventing another alliance between them. All East European Communists had also observed the results of party factionalization in Hungary. The year 1956 reinforced the value they attached to party unity, and thus to the original us-them dichotomy of Stalinism. Force was still available, but in terms of the new challenges and the new responses required — boosting productivity, convincing by persuasion — it was less likely to be effective than before. More and more, and in more and more places, regime violence ceased to be the weapon of first resort, as regimes struggled to replace it with party unity bolstered now by ideological conviction and economic growth.

The Soviet state and party had broader responsibilities than any individual East European state and party, and saw the issues more broadly. The reconquest of Hungary destroyed the spirit of Geneva in East-West relations and threatened a renewal of East-West tensions and thus a new surge of Western consolidation. In response, the Soviets proceeded after 1956 to revamp the whole structure of their imperial rule in Eastern Europe.[24]

Notes

1. There is of course an enormous literature on the Tito-Stalin split. Leszek Kołakowski's *Main Currents of Marxism, Vol. 3: The Breakdowm* (Oxford: Oxford University Press, 1978), 474-478, is a good summary of its significance for the Communist world as a whole, but the *locus classicus* is still Adam Ulam's older *Titoism and the Cominform* (Cambridge, Mass.: Harvard University Press, 1952).

2. Jiří Pelikán, ed., *The Czechoslovak Political Trials 1950-1954* (Stanford: Stanford University Press, 1971), 69-139.

3. For a useful account of the "Third Force" option and its demise in West European politics, see Wilfried Loth, *The Division of the World, 1941-1955* (New York: St. Martin's, 1988), 176ff.

4. For the "lost opportunity" thesis and how it thenceforth became a staple in West German politics, see William Hyland, *The Cold War Is Over* (New York: Times Books, 1990), 57ff., and the citations to West German scholarly literature on the topic in Norman Naimark, "Soviet-GDR Relations: An Historical Overview" (Cologne: Bundesinstitut für ostwissenschafliche und internationale Studien, Bericht 52-1989, mimeo). For readers of German, there are more recent considerations in Michael Lemke, "Chance oder Risiko? Die Stalin-Note vom 10. Marz 1952 im aussenpolitischen Konzept der Bundesregierung," *Zeitschrift fur Geschichtswissenschaft*, 2 (1991), 115-129, and Gerhard Wettig, "Die Stalin-Note vom 10. Marz 1952 als geschichtswissenschaftliches Problem," *Deutschland Archiv*, 2 (February 1992), 157-167.

5. The best work available in English is still Arnulf Baring, *Uprising in East Germany: June 17, 1953* (Ithaca: Cornell University Press, 1972); for a more recent recapitulation, see Victor Baras, "Beria's Fall and Ulbricht's Survival," *Soviet Studies*, 27, no. 3 (July 1975): 381-395. On the Soviet approach to reunification after Stalin's death, readers of German should now consult Gerhard Wettig, "Sowjetische Wiedervereinigungs-

bemühungen im ausgehenden Frühjahr 1953?," *Deutschland Archiv,* 9 (September 1992), 943-958. Newly published Soviet archives show that plotting to let the GDR pass under Western control was in fact one of several charges levelled against Beria in the Central Committee: see "New Evidence on Beria's Downfall," *Cold War International History Project Bulletin* (Washington, D.C.: Woodrow Wilson International Center for Scholars), no. 1 (Spring 1992), 16, 27.

6. On the recurrent destabilizing effect on Eastern Europe of Soviet domestic political preoccupation in the 1950s, the 1960s, and again in the 1980s, see Charles Gati, *The Bloc that Failed* (Bloomington: Indiana University Press, 1990), 60. We shall see the phenomenon at closer range as we go along.

7. Zbigniew Brzezinski, *The Soviet Bloc: Unity and Conflict,* rev. ed. (New York: Praeger, 1961), 221. For a convenient recent summary of the post-Stalin Soviet approach to Eastern Europe, see Michael Shafir, "Eastern Europe," in Martin McCauley, ed., *Khrushchev and Khrushchevism* (Bloomington: Indiana University Press, 1987), 156-179.

8. The classic work is still Michel Tatu, *Power in the Kremlin from Khrushchev to Kosygin* (New York: Viking, 1968); for the period after 1957, Carl A. Linden, *Khrushchev and the Soviet Leadership 1957-1964* (Baltimore: Johns Hopkins University Press, 1966), is also useful.

9. For a good recent summary of the reconciliation process, see Robert F. Miller, "Khrushchev and Tito," in R.F. Miller and F. Fehér, ed., *Khrushchev and the Communist World* (Totowa, N.J.: Barnes & Noble, 1984), 189-209.

10. Brzezinski, *Soviet Bloc,* 52ff.

11. On the Zambrowski episode, see Flora Lewis, *A Case History of Hope* (New York: Doubleday, 1958), 105-106; on Rákosi, see Gati, "Moscow and Imre Nagy," in *Hungary and the Soviet Bloc* (Durham: Duke University Press, 1986), 131, with citations to the Hungarian sources.

12. On the New Course in Bulgaria, see J.F. Brown, *Bulgaria Under Communist Rule* (New York: Praeger, 1970), 22-82. The 1953 figure for Romania is taken from John Michael Montias, *Economic Development in Communist Rumania* (Cambridge, Mass.: MIT Press, 1967), 27; that work remains the classic analysis of its subject. On the political process in Romania, see Ghita Ionescu, *Communism in Romania 1944-1962* (London: Oxford University Press, 1964), and "Transformation and Consolidation under Dej," with citations to the recent literature, in Michael Shafir, *Romania. Politics, Economics and Society. Political Stagnation and Simulated Change* (Boulder: Lynne Rienner, 1985), 41-46.

13. For pertinent comments on the role of party strength and character in these developments, written not long after, see Hugh Seton-Watson, "The East European Communist Parties, 1944-1958," in his *Nationalism and Communism. Essays 1946-1958* (New York: Praeger, 1964), 163-172.

14. That the intelligentsia was the linchpin of development is clear from both Lewis, *Case History of Hope* (for Poland) and Bill Lomax, *Hungary 1956* (New York: St. Martin's, 1976), despite Lomax's effort to ascribe that role to the working class.

15. This is clear from Nagy's privately circulated writings of the time, later reprinted as Imre Nagy, *On Communism: In Defense of the New Course* (New York: Praeger, 1957); and Charles Gati carefully establishes Nagy's role as Moscow's man in "Moscow and Imre Nagy, 1953-1956" in his *Hungary and the Soviet Bloc,* 127-155: It helps explain (though not excuse) the ferocity of Moscow's retribution.

16. Flora Lewis, "The Shadow of a Prisoner," in her *Case History of Hope*, 37-53; for a
     later counterpoint, see Jadwiga Staniszkis, "October 1956 as Ritual Drama: Case Study
     of Artificial Negativity," in her *Poland's Self-Limiting Revolution* (Princeton: Prin-
     ceton University Press, 1984), 278-281. Much new material on Gomułka and the politics
     of the time is appearing in Poland itself, but the standard English-language biography
     is still Nicholas Bethell, *Gomułka: His Poland and his Communism* (1969; London:
     Penguin/Pelican, 1972).
17. Because Kołakowski was a veteran of these processes, his account of de-Stalinization
     and the East European revisionism of 1953 to 1956 is especially valuable: Main
     Currents, 450-464.
18. The text is given in Paul E. Zinner, ed., *National Communism and Popular Revolt in
     Eastern Europe* (New York: Columbia University Press, 1956), 485-492. On the Soviet
     decision to intervene the second time, see Michael G. Fry and Condoleeza Rice, "The
     Hungarian Crisis of 1956: The Soviet Decision," *Studies in Comparative Communism*,
     16, nos. 1 & 2 (Spring/Summer 1983): 85-98. For some (bitterly anti-Kádárist) Hun-
     garian reconsideration, see Ferenc Fehér and Agnes Heller, *Hungary 1956 Revisited*
     (London: Allen & Unwin, 1983).
19. Lomax is eloquent on these developments, though he still fails to convince (me) that
     they signified working-class domination of the revolution: *Hungary 1956*, 146ff.
     Analysis of new material now emerging suggests that the Budapest fighters were
     "mostly young, unskilled workers, and, in some cases, students, soldiers and army
     officers," and that for all of them political motivation was "weakly defined": see Csaba
     Békés, "New Findings on the 1956 Hungarian Revolution," *Cold War International
     History Project Bulletin* (Washington, D.C.: Woodrow Wilson International Center
     for Scholars), Issue 2 (Fall 1992), 1, 2-3. This piece is disappointingly without documen-
     tation but promises it will appear in the 1992 Yearbook of the Institute for the History
     of the 1956 Revolution in Budapest. For a journalistic foretaste of what researchers
     from this project may turn up in Soviet archives on issues ranging across our whole
     period, see John-Thor Dahlberg and Cindy Scharf, "Sifting for Soviet Clues to the Cold
     War's History," *Los Angeles Times*, 25 January 1993.
20. The Soviet official history of 1956 continued to stress the few lynchings of Communists
     as if they were the whole revolution, and the high-security residential complex of the
     East German leadership that was discovered and dismantled in November 1989 amid
     general indignation had been set up in November 1956, after Budapest: Gati, *Hungary
     and the Soviet Bloc*, 152, and David Binder, "Where East Berlin's Elite Lived It Up,"
     in Bernard Gwertzman and Michael T. Kaufman, eds., *The Collapse of Communism*
     (New York: Times Books, 1990), 260-262. Memories were also long and green (or red)
     within the leadership: a former senior Polish official who was there told me that when
     the next steps in Poland were under discussion in Moscow in December, 1981 (a week
     before Polish martial law was declared), the Soviet hosts ran films of 1956 Budapest
     lynchings for their Polish comrades.
21. See Timothy Garton Ash, *The Polish Revolution: Solidarity* (New York: Scribner's,
     1983), 9-11, on the long-term significance of this neutralization. In Hungary, new
     documentation puts the movement at 2,100 workers' councils with 28,000 members
     throughout the country: see Békés, "New Findings on the 1956 Hungarian Revolu-
     tion," 2. By contrast, the demands of the East German workers in June 1953 were more
     direct and also more political: reduction in work norms, but also free and secret

elections, the release of political prisoners, the removal of Ulbricht and the like: Baring, *Uprising in East Germany*, 68-78.

22. On the development of a distinctively Yugoslav version of communism, I have found the following works useful: M. George Zaninovich, "The Yugoslav Variation on Marx," in Wayne S. Vucinich, ed., *Contemporary Yugoslavia. Twenty Years of Socialist Experiment* (Berkeley: University of California Press, 1969), 285-315; A. Ross Johnson, *The Transformation of Communist Ideology: The Yugoslav Case, 1948-1953* (Cambridge, Mass.: MIT Press, 1972); and Eric R. Terzuolo, "Soviet-Yugoslav Conflict and the Origins of Yugoslavia's Self-Management System," in Wayne S. Vucinich, ed., *At the Brink of War and Peace: The Tito-Stalin Split in a Historic Perspective* (New York: Columbia University Press, 1982), 195-218.

23. On Tito's dilemma, see Brzezinski, *Soviet Bloc*, 229-235.

24. For many years Leszek Kołakowski was one of the few who believed the system could not survive, so now that it is gone he may be forgiven for reaffirming that "(a)fter Stalin's death the totalitarian *will* to power survived, but its effectiveness and skill in enforcing slavery grew weaker and weaker, all the regressions and U-turns notwithstanding. A tyrannical regime, suddenly ashamed of mass slaughter, that seeks to replace it with selective terror is doomed": "Amidst Moving Ruins," *Daedalus*, 121, no. 2 (Spring 1992), 45. But this "truth," if that is what it is, was not only very unclear at the time, but revealed itself only slowly, through tortuous processes which I examine and define in what follows. Perhaps my problem with it is that lightning which takes more than thirty years to strike is, as Americans say, some lightning; perhaps it is only that historians have a different "truth" from philosophers.

SIX

THE IRON RING, 1956-1968

As the Cold War developed, it drew attention away from its place of origin. The Soviet invasion of Hungary was overshadowed in the West by the debacle at Suez, and the East-West tension of the years after 1956 was no longer focused in Europe. For the West, Eastern Europe continued to symbolize what Soviets would do if they were not contained but was no longer considered to be a prime arena of active competition. The Soviet Union launched *Sputnik* in 1957, opening the age of the intercontinental ballistic missile, ending American invulnerability, and bringing the Cold War home to Americans. Meanwhile, decolonization was creating new opportunities for the Soviet Union to expand its influence in the Southeast Asia, Africa, and Latin America, and the West felt compelled to respond. Berlin in 1961 was the last great East-West crisis in Europe, Cuba in 1962, the first of a series of confrontations in the Third World that were politically recognized as such (for Korea had been considered a confrontation at the core).

This shift of emphasis in the Cold War was possible in part because Stalinism made enough successful adjustments to sustain itself after 1956. The West had been vociferously indignant as Hungary and Poland rose, but in the end that had been the limit of its response. The worst fears of the Soviets and East European regimes had not been justified. The old parties had tried to reassert themselves in Hungary, where revolt had not come from feudal and bourgeois remnants but rather from the new working class and the remade intelligentsia. Economic success in the late 1950s allowed the regimes to relax the pace of industrialization and expand consumption, and this gave them and the Soviets a measure of confidence that East European workers and intellectuals could be satisfied by a new economic dispensation.[1] In trying to design such a dispensation without fundamentally changing Stalinism, the East European regimes experimented throughout these years. This period of innovation, 1956 to 1968, may be roughly but helpfully divided into two phases, 1956 to 1960 and 1960 to 1968. The years around 1960 were a major turning point in the history of Communist rule in the area.

The first phase, 1956 to 1960, is associated with the leadership of Nikita Sergeievich Khrushchev in the USSR. With his victory over the "antiparty group" in 1957, Khrushchev was firmly in power. Of course, his power was not as absolute as Stalin's had been, so the Soviet line fluctuated more than it had under Stalin. Khrushchev was personally interested in experimentation and considered it mandatory for all Communists, especially those in Eastern Europe. His experiments in foreign policy included stirring up a crisis in Berlin, putting missiles in Cuba, and preparing another offer to the West regarding German unification. At home, he experimented with combining party and government, with separating industrial and agricultural management, with a territorial approach to running the economy; he experimented with corn, with the Virgin Lands in Kazakhstan, with making all schools boarding schools. When he was overthrown in a palace coup in 1964, what were then called his "harebrained schemes" constituted the main charge against him.[2] The dour defensiveness of Stalinism was now out of favor in Moscow. Khrushchevian experimentalism was buoyant and optimistic in spirit. Soviet rates of economic growth were high, decolonization seemed to mark the decline of imperialism and open up new opportunities to beat it through the back door, and Khrushchev himself was borne by a renewed confidence in the future of socialism. He told Americans that his country would bury them. Surpassing capitalism in production was written into the 1961 Soviet Communist party program as a realistic target for 1980.

The broad purpose of de-Stalinization was to consolidate Communist rule by replacing force with assent wherever possible. Given his optimism about socialism's superior economic efficiency, it was natural for Khrushchev to regard economics and ideology as the keys to maintaining Stalinism without Stalin. The Khrushchev leadership believed that economics should be the means by which governments gained support from their people and by which the Soviet Union maintained the loyalty of its allies. Success at either of these levels required that economic relations between the Soviet Union and Eastern Europe be reformed to benefit both partners, rather than just the Soviets, as they had under Stalin. Such a positive sum outcome was difficult to achieve at first, as the Soviets had little to give. Pending the kind of growth in the Soviet economy that would produce the surpluses and markets that the East Europeans wanted, the Soviets could at least allow them some genuine autonomy for economic decisionmaking. The Soviets saw clearly that this was not without peril, for the habit of autonomy in economics could easily create the desire for autonomy in politics. The Soviets were willing to take that chance, for simultaneously they brought the same buoyant optimism to the task of reinforcing the ideological and institutional bases of the socialist camp.[3]

In the years after 1956 the Khrushchev leadership embarked on what might in retrospect be called a four-point program for revamping the structure of Communist rule and Soviet dominion in Eastern Europe. The program was framed within the standard ideological binarism. Monopoly capitalism in its imperialist form was still the enemy, and reform was to be a project of the united socialist camp. The significant debate of this period was among Communists, just as it had been in immediate de-Stalinization period between 1953 and 1956. The question was definitely not alternatives to socialism: The Soviets had shown in 1956 that they were determined to prevent such alternatives by force if necessary. The issue was how to make Stalinism work without Stalin; its crux was to do so using as little force as possible. The four parts of the Khrushchevian program were the following.

First, because the Soviets wanted to make their version of Communist ideology consensual rather than imposed, real rather than simply ritual, they allowed genuine debate, albeit within narrow limits. Politically, the goal was to construct and occupy an ideological middle ground between unrepentant Stalinists and genuine reformers, and exclude both from the new consensus. But to fashion such a consensus and then to maintain it, real discussion was required. East European Communists took up the debate — on the economy, on the meaning of socialist internationalism, on the legitimate limits of debate itself — with enthusiasm.

Ideological debate was also relevant to international politics. The reformers, now called revisionists, were still identified with the Yugoslavs, and the Stalinists, now called dogmatists, were coming more and more to be identified with the Chinese. These were the years of the last comprehensive conferences of the world Communist and workers' movement in Moscow, and the Soviets were struggling to maintain Moscow's leadership in the movement. They were ultimately unsuccessful, but the result in the meantime was to keep the regimes interested in wooing the intellectuals where they could, while repressing them only where they felt they must. In other words, after the trauma of 1956 they did not return to systematic repression.[4]

Second, Khrushchev tried to enliven the institutions of the socialist camp, the Warsaw Treaty Organization (Warsaw Pact) founded in May 1955 as a pendant to NATO and the Council for Mutual Economic Assistance (CMEA, or Comecon), which had been founded in 1949 as a vehicle for organizing the boycott of Yugoslavia.[5] As long as systematic Stalinist bilateralism dominated Soviet-East European relations in all fields, these multilateral institutions had been skeletons with very little flesh. After 1956 the Soviets accepted that they would have to listen and bargain rather than simply command, and they took the first tentative steps to give the Warsaw Pact and Comecon some real life.

It was coming to be recognized that the industrial products favored by the Soviet model engendered considerable duplication and tremendous losses in economies of scale in these small countries. Within Comecon, Khrushchev created an elaborate structure of commissions to encourage specialization in product lines, and in 1958 at Bucharest the organization formally adopted world market prices as the standard for valuing trade among the member countries. The new commitment to economic specialization meant that the Soviets recognized in principle that they would have to sacrifice for the common good. But just as they were unwilling to allow anyone but themselves (and the reprobate Yugoslavs) to exercise the right to national paths to communism they had formally granted in 1956, they were unwilling in the first years after 1956 to give up any product lines, which meant that specialization within Comecon was only for the states of Eastern Europe, and not very attractive to them.

Third, the Soviets did end some of their more exploitative trade practices. Because their economic exploitation of Eastern Europe had been a political issue in 1956, they canceled debts, allowed the East Europeans to buy back the Soviet shares of the joint companies that had been ruthless vehicles for resource transfer to the USSR, and allowed the terms of trade — the relationship of prices for products they sold to prices for products they bought — to shift against them in some areas. They also allowed countries with resources that could be sold in the West to develop some trade ties with capitalist economies. These changes in trade policy left the East Europeans with more resources, and because the Soviets were now allowing economic experimentation, the regimes had some discretion over how these resources were used. They were used partly to boost consumption, partly to shift investment out of heavy industry, and partly to reform. In 1958 the Poles and Czechoslovaks significantly decentralized investment decisions. That same year the Bulgarians embarked on a curious miniversion of the Chinese Great Leap Forward, completing agricultural collectivization on the basis of communes rather than collectives.[6]

Fourth, and most important, the late 1950s witnessed a new burst of industrialization throughout the area, and it was accompanied by a restructuring of the Soviet economy that made huge new resources of industrial raw materials available for trade with Eastern Europe. Soviet energy production had always been based overwhelmingly on coal, but a crash program in oil development that began in 1955 tripled Soviet petroleum output in five years. Massive if less spectacular advances also took place in the output of iron ore and other minerals. Such successes underlay Khrushchev's optimism about socialism and provided the key to maintaining Soviet rule with minimum force in Eastern Europe. Just as direct Soviet rule became intolerable, East European industrialization was reaching the point at which raw materials and markets were urgently needed, and the Soviet economy was changing so that it could supply these needs.[7] This essentially new economic link between Eastern Europe and the Soviet Union, which I will call the iron ring, was a crucial development for the next three decades of East European history. Its causes, character, and development therefore warrant investigation.

Recall that economic Stalinism required a closed economy to work at all, because central planning required state control of all significant economic resources. As domestic capital was perpetually short and labor was soon immobile, foreign trade soon became the one economic sector over which central planners had real discretion. But Stalin had preserved

Eastern Europe's national boundaries, so that all resource transfers across them were subject to international negotiation. Because they represented the overwhelmingly largest economy, and the predominant political power to boot, Soviet negotiators had the most bargaining power, but bargaining was still required.

Moreover, because convertible currencies would give foreign states that held them purchasing power in the internal markets of the issuing state, and thus the power to interfere with the functioning of its central plan, "socialist" currencies were inconvertible. And because their currencies were inconvertible and their prices were artificial, reflecting planners' priorities rather than supply and demand, Communist states tended to barter, to trade by negotiating exchanges of needed products.

Unlike capitalist firms, socialist states sold goods only in order to buy needed inputs for their planned economies, but they needed those inputs desperately if they were to avoid bottlenecks and breakdowns and maintain steady growth on the scale of whole nations. So they had both an aversion and a propensity to trade, and in practice this made trade susceptible to large, disturbing fluctuations. To reduce them, they all sought to negotiate agreements valid for at least a year and preferably longer and providing for balanced exchanges of quantities of goods, with no surpluses and no deficits. In the negotiations required to effect this bilateral balancing and keep it going, those who had surpluses of goods that others needed, and who were willing to take goods that could not be sold elsewhere, had the whip hand. Most often this meant the Soviets, but over the course of the 1950s other countries — and not necessarily the strongest by classic Western criteria — seized it too.[8]

Most of Eastern Europe was poor in oil, coal, and iron, the resources required for heavy industrialization, but at first the consequences were hidden. The regimes began industrialization by using agricultural collectivization as well as the natural pull of city living to shift labor into heavy industry. Industry was built using the existing technologies of the late 1940s and early 1950s, what raw materials the countries had, and what raw materials the Soviets could spare to supplement them. The result was rapid growth but persistently low productivity of both labor and capital. In the one area without rural underemployment, the Czech lands, labor was obtained first by collectivizing agriculture, then by forcing women into the labor force, where they reached a participation rate of over 85 percent. Once the reserves of peasants and women had been depleted, the Czechs used convict labor.[9] Throughout the process, they simply ran down the industrial plant inherited from capitalism by building heavy industry instead of the light industry that had supported capitalism between the wars. Between 1949 and 1964 less than 2 percent of the value of the stock of machinery was retired, and as it aged its productivity declined.[10] Elsewhere the Stalinist industrialization strategy, using the resources available, looked like just what the doctors ordered.

The initial results of industrialization were astounding. Tremendous rates of growth of national income and industrial production served as a superb advertisement for socialism to the less developed world and as a source of pride in socialism for the regimes. It was only around 1960 that some less welcome side effects of Stalinist industrialization began to heave into view.

The industrialization had all been based on massive inputs of unskilled labor, and by about 1960 the reserves of underemployed peasants were beginning to dry up. When that happened, capital/output ratios — the amount of capital needed to produce a given increment of production — rose. And because the region was as short of capital as it had always been, efficiency of capital investment became the overwhelming economic concern.

Meanwhile, the technologies of the 1940s and 1950s that had been exploited in the initial drive were becoming antiquated, and it was also becoming apparent that the Stalinist system resisted the technological innovation and diffusion that were needed to make capital more efficient. Because production (and bonuses) were determined by yearly quantitative output targets handed down by the central planners, the short-term dips in production that are needed to integrate new technologies appeared disadvantageous. Once production lines were in place, managers, workers, and planners had no incentive to change them. Moreover, there was no price mechanism to allow anyone to judge real economic costs, and therefore efficiency.

Most significant, Stalinist economics meant that East European industry built second-rate heavy machinery, in quantities far in excess of East European needs, and unsalable on hard-currency markets. Producing that machinery required raw materials that were not indigenous to Eastern Europe, and selling it required a peculiar kind of customer.

If East Europeans were to buy off their working classes and intelligentsias with higher living standards after 1956, they had to resolve these problems. Steady economic growth rates were needed to maintain Communist rule without much use of force. But given the structure of industrialization and the peculiar character of trade within the region, such growth (and the possibility of an economic dispensation for workers and intellectuals) came to depend on each regime's ability to fob off its surpluses of second-rate machinery onto others in return for the fuel and raw materials required to produce more machinery.[11]

This bind seized each country in turn as it reached a certain level of Stalinist industrialization. It created a counterintuitive distinction between "hard" goods — agricultural products and raw materials that could be sold on hard currency markets — and "soft" goods — goods, usually machinery, that could not find hard-currency buyers. Under the system of bilateral trade balancing, countries that still had hard goods to spare — Polish coal and hams, Romanian oil, Bulgarian fruits and vegetables — could force other socialist countries that needed such goods to buy their own surplus machinery. It put the less developed countries — Romania, Bulgaria, and to a lesser extent Poland — in the driver's seat of intra-Communist trade, and made the more developed countries — the GDR, Czechoslovakia, and increasingly Poland and Hungary — ever more dependent on the Soviet Union for raw materials and markets.[12] The countryside took a paradoxical revenge on the city. The Soviet Union, whose economy could still use second-rate machinery, and which now had new surpluses of raw materials coming on line, became the natural arbiter of each country's economic destiny, just as it lost its capacity for direct political control. In October 1956 delegations from the GDR, Czechoslovakia, Poland, and Hungary appeared almost simultaneously in Moscow, all begging for more raw materials and more markets for their machinery.[13]

Of course, this transition did not work out that neatly. Throughout this period, first under Khrushchev and then under the collective leadership of Leonid Brezhnev, Alexei Kosygin, and Nikolai Podgorniy that succeeded him in 1964, the Soviets were preoccupied with domestic affairs. This allowed the East Europeans some room to maneuver. They remained subject to the threat of Soviet force, which became reality in Czechoslovakia in 1968, but in general, even after Khrushchev's fall, the Soviets continued to experiment and to tolerate experiments to their west. Their Stalinist economy was facing some of the same problems as those of the East Europeans. The year 1962 saw the publication in *Pravda* of Professor Evsei Liberman's proposals for economic reform, and 1965 saw both a watered-down reform program based on them, but sponsored by Kosygin, and introduction of a farm program involving a tremendous boost in investment in agriculture, and associated with Brezhnev. Though tame, the Liberman proposals and the 1965 programs gave an ideological green light to economic reform in Eastern Europe. Confident of their economic power over the region, the Soviets were willing to accept experimentation.

The transition to Soviet economic hegemony over Eastern Europe through mutually advantageous trade rather than unilateral exploitation, just as Stalinist industrialization was starting to reach the natural limits of its efficiency, was the major reason why the years around 1960 constituted a major turning point for Communist rule in Eastern Europe. And two international developments, both in 1961, made this new economic basis for empire even more important to the Soviets.

The first was the Sino-Soviet split.[14] China's challenge to Soviet ideological primacy went far beyond Tito's insistence on the right to national paths to communism. Like Tito's, it was framed in socialist terms, so that it hurt; but it was more comprehensive, and it reached a pitch of vituperation that made Western anti-Soviet propaganda seem mild by comparison. The Chinese alternative was particularly appealing within the Third World, to which the Soviets were turning as the arena of the future in the competition between imperialism and socialism. The Chinese challenge therefore further diverted Soviet attention to the Third World and away from Eastern Europe. It also eroded Soviet ideological primacy within the world Communist movement, and thus decreased Soviet confidence in the persuasiveness of its version of communism. After 1956 the Soviets had expected ideology to serve as one means of making assent rather than just force the keystone of their rule. As ideology became less reliable, economics became even more important.

The second development, almost simultaneous with the first and not unrelated to it, was the stabilization of the German Democratic Republic following the building of the Berlin Wall in August 1961. Until then, the GDR's best labor had left in a steady stream for West Germany. When the wall stopped the hemorrhage, the GDR could be turned at last into a real socialist state, if not a real nation. The transformation of East Germany into a de facto state had three significant results for Eastern Europe. First, Czech and Polish fear of West German revanchism was tempered somewhat. This fear had been one source of domestic support for these two East European regimes, and it gave them a motive for fidelity to the Soviet Union, the country that had defeated the Germans and guaranteed the postwar status quo, which the others did not have. West German revanchism remained (and remains) an issue, but its importance had begun a long decline. Second, because a stable GDR was the last building block in the edifice of a reliably divided Europe, Soviet attention could continue to drift toward the Third World. Third, the GDR could produce the high-quality industrial goods that only Czechoslovakia had made up to then, and that gave the Czechoslovak economy a needed respite. Czech economic problems continued to fester, but the (very relative) relaxation of bloc demand provided economic and political space for emerging support for economic reform within that nation.

Czechoslovakia had felt the tug of the iron ring first, but as the 1960s progressed every regime had to decide how it would deal with the new, more economic shape of its dependence on the Soviet Union. Each was wrestling with the emerging problems of a new stage of development, as defined and dramatized by the events of 1956, and as the countries weighed their responses, they had some things in common.

First, even as they sought safe ways to make Stalinist rule less rigid and more attractive, most of the regimes wanted to complete the process of Stalinizing their economies. Every country except for Poland, which had decollectivized agriculture in 1956, completed the collectivization process. The years around 1960 witnessed conditions resembling civil war in Hungary, Romania, and Bulgaria, as the last private land was stripped from lowland peasants and they were driven into collectives (some private farming subsisted in the hills). Everywhere, finishing collectivization demonstrated ideological orthodoxy to the Soviets. More important, it was designed to give the regimes a one-shot surplus in hard goods to trade, in order to ward off the iron ring. Collectivization does not make agriculture more efficient, but it does deliver an agricultural surplus into the government's hands. In Poland, decollectivization had the same effect by temporarily boosting agricultural productivity.[15]

Second, the character of politics remained binary and very personal. In these small countries, where most members of the elite knew each other, where every leader depended on clienteles based on personal loyalty at home, and where Communists had to follow the fates of their particular Soviet patron(s), it was genuinely hard to define economic and political issues in terms other than personal power.

Third, the regimes began to face pressure for generational change from new men and occasionally women who had come of age under communism. We have seen their emergence in Hungary, where idealistic young intellectuals who had joined the party after the war led the struggle for reform. But the younger generation were not all liberals; they filled the ideological spectrum. Better educated, more energetic, but also more bureaucratic than the survivors of the Stalinist purges, they shared a desire for high positions in party and government, and now entered the fray of personal politics. It is easy to forget this development, for so many of the Communist leaders we are familiar with, including Brezhnev, Kádár, Honecker, Zhivkov, and Ceauşescu, were prewar Communists. But during the 1950s and 1960s the new generation, these *nouvelles couches montantes* of Communist politics, became cohorts with punches of their own.[16]

Despite these shared traits, some of the common patterns that Stalin imposed upon Eastern Europe in the late 1940s and early 1950s now began to fade. Diversity was controversial in principle, but in practice some diversity became a rule of East European economic and political development. The iron ring of growing dependence on the Soviet market to keep growth rates up generated several distinct responses.

Two countries, East Germany and Bulgaria, chose to snuggle into it. The GDR probably had little choice. It was industrial, so that the tug of the iron ring was especially powerful, and moreover it was scarcely a country. Its main enterprise in the 1960s was nation-building, which required Soviet economic and political help. Trade with West Germany was economically helpful but ideologically dangerous. To reassure the

Soviets, the GDR set out to make itself the Soviet Union's most reliable industrial trading partner.[17]

Bulgaria probably did have a choice. Because it was still industrializing, Stalinist economics were producing high rates of growth without much Soviet help. Bulgaria also had agricultural hard goods that it could trade west and south. Instead, Bulgaria chose to remain the Soviet Union's most faithful and obedient ally. We have little historical evidence at our disposal to evaluate this choice. Bulgaria had its only postwar political crisis in this period, a coup attempt by army officers in April 1965; but the details remain murky.[18] The party was strong and had to contend with little of the national anti-Russian feeling that fed anti-Sovietism in the other countries. Bulgaria did not cease to industrialize, but it did accept the agricultural vocation that Khrushchev had called for, and it tried seriously and with some success to make collectivized agriculture work efficiently. And it extracted benefits in return, even beyond Soviet political support: It had the most favorable terms of trade of any bloc country, and in these years it was singled out for the specialization in electronics manufacture that gave it a disproportionate share in intrasocialist trade in that sector by the 1980s.

Romania had roughly the same options as Bulgaria. Some mileage was left in Stalinist industrialization, and the country still produced "hard" goods, oil as well as food. But when Khrushchev proposed in 1962 to turn Comecon into a supranational organization managing the economic development of the world socialist camp on the basis of comparative advantage, in Romania he provoked not creative acquiescence, as in Bulgaria, but defection. Though Khrushchev's proposal meant that the Soviet Union was willing at long last to submit to collective decisions, the Romanians refused to have any part of it.

The reasons for this refusal are to be found in the unique history and character of the Romanian party. Remember that Romania had been the laughingstock of Eastern Europe: late with a reconstruction plan, over-ambitious in the first Five-Year Plan, late with collectivization. Gheorghe Gheorghiu-Dej's talent for power, however, was no joke. As a friend of mine who knew him put it, he walked the streets in his cloth cap, but at heart he was a Byzantine beast. He had purged his most prominent Stalinist competitors in 1952, so when Stalin died he could claim that

Romania needed no further de-Stalinization. He had kept his anti-Tito polemics relatively moderate, and Tito did not demand his head as the price of reconciliation after 1953. In 1956 Dej helped Khrushchev with Hungary: Soviet troops entered Hungary through Romania, Imre Nagy and the other revolutionary leaders were taken to Romania after leaving the Yugoslav Embassy in Budapest, and the Romanians gave the new Kádár regime immediate and considerable political and financial help. In 1957 Dej succeeded in ridding himself of the last major Jewish Stalinist and the first major liberal in his leadership at the same time. By 1958 Khrushchev was so confident in Dej's rule that he withdrew Soviet troops from Romania.[19]

In this context, from the point of view of Romanian Communists, Khrushchev's proposals to reform Comecon seemed to threaten their nation's emerging strength and independence. Dej took the socialist division of labor proposed for Comecon as an attack on Romania's industrial vocation. Arguing that forced-pace industrialization was the correct Romanian national path to socialism, he used Khrushchev's proposal to gain the support of the rising generation of Communist bureaucrats. He used a similar line with the people, treating heavy industrialization as the key to Romanian independence. At the same time, Dej freed thousands of political prisoners and gave intellectuals a wider role in party and national life. He was thereby able to combine nationalism and the desire of Romanians for independence with an orthodoxy that was Stalinist without the name, and he gave the Romanian party a national role and a national base for the first time in its sorry history. Nicolae Ceauşescu used this program of national Stalinism to succeed Dej upon his death in 1965, then to overcome his more senior competitors within the party, and then to gather the party and nation around him to break ranks with the Soviets and the other regimes that invaded Czechoslovakia in August 1968. The crowds flocked to cheer him, the intellectuals joined the regime, his opponents were rendered "impotent and obsolete," as President Reagan hoped the Strategic Defense Initiative would make nuclear weapons, at a stroke. For one precious moment Ceauşescu was the Communist leader of a united country.[20]

That moment had come for Imre Nagy and Hungary in the last week of October 1956, before the Soviet tanks returned to Budapest. Nagy's successor, János Kádár, had to rebuild a Stalinist party and Stalinism itself against a cowed but hostile people before he could even contemplate reaching out to them for new support. When the time came to rebuild the party, he knew that he could not do so on the old bases of force and ideology.

When order was restored in the early 1960s, Hungary found itself a medium industrialized country, more dependent on trade than ever, and lacking hard goods. Hungary had few defenses against the iron ring. Neither Romanian-style national Stalinism nor a Bulgarian-style agricultural vocation were available. GDR-style subservience to the Soviets probably was, but Kádár instead chose a fourth variant. While continually proclaiming his political subservience to the Soviet Union, Kádár slowly built a party consensus among the new generation of Communist bureaucrats for substantial, decentralizing reform of economic management. To the Soviets, Kádár maintained that such reform was not political, except insofar as it gained the acquiescence of the population by improving its standard of living. He argued that economics was his only option in gaining support for Communist rule after the trauma of 1956.

The Soviets grew to trust Kádár after he successfully "normalized" Hungary following 1956. While they remained suspicious, therefore, they were still willing to accept his New Economic Mechanism (NEM), introduced in 1968, a package of marketizing economic reforms, especially as Kádár treated it neither as an ideological advance nor as a model for other East European states. Moreover, in 1968 the Soviets were preoccupied with both Poland and Czechoslovakia. As the NEM was implemented with some success, Hungarians slowly became grateful to Kádár, not so much as leader of the party but as a national father figure who was clever with the Russians and left them alone to prosper modestly if they could.[21]

Like Imre Nagy, Władyslaw Gomułka had his shining moment as the Communist leader of a united nation in October 1956, and the Soviets chose to gamble on him rather than crush Poland. That gamble paid off well, for Gomułka was and remained a Stalinist. Like Hungary, Poland was a medium-level industrialized country, and could feel the iron ring encircling its economic options. Unlike Hungary, however, Poland had "hard" goods — coal, agricultural products, sulfur and later copper — that were salable for hard currency. Also unlike Hungary, Poland had some access to Western markets and credits, as a result of the liberalization of 1956, the main features of which, considerable freedom for the Catholic church and the decollectivization of agriculture, remained intact. Gomułka had more room for economic maneuver than Kádár.[22]

On the other hand, Gomułka faced three difficulties that Kádár did not. First, as long as West Germany and its allies did not recognize Poland's western borders, he was bound over to the Soviets and the East Germans who guaranteed them. Although over the long term the wall decreased Polish fears of West German revanchism, during and immediately after it was built Gomułka was forced by the rise in East-West tension to proclaim Poland's loyalty to the Soviet Union and the GDR, which soured its relations with the West. Also, the stabilizing GDR became a powerful competitor for Soviet favor and toleration, limiting Gomułka's leverage with the Soviets. Second, Gomułka had become the Communist father of his nation under false pretenses. Hungarians and Romanians had known what Kádár and Ceauşescu represented, whereas the Poles had invested Gomułka with a passionate, almost mystical aura of liberalism and patriotism. Gomułka in power proved to be a bitter disappointment, particularly to intellectuals, as the freedom of expression that had flowered in 1956 began to be eaten away by the regime after 1957. As his support among the people and the intelligentsia waned, Gomułka was forced back onto almost pure party rule. Third, his strength of 1956, compared to Nagy, turned into his weakness after 1956, compared to Kádár: He did not have Kádár's luxury of building a new party around himself from a younger generation of Communists. The Polish party had not collapsed in 1956, as had the Hungarian party. Gomułka had been brought to power by, and was beholden to, a coalition of Stalinists and ex-Stalinist liberals, of Jews and non-Jews. The new generation of Polish Communists was outside and starting to pound on the door. Gomułka had to walk a very narrow and tortuous path.

In 1958, while Poland still had hard goods and some trade with the West, Gomułka tried economic reform, moving some investment decisions out to enterprise managers. The result was catastrophic, because the reforms were implemented in a system that was still basically Stalinist. Investment capital had no cost for managers, and managers had limitless needs for investment capital, so it was quickly absorbed and dispersed in construction projects that would take years to build. Gomułka was forced to recentralize in 1960 and was almost immune to domestic economic reform proposals for another decade.

After his bitter experience with domestic reform, Gomułka supported Khrushchev's 1962 Comecon reform proposal. He was willing to gamble on Poland's industrial future and therefore wanted to increase its bargaining power by multilateralizing Comecon. But after the Romanian defection and Khrushchev's fall in 1964, Comecon reform was dead, and meanwhile, Poland's economic access to the West was shrinking. Without either Comecon or domestic reform, and lacking a Western option, the Polish economy fell into stagnation as the iron ring of dependence on the Soviets tightened around it.[23]

Economic downturn transformed the pressure for generational change within the party into a full-fledged political crisis. As the working class became increasingly disaffected by continuing economic failure, and as the intelligentsia remained disappointed and repressed, a coalition of young Communists bid for power under the leadership of Interior Minister Mieczysław Moczar. Moczar had suffered with Gomułka during and after the war. The essence of his coalition's bid for power was raw nationalism, but it was cloaked and covered by that most traditional of East European political appeals: anti-Semitism. Nationalism as an agent of change required a scapegoat, something to symbolize its opposition to the current system and to make that system appear alien. The Soviets, the obvious candidate, were out of the question. Anti-Semitism was the next best thing, as it struck both at the Jewish Stalinists whom the Soviets had brought with them and at the revisionist forces those same Jewish Stalinists had led after their conversion to reform communism following Stalin's death. And best of all, anti-Semitism would also serve to keep workers and intellectuals apart.

It was the 1967 Arab-Israeli war and the strong Soviet hostility to Israel on foreign policy grounds that gave this anti-Semitism the fashionable new label and cover of "anti-Zionism." Moczar's purging began that year, but it became rolling thunder when the closing down of a classic patriotic play provoked student protests in March 1968. The rationale for the witchhunt was antirevisionist, but the real targets were Jews and anyone who could be associated with them. Gomułka rolled with the punch, accepted the purges of Jews, and regained control of the situation by July. He saved himself by enrolling in GDR leader Walter Ulbricht's anti-Czechoslovak crusade. Poland's help in the invasion of Czechoslovakia the next month convinced the Soviets that they wanted no more trouble in Poland and prompted Brezhnev's personal endorsement of Gomułka at the Polish Party Congress that December. There Gomułka finally brought a group of new-generation technocrats beholden to him, the so-called Young Turks, into the Politburo. It was too late. By then, Gomułka's 1956 coalition had been destroyed, the party was seriously discredited, and the whole political system was demoralized.[24]

Whereas 1968 brought triumph to Ceauşescu and tragedy to Gomułka, it brought first triumph and then tragedy to Czechoslovakia and its Communist party. As elsewhere, the antecedents were both recognizably common to all the Stalinist systems and specific to the country involved. As the area's most industrialized country, Czechoslovakia had been the first through the iron ring, in the early 1950s, and we have seen how drastic reductions in machinery imports from Czechoslovakia by its socialist partners had produced the socialist equivalent of near crisis. Like Poland, Czechoslovakia had tried decentralizing investment decisions in 1958, with the same results: Given the bottomless demand for capital and the fact that under the prevailing system it had no cost, all there was promptly disappeared into new plants that would take years to complete and into the pockets of the population, but with nothing new for them to buy. The resulting tensions in the economy forced rapid recentralization, and in 1962 Czechoslovakia became the first socialist country to see its national income actually decline. As the regime was as committed as the others to rising living standards in order to preserve itself, this came as a tremendous shock to the whole political system. It encouraged a broad discussion of economic reform among Communists that continued throughout the 1960s.[25]

As this discussion continued, it was clear that the Czechoslovak regime would have special problems adjusting. The terrifying and thorough purges of the early 1950s had already brought the new generation of bureaucrats (who were just beginning to gain power elsewhere a decade later) to power. Antonín Novotný, Czechoslovakia's leader, was one of them. His generation had been traumatized by the purges and was simultaneously afraid of a rehabilitation process that would discredit them. In 1963 Novotný finally removed the last of Gottwald's Politburo and established the kind of authority that Dej had achieved in Romania in 1952. When Khrushchev fell in 1964, Novotný was the only East European leader with the courage to complain in Moscow. His regime proceeded to encourage the ongoing economic debate, which it hoped would produce an economic reform that could remedy the economic weakness revealed by the downward dip of 1962. The immediacy of Czechoslovakia's economic problems and the determination of many dedicated Communists to resolve them pushed many of these Communists back into a political (rather than a strictly economic) understanding of development. They saw — or claimed to see — that in Stalinist conditions economic reform was a recipe for technocracy and that for economic reform to be effective, it had to be preceded by a broadening of the political system. The party had some time to debate this. The economy picked up again beginning in 1964 and 1965, removing for the time being the party's concern about the loyalty of the working class. Within the party and within the intelligentsia the momentum for both economic and political reform continued to build. When Novotný's attempts to slow it down made him intolerable by the end of 1967, Brezhnev refused to save the man who had complained about Khrushchev's ouster in 1964, and allowed the rise of the Slovak Alexander Dubček.[26]

From that point onward, the Prague Spring and its aftermath read like a primer on Stalinism's re-creation of personal politics. When Brezhnev asked the Czechoslovaks in December 1967 who was number two after Novotný, and was told no one was, he indicated that anyone would do.[27] Alexander Dubček, who had spent much of his adult life not only in the party but in the USSR, looked acceptable, and became first secretary in January 1968. In the desert of organized forces that Stalinism produces, over the months that followed Dubček became the indispensable personal force that held the whole burgeoning reform movement together. Dubček was himself convinced that personal connections were going to be decisive in reforming the system. He spent the time that should have been spent developing a party reform program on placing personnel. While he did so, the freedom of expression he allowed pushed the Prague Spring out of his hands. It took until early April to produce and get Central Committee approval for the party's new Action Program, and before it could be fully implemented it was superseded as the national program, as far as the unleashed intelligentsia was concerned, by Ludwík Vaculík's *2000 Words*, published in late June. Dubček was fairly remote from these issues; instead, he invested his confidence in his own ability to convince Brezhnev that he was neither antisocialist or anti-Soviet.[28]

The Soviets also understood these events in personal terms. Dubček was one of theirs, and in the first months they showed their concern and suspicion that events were getting out of hand carefully, for fear that he would slip into the clutches of "antiparty" elements. But *2000 Words* stung them into more forceful action, and July was marked by mounting Soviet and Warsaw Pact warnings, demands, troop movements, and finally the meeting of the two Politburos at the border town of Cierná-nad-Tisou. There they felt they finally got reliable commitments from Dubček and his colleagues to keep reform within systemic bounds, and most of them went off to their August vacations. And yet the momentum of reform carried onward and upward: On August 10 the Czechoslovaks proclaimed new and spectacularly un-Leninist party statutes — elections by secret ballot, factions within the party — and announced an Extraordinary Party Congress to ratify them, beginning September 9. The Soviets felt betrayed, just as they had felt betrayed by Imre Nagy in 1956, and during the night of August 20-21 they and five of their Warsaw Pact allies — all except Romania — invaded Czechoslovakia. A friend of mine was at the downtown Moscow airport on the night of August 20, when Soviet leaders suddenly returning from vacation walked off the plane with what he said were tears in their eyes. Having spent some time with them myself, I find public tears hard to imagine, but the decision to intervene was clearly not an easy one. The Soviets were not looking for trouble and felt that the Czechs had forced the decision on them. Still, the Soviets were also more serious than Dubček. Kádár's question to Dubček — "Don't you really understand the kind of people you're dealing with?" [29] — may stand as the epitaph for the Czechoslovak reform movement.

Like 1956, 1968 had its lessons. For both rulers and ruled, the invasion of Czechoslovakia proved once again that the Soviets would use force to prevent developments they defined as contrary to their vital interests. The line they drew in 1968 to define their vital interests was the Leninist hegemony of the local Communist party. This definition of Soviet interests meant that political reform which disturbed the now-traditional character of party rule would not be tolerated. If the price of national leadership was to change that character, it was too high for the Soviets. In a sense, they now defined their interests even more retrogressively. In November 1956 they had crushed the Hungarians, but at the end of October their government declaration had admitted at least a theoretical legitimacy for national paths to communism. After 1968 they issued what the West called the Brezhnev Doctrine, asserting the right to intervene to save socialism wherever they judged it to be threatened, and wherever they could get a few compliant locals to call them in.

The overarching message of Prague in 1968 was that the whole struggle over reform communism and national communism — in fact all the debate within the party and between the party and the intelligentsia over ideological issues and socialism — had been a sham. Enthusiasm about purifying socialism was bitterly disappointed, not for the first time, but for the last. Ideology could no longer be taken seriously.[30] Both rulers and ruled knew that henceforth they would have to reach beyond the narrow confines of the party and the intelligentsia, of thinkers and thoughts, for the system's salvation — or for its destruction.

Notes

1. For convenient data on the economic buoyancy of the late 1950s, see Maurice Ernst, "Postwar Economic Growth in Eastern Europe" and Josef Goldmann, "Fluctuations and Trends in the Rate of Economic Growth in Some Socialist Countries," in George R. Feiwel, ed., *New Currents in Soviet-Type Economies: A Reader* (Scranton, Pa.: International Textbook Co., 1968), 75-121.
2. For some recent appreciations, see George W. Breslauer, *Khrushchev and Brezhnev: Building Authority in Soviet Politics* (London: Allen & Unwin, 1982), and Ferenc Fehér, "The Social Character of Khrushchev's Regime," in Ferenc Fehér and Agnes Heller, *Eastern Left, Western Left. Totalitarianism, Freedom and Democracy* (Atlantic Highlands, N.J.: Humanities Press International, 1987), 77-103. As an antidote, William Hyland's very harsh judgment: *The Cold War Is Over* (New York: Times Books, 1990), 102-103. Even harsher, and brilliantly and poignantly argued from the longer perspective of after the fall, is Ken Jowitt's judgment that Khrushchev's alterations— and especially his renunciation of class war against society as a whole—were the

beginning of the end for Leninism in general: *New World Disorder. The Leninist Extinction* (Berkeley-Los Angeles, Calif. and Oxford: University of California Press, 1992), 249-283. In other words, whereas for Kołakowski (see note 24 to Chapter Five) the spring broke when Stalin's immediate successors gave up mass terror, for Jowitt *c'est la faute à Khrouschtchev*. I still think the processes were more specific (and open-ended); but Jowitt is a political scientist.

3. The approach had already begun to emerge before 1957: Brzezinski, "Khrushchev's Conception of the Communist Camp," in his *Soviet Bloc: Unity and Conflict*, rev. ed. (New York, Praeger, 1961), 168-176; but it was really put in place thereafter. For intelligent meditation on regime problems in the post-revolutionary period, see Richard Lowenthal, "The Ruling Party in a Mature Society," in Mark G. Field, ed., *Social Consequences of Modernization in Communist Societies* (Baltimore: Johns Hopkins University Press, 1976), 81-120. Contemporary scholars tended to feel that as time went on it would get easier to achieve value consensus, but that this would make it harder to justify the Party's political monopoly.

4. There is good contemporary material on revisionism to be found in Leopold Labedz, ed., *Revisionism. Essays on the History of Marxist Ideas* (London: Allen & Unwin, 1962), 215-280. In the aftermath, there are now two books on Marxist revisionism from egg to earth: Raymond Taras, ed., *The Road to Disillusion: From Critical Marxism to Postcommunism in Eastern Europe* (Armonk, N.Y.: M.E. Sharpe, 1992), and James H. Satterwhite, *Varieties of Marxist Humanism. Philosophical Revision in Postwar Eastern Europe* (Pittsburgh, Penn.: University of Pittsburgh Press, 1992). One question about such studies is whether they are Hegel's owl of Minerva, which takes wing only when night has fallen, or simply validate "Gałeski's rule" (see note 5 to Chapter 1) that academic interest in a given subject prospers best in the countries where there is the least of it (he was referring to peasant studies in the U.S. and the U.K.). Perhaps it is both. For retrospective appreciations by veterans, see Adam Michnik, *Letters from Prison and Other Essays* (Berkeley: University of California Press, 1985), 46-48 and 137, and Bronislaw Geremek, "Between Hope and Despair," *Daedalus*, 119, no. 1 (Winter 1990): 100-101.

5. On the Warsaw Pact, see the brief recent history by Malcolm Mackintosh, "The Warsaw Treaty Organization: A History," in David Holloway and Jane M.O. Sharp, *The Warsaw Pact. Alliance in Transition* (Ithaca: Cornell University Press, 1984), 41-58, and especially Dale A. Herspring's survey, "The Soviets, the Warsaw Pact, and the Eastern European Militaries," in William E. Griffith, ed., *Central and Eastern Europe: The Opening Curtain?* (Boulder: Westview, 1989), 130-155. On Comecon, the classic early work is Michael Kaser, *Comecon*, 2nd ed. (London: oxford University Press, 1967) and there is interesting material on the lean years between its founding and the mid-1950s in Iván Berend, "The Problem of Eastern European Economic Integration in a Historical Perspective," in Imre Vajda and Mihály Simai, eds., *Foreign Trade in a Planned Economy* (Cambridge: Cambridge University Press, 1971), 14-23, and Jozef M. Van Brabant, *Socialist Economic Integration. Aspects of Contemporary Economic Problems in Eastern Europe (Cambridge: Cambridge University Press, 1980), 16-54.*

6. For a summary of the Khrushchev-era reforms in industry, see Jan Marczewski, *Crisis in Socialist Planning: Eastern Europe and the USSR* (New York: Praeger, 1974), 58-120, which includes a convenient chart (omitting Czechoslovakia, however) at 58-59. On the Czechoslovak reforms, see "The 1958-69 Reform and its Aftermath," in George

R. Feiwel, *New Economic Patterns in Czechoslovakia. Impact of Growth, Planning, and the Market* (New York: Praeger, 1968), 103-128, and "Emergence of an Economic Reform Movement in Czechoslovakia: 1958-1963," in John N. Stevens, *Czechoslovakia at the Crossroad. The Economic Dilemmas of Communism in Postwar Czechoslovakia* (New York: Columbia University Press, 1985), 58-97. On the Polish reforms of 1956 to 1960, see Teresa M. Piotrowicz, "The Polish Economic Pendulum," in her *Communist Economy Under Change* (London: Institute for Economic Affairs, 1963), 83-124. On the Bulgarian Great Leap Forward, see John R. Lampe, *The Bulgarian Economy in the Twentieth Century* (New York: St. Martin's, 1986), 149-154. Bruce McFarlane has advanced the interesting idea that the cycle centralism-decentralization-turmoil-recentralization was practically a law of life in Stalinist economies, and defined their political cycles: "Political Crisis and East European Economic Reforms," in Paul G. Lewis, ed., *Eastern Europe: Political Crisis and Legitimation* (New York: St. Martin's, 1984), 176-199. But of course it took life some time to teach the law.

7. For vivid data on 1955 to 1965 increases in Soviet oil and gas production and exports to Eastern Europe, see Robert W. Campbell, *The Economics of Soviet Oil and Gas* (Baltimore: Johns Hopkins University Press, 1969), 225-249; on the impact in Eastern Europe, see Alfred Zauberman, *Industrial Progress in Poland, Czechoslovakia and East Germany* (London: Oxford University Press, 1964), 128-170. For a recent retrospective view, see Paul Marer, "The Economics and Trade of Eastern Europe," in Griffith, *Central and Eastern Europe*, 37-73.

8. On the role of foreign trade, see Franklyn D. Holzman, "Foreign Trade Behavior of Centrally Planned Economies," in Henry Rosovsky, ed., *Industrialization in Two Systems. Essays in Honor of Alexander Gerschenkron* (New York: John Wiley, 1966), 237-265, and at more length, his *Foreign Trade Under Central Planning* (Cambridge, Mass.: Harvard University Press, 1974). For prescient analysis dating from 1944, see Jacob Viner's classic "International Relations between State-Controlled National Economies," in his *International Economics Studies* (Glencoe, Ill.: Free Press, 1951), 216-231.

9. And they were still doing it when the "velvet revolution" came: Craig R. Whitney, "A Casualty of Amnesty: A Plant Using Convicts," *New York Times*, 1 April 1990 (the Škoda plant at Mláda Boleslác), and Tony R. Judt, "Metamorphosis: The Democratic Revolution in Czechoslovakia," in Ivo Banac, ed., *Eastern Europe in Revolution* (Ithaca, N.Y. and London: Cornell University Press, 1992), 114.

10. See Feiwel, *New Economic Patterns*, 22, 25; data on the age of foundry equipment in different industries in 1964 showed just under half to be over ten years old.

11. The *locus classicus* on how this worked is still John Michael Montias, *Economic Development in Communist Rumania* (Cambridge, Mass.: MIT Press, 1967), and especially its summing up, 231-247.

12. "I am tempted to conclude, then, that [Czechoslovakia and the GDR] are exploited by all the others": Peter J.D. Wiles, *Communist International Economics* (Oxford: Blackwell, 1968), 247. The classic account of the 1953-1957 crisis for Czechoslovakia is John Michael Montias, "Economic Nationalism in Eastern Europe: Forty Years of Continuity and Change," *Journal of International Affairs*, 20, no. 1 (1966): 45-71. The comparison is to the beggar-my-neighbor policies of the 1930s. Montias shows that between 1953 and 1957 Czechoslovakia's exports to Romania dropped by two-thirds, compared to one-third between 1928 and 1933, and that between 1953 and 1956 its

machinery exports to Hungary, Romania, Bulgaria, and Poland dropped by over half. The reverse effect, on Romania, is described by Montias in his "Background and Origins of the Rumanian Dispute with Comecon," *Soviet Studies,* 16, no. 2 (October 1964): 125-151. And for a short, sharp retrospective on these years (in response to Montias), see Wiles, "Foreign Trade of Eastern Europe: A Summary Appraisal," in Alan A. Brown and Egon Neuberger, eds., *International Trade and Central Planning* (Berkeley: University of California Press, 1968), 166-176.

13. Frederic C. Pryor, *The Communist Foreign Trade System* (London: Allen & Unwin, 1963), 33n.

14. The classic early account is William E. Griffith, *The Sino-Soviet Rift* (Cambridge, Mass.: MIT Press, 1964); more recently, see Alfred D. Low, *The Sino-Soviet Dispute. An Analysis of the Polemics* (Cranbury, N.J.: Associated University Presses, 1976), which takes the story through 1969.

15. For a summary, see "Collectivization in Eastern Europe," in Karl-Eugen Wädekin, *Agrarian Policies in Communist Europe. A Critical Introduction* (The Hague: Allenheld/Osmun/Martinus Nijhoff, 1982), 63-82 and 141; for the effects on Romania, see Montias, *Economic Development,* 87-134; for the Bulgarian Great Leap Forward, see J.F. Brown, *Bulgaria Under Communist Rule* (New York: Praeger, 1970), 83-95; and for the Polish exception, see Andrzej Korbonski, *The Politics of Socialist Agriculture in Poland: 1945-1960* (New York: Columbia University Press, 1965) and his "Peasant Agriculture in Poland Since 1956: An Alternative to Collectivization," in Jerzy F. Karcz, ed., *Soviet and East European Agriculture* (Berkeley: University of California Press, 1967), 411-431, which takes the story through 1965.

16. Paul Neuberg, *The Hero's Children. The Post-War Generation in Eastern Europe* (New York: William Morrow, 1973) is still full of insights on elite generational change in general during the 1960s, and Zdeněk Mlynář, *Nightfrost in Prague: The End of Humane Socialism* (New York: Karz, 1980), passim, conveys the smell and feel of it in Czechoslovakia.

17. For the GDR's situation as it later looked, beginning in the 1970s, see Werner Klein, "The Role of the GDR in Comecon: Some Economic Aspects," in Ian Jeffries and Manfred Melzer, *The East German Economy* (London: Croom Helm, 1987), 261-279.

18. On the April conspiracy, see Brown, *Bulgaria Under Communist Rule,* 173-195. It is hoped that more will come to light in the reformed Bulgaria of the 1990s.

19. On Romanian help over Hungary, see Robert R. King, *Minorities Under Communism. Nationalities as a Source of Tension among Balkan Communist States* (Cambridge, Mass.: Harvard University Press, 1973), 82-85. J.F. Brown also points out that after 1956 there was a serious crackdown in Romania itself, mainly against the Hungarian minority which had sympathized with the Hungarian revolution, and which began an erosion (that continued until 1989) of the distinct Hungarian minority institutions granted in the early postwar period: *Surge to Freedom. The End of Communist Rule in Eastern Europe* (Durham, N.C. and London: Duke University Press, 1991), 14. Just as Montias remains good on the economic side, Kenneth Jowitt, *Revolutionary Breakthroughs and National Development. The Case of Romania, 1944-1965* (Berkeley: University of California Press, 1971), 135-231, is still very good on Romanian politics in this period.

20. For a useful brief review of Romanian party history as background to Ceauşescu's rule (which omits the politics of consolidation in the late 1960s, however), see Vladimir Tismaneanu, "Ceauşescu's Socialism," *Problems of Communism,* 34, no. 1 (January-

February 1985): 50-66, and, at greater length, his "The Tragicomedy of Romanian Communism," *Eastern European Politics and Societies*, 3, no. 2 (Spring 1989): 329-376. For historical background on the soporific effect of state-sponsored nationalism on the Romanian intelligentsia, see Michael Shafir, *Romania. Politics, Economics and Society. Political Stagnation and Simulated Change* (Boulder: Lynne Rienner, 1985), 144-150, with citations to further readings. For a longer treatment of this critical period that includes some sense of the argument within the leadership over economic strategy, see Mary Ellen Fischer, *Nicolae Ceaușescu. A Study in Political Leadership* (Boulder: Lynne Rienner, 1989), 83-159. But J.F. Brown also usefully recalls that Romanian obstinacy checked a streak of supranationalist millenarianism in Khrushchev, or at least kept it at bay in practical terms, and thereby saved the rest of us a lot of potential trouble: in the work cited above, 17-21. A former senior Polish communist, very much of the post-1956 generation, reminded me in a private conversation in early 1993 just how passionately he and others like him believed in heavy industry as the key to Poland's modern future; if it was true in Poland, it was true in spades in Romania; and the resulting economic structures are a problem for them all, now that communists like him are gone.

21. Bill Lomax has recently developed and documented the theory that the germs of later liberalism were all present in the tough early days of the Kádár regime, although Kádár was then an impotent and inexperienced figurehead: "The Hungarian Revolution of 1956 and the Origins of the Kádár Regime," *Studies in Comparative Communism*, 18, nos. 2 & 3 (Summer/Autumn 1985): 87-114. For a balanced assessment, see Charles Gati, "Moscow and János Kádár since 1956: An Overview," in his *Hungary and the Soviet Bloc* (Durham: Duke University Press, 1986), 156-178.

22. On Poland's accession to industrialized status, see Zauberman, *Industrial Progress*, 275ff.

23. On the struggles over economic reform after 1956, see Janusz G. Zieliński, *Economic Reforms in Polish Industry* (London: Oxford University Press, 1973), 1-14 and passim; Włodzimierz Brus, "The Political Economy of Reform," in Paul Marer and Włodzimierz Śliwiński, eds., *Creditworthiness and Reform in Poland* (Bloomington: Indiana University Press, 1988), 67-70; and the chapter titled "The Economic Reform Deadlock in Poland," in Paul M. Johnson, *Redesigning the Communist Economy: The Politics of Economic Reform in Eastern Europe* (New York: Columbia University Press, 1989), 121-138.

24. Lendvai, *Anti-Semitism Without Jews* (Garden City, N.Y.: Doubleday, 1971), 89-242 ("Nightmare in Poland") remains an excellent account, but it should be supplemented by Michael Checinski, *Poland. Communism, Nationalism, Anti-Semitism* (New York: Karz-Lohl, 1982); by Aleksander Smolar's masterful "Jews as a Polish Problem," *Daedalus*, 116, no. 2 (Spring 1987): 31-74, which take the problem much farther back; and by the essays in Antony Polonsky, ed., *My Brother's Keeper* (London: Routledge, Chapman and Hall, 1990). See also Josef Banas, *The Scapegoats. The Exodus of the Remnants of Polish Jewry* (London: Weidenfeld and Nicholson, 1979). In "Shadows of Forgotten Ancestors (1973)," reprinted in *Letters from Prison and Other Essays* (Berkeley: University of California Press, 1985), Adam Michnik gives some personal recollections of the resonance of anti-Semitism in 1968. For a recent revisiting of the 1968 crisis in terms of party legitimation, see Andrzej Flis, "Crisis and Political Ritual in Postwar Poland," *Problems of Communism*, 37, nos. 3-4 (May-August 1988): 43-54. Coming on top of the domestic softening-up of the 1980s, the collapse of 1989 has multiplied sources on 1968 in Poland and permitted a judicious new historical synthesis on the political crisis of that year based on excellent documentation and previously

unpublished interview material: Jerzy Eisler, *Marzec 1968 (March 1968)* (Warsaw: Państwowe Wydawnicstwo Naukowe, 1991). It deserves translation.

25. For a good analysis of the causes and course of the 1962-63 Czechoslovak economic crisis, see Wiles, *Communist International Economics,* 112-122.

26. The insider account is Zdeněk Mlynář, *Nightfrost in Prague,* but Galia Golan's reconstructions, *The Czechoslovak Reform Movement: Communism in Crisis, 1962-1968* (Cambridge: Cambridge University Press, 1971) and *Reform Rule in Czechoslovakia: The Dubček Era, 1968-1969* (London: Cambridge University Press, 1973), are still useful, and Judy Batt's *Economic Reform and Political Change in Eastern Europe* (New York: St. Martin's, 1988), 171-232, should now be consulted. In the wake of the regime's collapse, 1968 in Czechoslovakia is getting some urgent reconsideration: see Jan Moravec, "Could the Prague Spring Have Been Saved? The Ultimatum of Cierna nad Tisou," *Orbis,* 35, no. 4 (Fall 1991), 587-595; Jiří Valenta, "The Search for a Political Solution," *ibid.,* 581-587, and Valenta, "The Last Chance," *ibid.,* 595-601. And for a preview of the extensive new documentation now becoming available, see Mark Kramer, "New Sources on the 1968 Soviet Invasion of Czechoslovakia," *Cold War International History Project Bulletin* (Washington, D.C.: The Woodrow Wilson International Center for Scholars), no. 2 (Fall, 1992), 4-13, which includes the text of the hardliners' August "request" to Brezhnev for intervention, and promises to review interpretations in a future issue.

27. Mlynář, *Nightfrost in Prague,* 71n.

28. *Ibid.,* 101-104, 120-124; but his whole chapter on the Prague Spring, 77-145, is well worth reading. For wrenching evidence of personalism at leadership level during the 1968 Czechoslovak crisis, see the memoirs of Gomułka's interpreter, Erwin Weit, *At the Red Summit: Interpreter behind the Iron Curtain* (New York: Macmillan, 1973), 193-217. On divided counsels within the Soviet leadership, see Jiří Valenta, *Soviet Intervention in Czechoslovakia, 1968. Anatomy of a Decision* (Baltimore: Johns Hopkins University Press, 1979). For how it felt watching it as a Western correspondent in Moscow, see Anatole Shub, *An Empire Loses Hope* (New York: Norton, 1970), 369-442.

29. Mlynář, *Nightfrost in Prague,* 157.

30. Peter Wiles characterizes the effect as a shift from "the once half-accepted theocracy to a 'Logocracy'"; the latter "still makes enormous moral claims, but they have become totally invalid": in Jan Drewnowski, ed., *Crisis in the East European Economy. The Spread of the Polish Disease* (London: Croom Helm, 1982), 11. For the same testimony in different words from someone who helped with the shifting, see Adam Michnik, "The Prague Spring Ten Years Later (August 1978)," reprinted in his *Letters from Prison,* 155-159. For a sensitive short account of the whole 1956 to 1970 period and its 1968 culmination in Poland, see Neal Ascherson, *The Polish August. The Self-Limiting Revolution* (New York: Viking, 1982), 81-105. Leszek Kołakowski, while clear about Poland (*Main Currents of Marxism: Vol. 3: The Breakdown* [Oxford: Oxford University Press, 1978], 466-468), is somewhat more sanguine about socialism's staying power in Czechoslovakia, incorrectly as it turned out: 69-70. On the critical role of 1968 for the East European intelligentsia and the opening up of the split with Western leftists, see the introduction to Fehér and Heller, *Eastern Left. Western Left,* 1-47, and Ferenc Fehér, Agnes Heller, and György Márkus, *Dictatorship Over Needs* (New York: St. Martin's, 1983), 290ff. This work also includes some pertinent meditation on the "anti-Bolshevik Bolshevism," which they see as one plausible historical alternative.

THE PERSONALITY OF THE OLD REGIME

When the hollowness of communism was revealed to East Europeans in 1968, what were they left with? The easy answer is that they were left with nothing because that was what communism had offered them to start with, that it in fact offered them nothing from start to finish. There has always been an argument to be made that the East European Communist regimes were doomed from birth, from the moment they were artificially grafted onto the bodies politic of the area. That argument is especially attractive after 1989, but it has always been there, because it has always contained a modicum of truth: In terms of the traditions and political cultures of the peoples and nations of Eastern Europe, these regimes always were bizarre and artificial, they were imposed and maintained by force, they never fit quite right. During my first tour in Poland in the late 1960s, there was a joke about the peasant in the back of the hall asking the Central Committee lecturer on the podium whether Marxism-Leninism was scientific or humanistic. "Profoundly humanistic," the lecturer replied; at which the peasant turned to his buddy and said in a whisper, "I knew it; because if it was scientific they would have tried it on animals first." And it was already an old joke.

And yet these odd regimes lasted forty years. Forty years may be only a blink in the eye of God, to be sure, and is certainly less than a lifetime; but it is longer than the French Revolutionary and Napoleonic period, twice as long as the interwar period, almost as long as the Second German Reich, which ended in 1918. It was long enough in any event for the regimes to generate a body of Western scholarship about postrevolutionary stabilization, normalization, even legitimation. In the aftermath of the whirlwind that swept them away in 1989, or at least pulled them out of the ground to reveal their poisoned roots, some of this scholarship does not bear rereading. But even at its most obsolete that scholarship also reflects its modicum or parcel of truth: the truth that by the 1960s these regimes had become part of a functioning status quo, that they had roots, that they constituted a system, a curious system, in many ways an unnatural and hateful system still, but still a system, one that worked more or less well or badly, but one that worked. It was the quotidian reality of the Eastern Europe in the years following 1968.

The reality of contradictory truths presented Westerners who cared about the area — academics, but also those of us who lived and worked in the area and the policymakers we served — with a genuine dilemma. If you limited your analysis to what was bizarre and unnatural, it was hard to understand how the regimes survived; if you went beyond it to ask how they functioned on a day-to-day basis, you risked losing sight of how odd they were. I believe that dilemma is likely to survive the regimes themselves, now that (or to the extent that) they are safely consigned to the lumberroom of history; it will survive as an analytical and intellectual problem for those who seek to understand what made them survive, and how they were swept away, and what is likely to follow them. So before I go on to examine the mechanisms of their slow destruction after 1968, I should like in this interlude to recall the lived experience of how my family and I came to cope with the dilemma at the time.

We arrived in Eastern Europe in 1968 and spent most of the 1970s in the region, and I returned to it frequently beginning in the mid-1980s. Compared to the West in which we had grown up, we found a dark and quiet world. The cities we lived in had few shops and little neon; they were truly "cities of silence and darkness," as one Westerner called them. But by talking to people and looking at pictures, we learned that they had always been that way, and we found that to explain the grimness, we had to pursue the darkness to its roots.

The apostles of light were, of course, the intelligentsia. They were better able to see Westerners than officials or ordinary people, and were attractive to Westerners, because they tried to put themselves above classes, to talk in terms of broader human values, to escape the stultifying provincialism of East European life. At the same time, they were the self-conscious carriers of each nation's historical consciousness, fascinated with comparing past and present. Friendship with intellectuals was not just a human pleasure but also a historical education.

But we soon discovered that their sense of history did not make them really impartial. On the contrary, intellectuals were ruthlessly engaged in the political and social process. Of course, the regimes insisted that art and language, the tools of the intellectual, were inherently political. East Europeans could still go to jail for things they said. It seemed "natural" for Stalin to pursue the poet Osip Mandelstam to the ends of the earth and kill him, both for those who identified with the pursuer and for those who identified with the pursued. For like the regimes, the intellectuals insisted that to live the life of the mind or of art was to live politics. They did not of course welcome persecution, but they defined it as a necessary contour of their freedom. The specific issues — censorship, granting or withholding passports, professional advancement, university education for one's children — seemed rather mundane, and it could be boring to sit night after night in smoky apartments with slightly wild-eyed longhairs bent on convincing me that the fate of mankind depended on my support for their passport, or my buying their crummy paintings. But there were magnificent people among them, and they all believed passionately that they were the fulcrum of the world, and the regimes agreed.

After 1956 the regimes tried to keep intellectuals and workers apart. We arrived in Poland in August 1968, just before the invasion of Czechoslovakia, and we learned that after the student revolt that spring, the regime had fanned agitators out into Polish factories to lambaste the privileged Jews whose children, they claimed, were rioting in Warsaw. The agitators worked like preachers. "Do you have cars!?" they would roar. "No!!" the crowd would roar back. "The Jews have cars!" they would reply. "Are your children in university?!" "No!!" "The Jews' children are in university!" And, sadly, the tactic worked. It discredited the party for the long run, but in the short run that counts in politics, it did help separate workers and intellectuals. The intellectuals we met when we arrived were demoralized. Nothing would happen, they said, without a change in Moscow. "What about the working class?" I would ask. "You are naive," came the reply, "they are not really workers. They are peasants in factories. They raise pigs in their bathtubs. They are ready to sell their birthright for a mess of pottage."

To understand the gap between intellectuals and the masses whose national soul they claimed to keep, we had to go beyond the intellectuals, and outside the cities. In Poland in our time 3 million workers still lived at home in their villages, and every third urban worker was a peasant's child.[1] That meant that you could learn a lot about the workers by learning about the countryside. And it turned out that the countryside came right into the American Embassy.

Most of the Poles who came to the United States were peasants, so when I was an American consul for the year 1968-69 most of the people who came into the embassy for visas to visit their relatives were also peasants. I interviewed about twenty of them every working day for a year. We also went out looking for them, traveling around the country, trying to meet and understand a brand of humanity, the peasants, that constitutes the majority of humanity still, and about which most Americans are unaware. We did the same in the Soviet Union and Romania.

We found that the dark and silent capitals of Eastern Europe are bright and gay compared to the villages, and we also found that this different way of life produces people different from us, and different from our intellectual friends. In the consulate we used to get the court records of applicants who had been convicted, and I found that a majority of the convictions were for aggravated assault, with fence staves or more rarely with knives. The fights would start after dances on Saturday night, usually between groups of young men from different villages. Guns were rare, but deaths were fairly common, and violence was traditional and almost casual.

It was just part of life. Not long before we came to Poland a group of southern mountaineers had been tried and convicted of murder for fatally beating a Warsaw intellectual who had been strolling in their hills. The scandal in Warsaw was that they could not understand why they were in court. He had insulted them, they had beaten him, he had died; they had not meant to kill him, it was unfortunate, but it was not actionable. It was the sort of thing that happens. It should be beneath the law.

Still, we found that it was important to realize that there was almost always a provocation buried in the event. The intellectual had insulted the mountaineers. It is often said that the peasants' ideal is to be left alone. We found their hospitality so generous that it would be fairer to say that the real dream is mastery of one's own fate, a dream that has very rarely become a reality. In the main, the preferred response to outside intervention is massive indifference, with violence only the counterpoint. And yet the outside world keeps crowding in. It always has, and it did so even more under communism. If indifference does not work, how is the peasant to keep himself and his family afloat, to promote his mastery over destiny?

The answer is that he goes to the city. For peasants, we discovered, the essential unit of social consciousness was not the individual, not the nation, but the family. So long as the land was surest way to support a family, they remained famously attached to it. But as soon as other ways opened up, they sent their sons and daughters into the factories, the service sector, or the city schools. Collectivized or not, they left their little plots by the millions. Already in our time perhaps a quarter of the agricultural work force was female, a very high percentage was over fifty years old, and the smaller the plots got, the more women and older people were working them: the younger males had gone to town.

Where they could, those who left for the city kept up their ties to their families in the village. In Romania we discovered that almost everyone in Bucharest had a way, outside the official market, to get most of a pig on the table at Christmastime; in our time, at least, you could still send fresh pork through the mails in the holiday season. Most inhabitants of East European capitals retained thick ties of blood, goods, and affection with their family seats. Their families were the reason they were in the cities to begin with.

It was these people that the Communist regimes had to use to build socialism. Already in our time we found that they filled the lower ranks of the power structure. Disbelieving, but willing to serve. A Western journalist covering the Warsaw student disturbances of 1968 told a wonderful story that was true, even if not quite true. Warsaw University is a compound, and the police closed it and were beating the students inside. Some students were escaping across the street into Warsaw's largest sanctuary, the Church of the Holy Cross, and priests at the door directed them into cupboards and recesses under the eaves. The students were pursued by plainclothsmen of their own age, dressed as students. The journalist said that he asked a priest how he could distinguish between the hunted and their hunters. "That's easy," the priest replied, "every policeman who comes into this church crosses himself."

And by the 1970s ex-peasants also manned the command posts of power. I once sat next to the Romanian foreign minister at a table for twelve. He was a very cultivated man, one of the smartest statesmen in Europe. His plate was clean before the last guest had been served. When he looked up and saw that others had noticed, he explained with a smile that he was one of six or seven boys in a peasant family which ate from a common pot and that those who ate slowly got no seconds. The minister's assistant, a professor of literature turned talented diplomat, was from a neighboring village, and became first a deputy foreign minister and then an ambassador under the post-1989 regime. The assistant's deputy, I discovered, was from another neighboring village, whence also hailed the ambassador who headed the ministry's European security task force. The rule of the Ceauşescu family that seemed so bizarre at the end to most of the world did not seem so bizarre to me. I thought it differed in degree, rather than in kind, from the other personal networks that held these countries together.

Such networks extended across whole national societies. Not long before we left Romania I was walking down a village street on a glorious spring Sunday morning toward a wooden church we were visiting, when an old man came up to me. "Where are you from?" he asked. "An American," I said. "But where are you *from?*" he repeated. "From Bucharest," I said. "Where in Bucharest?" "Well, the First Ward, near the Aviator's Monument." "The reason I'm asking," he said, "is that we have our boys in Bucharest, from this commune. If you're ever in trouble, they'll look after you. You can count on them."

I was grateful as an American to be invited practically sight unseen into one of the thousands of great and small networks that bind city and country together. Where they can be, these are networks of blood ties. But the scale of the outmigration has been so large that "life itself," as the Soviets used to say, has often outrun the kinship tie, and the people have created larger networks based on something more than blood but with the same capacity to furnish trustworthy mutual aid. When that does not work, there is always corruption. The area is famous for it, and justly so.

Of course, the economics of scarcity always produces parallel markets and endemic corruption. But "corruption" is also a natural extension of village life into the cities. It personalizes human relationships to mutual advantage in new, impersonal and often inhuman environments. It keeps the old village forms, hierarchical but also personal, alive in the new world of building socialism.[2]

I once ran through several centuries of such forms in about five minutes as a consul in Warsaw. The man was poor and from an isolated village in a backward part of the country. We started as an American official and a Polish applicant engaged in a visa interview. When I discovered he did not qualify under U.S. law, we moved to another plane. I was shown an envelope, in his jacket pocket, with bills peeking out. That did not work. Properly offended, I came from behind my desk to show him the door. At that point, he went down on his knees, and back in time, to embrace my knees, in the ancient gesture of fealty and obedience of the Polish serf to his lord. I was so terrified I almost used the knee, but got him out without breaking the original, official mold of the interview.

More than a remnant of the past, patron-client networks were the very stuff of the present, throughout society. On the eve of our departure from Romania, I asked the head of a large academic institution whether the leadership's rediscovered recognition of basic research would have practical effects on resource allocations. This man was so clever that he was reputed to have worked during the war for both the NKVD and British intelligence. He told me that he did not know about others, but his own large academic institution was in good shape. He had the right personal connections, and he would get the funds and people he needed. I told him my story of the old man and his boys in Bucharest. A Central Committee member with ministerial rank, he was tickled pink.

We also discovered that the worship of form — the one right way of doing things — existed alongside this personal networking, perhaps as an antidote to it, perhaps from the same impulse to give yourself some framework of security in a very insecure world. It too permeated whole societies, all the way to the top. For instance, it helped explain the censorship. For the illiterate peasantries of historic Eastern Europe, the word was the monopoly of priests, and it was holy. The Communist authorities treated it that way too. In the spring of 1971 I sneaked into the back of a classroom at Warsaw University to hear Mieczysław Rakowski speak to students. In 1989-90 he became the Polish party's last general secretary, but then he was editor of Poland's most liberal paper, and he had been forbidden contact with students since 1968. They were pressing him hard on the issue of censorship, and as a Central Committee member mindful of his duty to the party he defended the institution. But he went on to explain how intensely the Polish Communists of the previous generation, those who had come from underground to power in 1944-45, had worshipped the written word. You must remember, he said, that when they were young it was more important to throw a pamphlet into a streetcar than to organize a successful strike. They went down on their knees before anything printed.

So things that had one function for us — the written word, the law — clearly had other functions in Eastern Europe. We discovered that the regimes were drunk on law. They were chronic lawbreakers, of course, but they genuinely tried to cram every aspect of life into a legal framework. It had, after all, not been that long since millions of people had been sent to the camps and death according to the letter of the law, on the strength of confessions to imaginary crimes that had been extracted individually, patiently, insistently, horribly. Why had these millions of men and women been subjected to judicial farce when they were condemned already? Now, of course, the law was not so deadly, but the legal impulse was alive and well. It turned out, for instance, that officials genuinely believed that central planning of the economy would make the "socialist system" superior to ours, and the feature they were proudest of was that the plan had the force of law. Putting the plan into law evidently gave it a substance it would not otherwise have.[3]

We discovered that dealing with the past came easier to East Europeans than to us, but that dealing with the future was incomparably more difficult. In these societies, we found, it is hard to project the future except in terms of salvation, or the apocalypse. Speaking before the U.S. Congress, Václav Havel dropped the apocalypse, but otherwise his deontological and historical vocabulary consisted of precisely these terms, salvation through moral honesty.[4] The future is not a matter of programs, it is a matter of faith and virtue. Why, I had to ask, should this be so? Because, the answer came back, in contemporary Eastern Europe that kind of faith and virtue was extraordinarily difficult to come by.

The problem was not poverty of imagination. East Europeans imagine vividly and nimbly about the past and the present. But they have trouble conceiving a concrete future. At one point local Polish passport-issuing offices began to write the destination and duration of travel in ink into passports that were officially valid for extended periods and for travel to all countries. This created a problem under U.S. law, so I asked the first fifty visa applicants with such passports what they thought the insertion meant. All the intellectuals and most of the workers I asked had some kind of answer: They are trying to scare me, they want me back, it's a bookkeeping exercise, it means nothing. The peasants were different. None of them knew what the notation meant. To get beyond their natural mistrust of officials, I forced the line of questioning into the future. What if you wish to extend? What if Uncle Staś takes ill, and you want to take care of him? I do not wish to extend, came the answers, Uncle Staś is perfectly well. I could not goad their imagination beyond the present. For millions of East Europeans there was no future.

As peasants left their village to constitute new socialist nations, they took their formalism and their moralism with them. It was reflected in every walk of life, from the incessant, driven advice on child raising to the hectoring public style of the regimes, from the legalism of the regimes to the legalism of the dissidents, and to the universal tendency to judge politicians not by whether they were effective but by whether they were good or bad men.

I learned that the first generation of Communists in power had believed they were bringing enlightenment to the functional equivalent of heathens, that they bore the torch of truth and freedom to benighted races. In 1969 a Jewish secret policeman came to me looking for some haven for his son from the anti-Semitism that was reaching gale force in Polish politics. He had a high-school diploma, had spent the war in the Soviet Union, and was very bright; he had been a secret policeman all his adult life. I asked him why he had done it. We thought that if we had a generation we could civilize these Poles, he told me. We have found that it is impossible.

It turned out not to be so impossible, but then it was hard to tell. Rather than a clear victory for anyone, stalemate prevailed, stalemate between the ideals and the reality, stalemate between the old and new people. Gomułka had been one of the founding fathers of postwar Poland, and in the terrible spring of 1968 a well-known intellectual flung the epithet "*Ciemniacy!* Dark people!" at those in power. Gomułka picked it up like the firebrand it was and hurled it back. Yes, he shouted from the tribune of the Sejm, we are the dark people! It is we dark people who have brought a new and better society. Our analysis, our approach, was correct. History has proved us right. We have brought full employment, education; we have given Poland security, the recovered territories, relief from the foreign policy dilemma that threatened her extinction for centuries. Only we dark people could have done that, and can keep doing it.

> It is easy to imagine what the fate of the Polish
> people would be if the glittering people *(jaśnieoświeceni)* had
> come to power in 1944 instead
> of the "dark people." It would be a Poland without the
> Western Territories, quarrelling with
> the Soviet Union, poor, backward, and over-
> populated, dependent on Germany, on the
> imperialist powers, it would be a pawn in their
> game, it would be a nothing, because there would be no
> place for such a Poland in today's Europe![5]

Neither side won. When Gomułka fell two years later a Warsaw cabaret singer who is now famous, Jan Pietrzak, celebrated the event with the refrain "Peasant understanding is no longer enough, we need workers' understanding." At the time it seemed there was no viable alternative in East European politics to Gomułka's "peasant understanding," transported into the cities and engraved on whole nations. What we saw in Eastern Europe in the 1970s was replication in country after country of the American big-city machine, this time on the scale of nations, Tammanies that used ideology as a cement on election day but held power day-to-day by patronage, delivering favors in return for support. The American big-city machines lasted almost a century, and the future of Eastern Europe looked like Chicago: "Nobody gets everything, nobody gets nothing, everybody gets something." [6] Gomułka had held off both the intellectuals and the genuinely dark forces in Polish politics, but he fell, and meanwhile he had drastically narrowed the party's options for the next phase and the next conflict. Nor were the intellectuals victorious: In 1970 the workers rose without them.

In the spring of 1971, after the workers had risen and thrown Gomułka out, I asked my intellectual friends where they had been. They had been nowhere. In the course of the 1970s, they began to reach out to the working class that had betrayed them in 1968 and that they had betrayed in 1970. The coalescence of workers and intellectuals was the soul of the Solidarity miracle. A miracle it was: In our time we would not have believed it. When you ask yourself why American specialists have been surprised at the collapse of communism in Eastern Europe, that is part of the answer.

Notes

1. Timothy Garton Ash, *The Polish Revolution: Solidarity* (New York: Scribner's, 1983), 129.

2. On the general phenomenon, see Kenneth Jowitt, *The Leninist Response to National Dependency* (Berkeley: Institute of International Studies, University of California Press, 1978), and most recently, Moshe Lewin, "The Rise of the Cities," in his *The Gorbachev Phenomenon: A Historical Interpretation* (Berkeley: University of California Press, 1988), 30-42. On how it works on the ground in the villages, see C.M. Hann, *A Village Without Solidarity. Polish Peasants in Years of Crisis* (New Haven: Yale University Press, 1985), 87-91.

3. The role of the law in these postpeasant Communist societies needs more study. Kołakowski's answer as to why the butchers insisted on legal form was that it made the victims accessories, and enforced complicity in the general campaign of falsification: George Urban, ed., *Stalinism. Its Impact on Russia and the World* (New York: St. Martin's, 1982), 259-260. This is true as far as it goes, but it does not go far enough. It does not explain (to me) why the Stalinists worked so hard to create the "socialist legality" that sometimes encompassed them too: see Robert Sharlet, "Stalinism and Soviet Legal Culture," in Robert C. Tucker, ed., *Stalinism. Essays in Historical Interpretation* (New York: Norton, 1977), 155-179. Latter-day examples could be comic: Gierek used a 1932 law to imprison the KOR activists in 1976 (Keith John Lepak, *Prelude to Solidarity: Poland and the Politics of the Gierek Regime* [New York: Columbia University Press, 1988], 213), and given Romanian culture's attachment to things French and Ceaușescu's extremism, it was perhaps inevitable that his regime was law-mad, down to the law requiring registration of private typewriters (see Celestine Bohlen, "Rumanians Moving to Abolish Worst of Repressive Era," *New York Times,* 28 December 1989).

4. See "Excerpts from Czech Chief's Address to Congress," in *New York Times*, 22 February 1990. In his highly intelligent survey "The Political Traditions of Eastern Europe," Georges Schöpflin suggests that by the 1980s living under communism had ironically wrought a congruence of the political values of the intelligentsia with those of the poorest old-regime peasants: *Daedalus*, 119, no. 1 (Winter 1990): 82-83.

5. To break my English-language rule one more time, this is taken from "The Party's Position — In Accord with the Nation's Will," *Trybuna Ludu*, 20 March 1968 (my translation).

6. Cited in Walter D. Connor, "Social Change and Stability in Eastern Europe," *Problems of Communism*, 26, no. 6 (November-December 1977): 31.

SEVEN

GOULASH COMMUNISM, 1968-1980

The Stalinist system remained in place after 1968, but it was drained of emotional and intellectual content in a part of the world where politics was still very much a question of emotions and ideas. After 1953 Stalinism could no longer be maintained by naked force alone, and after 1968 reform of socialism was discredited as an alternative or makeweight. As the Polish intellectual and former Communist Leszek Kołakowski said after he left Poland in 1969, talking about democratic socialism became like talking about fried snowballs.[1] As the 1970s progressed, the theory of the two camps and fear of German revanchism joined ideology as former sources of support that were no longer available. Increasingly, the regimes justified their rule in terms of goulash: steady increases in the standard of living in a context of comprehensive social security.

There was of course also the weight of inertia. The system had now been in place for two decades, and Soviet determination to keep it in place was dramatically demonstrated in Prague, and remained in force. Inertia and the shadow of Soviet intervention created a feeling, shared by regimes, populations, and the West, that socialism was the destiny of the region. This sense that Soviet-sponsored Stalinism was fate for Poland, Czechoslovakia, Hungary, East Germany, Bulgaria, and Romania is one key to understanding why the region appeared so stable in the 1970s.

The invasion of Czechoslovakia proved that the area was no more independent of the outside world after 1968 than it had been before. As after 1956 the Soviets strove to refine the preinvasion status quo. After

1956 Stalin's heirs wanted to rein in the police in order to secure rule through the party. After 1968 the Soviet leadership did not want to give up the opportunities they saw in expanding ties with the West. The reasons for this Soviet choice, and the international preconditions for their post-1968 attitude toward Eastern Europe, are to be found in Cuba, Vietnam, and Germany.

Just as the years around 1960 were a turning point in the "domestic history" of Communist Eastern Europe, the Cuban Missile Crisis of 1962 was a turning point in the Cold War. Thereafter, the United States and the Soviet Union believed that the Third World would be the main ring of active competition. The Soviets drew one more conclusion. They believed that it was their inferiority in strategic nuclear weapons that had forced them to yield in the 1962 confrontation. The Soviets had always had conventional force superiority on the central front in Europe. In order to counterbalance their conventional threat cheaply, the West had decided to rely heavily on nuclear weapons. In the 1950s this reliance was formulated as a policy of "massive retaliation": A Soviet conventional attack would face a Western nuclear response. After Cuba the Soviets embarked in earnest on a strategic force buildup. By forcing the extra resources needed from an economy probably less than half the size of America's, by the end of the decade they had attained strategic parity with the United States.[2]

The United States immersed itself in global competition with the Soviets, using the two tracks, military and developmental, that had proven so successful in containing Soviet expansion in Europe in the 1940s and 1950s. Applied close to home in Latin America, this two-track approach met with little in the way of Soviet response. But when it was implemented in Asia, where both superpowers were interested, and where the U.S. ability to project power was reduced, the result was Vietnam.

The U.S. preoccupation with Vietnam intensified throughout the 1960s. After the commitment of major U.S. ground forces in February 1965, it became a fixation; and from the Tet offensive in January 1968, it was an obsession. President Lyndon Johnson tried to fight a major land war in Asia without a secure mandate from the political system and without raising taxes, and gradually the issues involved in fighting the war attached themselves to larger issues in American politics and society. By conviction and distraction, the United States turned away from Europe.

The turn of American attention to Vietnam had several consequences in Europe. First, U.S. support for arms control and détente with the Soviet Union increased. As long as the Soviet Union had been driven by its sense of inferiority in the military competition, it had promoted general and complete disarmament. Faced with the Soviet strategic buildup and fighting an expensive war 13,000 miles from home, the United States began to see arms control as a way of stabilizing the strategic balance. The better to fight the war in Vietnam, the United States began to seek ways to reduce tensions in Europe. Here the milestones were President John F. Kennedy's American University speech in mid-1963, President Johnson's endorsement of bridgebuilding in May of 1964, and his adoption of peaceful engagement in November of 1966.[3]

At the same time, the United States hoped to maintain its leadership in Western Europe by co-opting and controlling the desire of its alliance partners to assert specific West European interests in relations with the East. By the 1960s Western Europe had completely recovered from wartime damages, was economically prosperous, and was growing restless with U.S. leadership. America's preoccupations with Vietnam and with its burgeoning domestic divisions increased the restlessness. Western Europe began to flex its muscles by promoting a European version of détente that gave pride of place to the regional interests of Europeans.

In its early stages, this version of détente was associated with French President Charles de Gaulle. In 1966 de Gaulle expelled American forces from France and withdrew his country from NATO's military organization. Beginning with his June 1966 trip to Moscow, he and other French leaders fanned out across the East to promote the idea of trading greater West European autonomy from the United States for greater East European autonomy from the Soviet Union. The Soviets seemed willing to play along, especially as de Gaulle was willing to put money up front, as it were, by taking steps to decrease French dependence from the United States before the Soviets did anything of significance to increase the independence of East Europeans. Many West Europeans came to believe that the Soviets were willing to make this exchange and that both parts of Europe could reduce their dependence on the superpowers together.

This perception undermined U.S. leverage with the Soviet Union over Europe, for not only did the Soviets have a new partner with which to negotiate, but that partner could and did reduce the U.S. role in Europe. The Soviets were as passionately resistant to bridgebuilding and peaceful engagement as they were quietly receptive to the Gaullist paradigm. The result of the clash between the U.S. and European conceptions of détente was a compromise. A major policy review within NATO in 1967 adjusted both the alliance's military strategy, from massive retaliation to flexible response, and its political purpose, from pure defense to the twin pillars of defense and détente. NATO's purpose was now more than simply deterring the Warsaw Pact: It was also to be a forum for negotiating concrete steps to reduce the tensions that made deterrence necessary. The United States preserved political support for adequate defenses by accepting a redefinition of their purpose.

For most of the 1960s, de Gaulle had the European détente stage practically to himself. Britain and West Germany were the only other states that could aspire to compete with the United States in East-West relations, and they had fatal disabilities for such a role. Britain had sacrificed its potential for European leadership by its determination to preserve a special relationship with the United States, its preoccupation with decolonization, and its ambivalence about the European Community. For different reasons, the Federal Republic of Germany (FRG) had never had such a leadership role. The new West German state was presumptively an object of suspicion in international relations. Also, it had no nuclear weapons, and was thus dependent on the U.S. nuclear guarantee for its security. Most importantly, the FRG prevented itself from leading Western Europe by its approach to the East. Following a policy known as the Hallstein Doctrine, the FRG not only refused to recognize the GDR, but (except for the Soviet Union, with which it had had relations since 1955) it refused to have relations with any other state that recognized the GDR. Attracted by de Gaulle's vision of European détente, the rest of Western Europe began to see West Germany and not the Soviet Union as the main source of tensions in Europe.

The FRG's singular immobility on East-West questions allowed the Soviet Union's client regime in East Berlin to exploit the German national question. Strange as it seems in retrospect, until late 1966 it was the GDR that talked most about German reunification. East Germany also took the initiative to promote talks with the West German Social Democratic

Party, the SPD. Its confidence in the attractiveness of its version of socialism outweighed its fear of capitalist infection.

That confidence evaporated, however, when West Germany moved to reduce its isolation in the West by accepting the possibility of relations with the East. The Social Democrats entered government for the first time in December 1966, in a grand coalition with the Christian Democrats. This new government dropped the Hallstein Doctrine and adopted what was called a policy of movement. In the interest of reducing tensions, West Germany would establish relations with East European countries even though they continued to recognize the GDR. The first fruit of this policy was maverick Romania, which demonstrated its independence once again by establishing relations with West Germany in January 1967. The GDR immediately dropped all talk about reunification and joined Poland in pressing the Soviets to prevent an increase in West German influence. So long as the FRG refused to recognize the new Polish frontier, Poland felt obliged to stay in lockstep with the GDR on the German issue. In April 1967 the Warsaw Pact adopted a kind of reverse Hallstein Doctrine: Except for Romania and of course the Soviet Union, no Warsaw Pact country would establish relations with the FRG until it recognized the GDR. The policy of movement ground to a halt, and France remained the leader of European détente.[4]

The invasion of Czechoslovakia ended the possibility of European détente in its Gaullist version, but this was not immediately apparent. The planned summit between President Johnson and Premier Kosygin in Leningrad to begin negotiations on nuclear arms was postponed because of the invasion, but the Soviet arms buildup continued, the United States remained obsessed with Vietnam, and the West Europeans remained restless, so the West remained committed to détente. The Soviets also continued to want improved East-West relations. In the foreign policy they adopted in the aftermath of the invasion, Khrushchev's heirs implemented institution-building, bolstering Comecon and the Warsaw Pact, but these were at most palliatives. For Leonid Brezhnev and his like-minded colleagues, the cure to instability in Eastern Europe was, in Soviet political language, a "grandiose" program of peace through disarmament and expansion of contacts with the United States and the whole West.

Like Khrushchev, they were basically optimists.[5] They believed that after a quarter century of struggle, and after a decade of strategic armament while the United States was mired in Vietnam, they had achieved equality with the United States as leaders of the struggle of the two camps. They also believed that this struggle was going rather well, that the "the world correlation of forces" between socialism and imperialism was shifting in their favor. Further, they thought that by offering to reduce tension through negotiated steps they could persuade the West to accept this worldwide trend, beginning in Europe.

Meeting in Budapest in March 1969, the Warsaw Pact tried to invigorate détente by appealing for a European security conference that would ratify the postwar territorial settlement and multiply East-West ties in Europe. During 1969 the Soviets (like the Americans) continued to feel the push of international military and prestige considerations to reduce tensions in Europe. The conference of Communist and workers' parties they held in Moscow in June did not ratify Soviet primacy in the socialist world, as they had hoped it would, and in August serious fighting broke out on the Soviet-Chinese frontier.

Despite the obvious willingness of the Soviets to negotiate the future of Europe, the Western response to the Budapest Appeal was ambivalent. The invasion of Czechoslovakia had invalidated de Gaulle's European version of détente. It was no longer possible to assume that the Soviets were willing to give the East Europeans more autonomy in return for greater West European independence from the United States. The Soviet response to France's partial disengagement from NATO in 1966 and 1967 had been the tanks in the streets of Prague: The Soviets had vividly demonstrated that they would keep the East in line no matter what the West did. Asserting their independence from the United States, West Europeans now realized, might merely weaken the American commitment to Europe without affecting Soviet behavior.

Still, Western enthusiasm for détente per se did not diminish. Arms control and reduced tensions were as attractive as ever. The invasion of Czechoslovakia did mean that the U.S. role in Europe would continue to be important to the Europeans, and this reduced the incentive for West European states to pursue relations with the East independently of and if necessary in contradiction to U.S. interests. In these conditions, West

Germany, now under a coalition government led by the Social Democrats and Willy Brandt, saw the chance to lead a scaled-back European effort to improve relations with Eastern Europe, in the ruins of the Gaullist approach.[6]

The *Ostpolitik*, or Eastern policy, that was initiated in 1969 by the Brandt government went far beyond the previous coalition government's policy of movement. Brandt offered to recognize the postwar settlement, including Poland's western frontiers and the legitimacy of the GDR, in the hope of breaking down barriers between the two Germanies, improving the living conditions of Germans in the GDR and elsewhere in the East, and increasing the likelihood of eventual reunification.[7]

Ostpolitik appealed to the Soviets for a whole variety of reasons. First, West German acceptance of the postwar settlement would remove the major barrier to its acceptance by the remainder of the West, and it would do so without endangering Soviet relations with the United States. Second, it put the Soviets directly in touch with the rising star of the West: The West German economy was beginning to move out ahead of the others, and with the Gaullist concept of détente discredited and de Gaulle retired (in 1969), West Germany was fast becoming the most important European state on East-West issues too. Third, the Soviets had demonstrated in Czechoslovakia that they were determined to keep Eastern Europe within bounds acceptable to them, and then made that determination a matter of "principle" by proclaiming the "Brezhnev Doctrine," so they had less fear of an East European ripple effect from Soviet-West German rapprochement and less need of the German threat to justify Communist rule in the area. Accordingly, negotiations between the Soviet Union and the FRG began in December 1969, the same month as the Strategic Arms Limitation Talks (SALT).

Polish leader Gomułka had been the GDR's staunchest East European supporter throughout the 1960s, but now he smelled the rat of Rapallo — the threat of a Soviet-West German deal over Poland's head — in Soviet receptiveness to Brandt's *Ostpolitik*. Having spent the entire period of his rule building his credibility with the Soviets, he now moved quickly, in May 1969, to offer negotiations for a new Polish-West German treaty, before the FRG recognized the GDR and even before Soviet-West German negotiations began.[8] The West Germans preferred to finish first with the Soviets, which they did in August 1970. In December they signed a treaty with Poland that normalized relations in return for a somewhat qualified West German acceptance of the Oder-Neisse frontier.

Meanwhile, the United States had made settling the status of Berlin a precondition for the opening of the European security conference that would extend West German recognition of the postwar territorial settlement to all of Europe, East and West. Once again the Soviets were receptive. U.S.-Soviet-British-French quadripartite talks on Berlin began in March of 1970 and were completed in September 1971. The agreement on Berlin, like the Polish recognition of the FRG, took place before a single Western state recognized the GDR. Compared to their previous policy, the Soviets and Poles were now stabbing the GDR regime in the back. The East Germans fought against the entire process. GDR resistance was so stubborn that East German leader Walter Ulbricht had to be retired and replaced by Erich Honecker in May 1971. Even then, the GDR and the now-normalized Czechoslovaks under Gustav Husák fought tenacious delaying actions. The basic treaty establishing relations between the FRG and GDR was not signed until December 1972. The Czechs held out even longer, and the treaty by which the FRG declared the Munich agreement of 1938 null and void and by which mutual relations were established had to wait until December 1973.

In this way the FRG entered East-West politics as an active participant, and the German specter that had haunted the politics of Eastern Europe for a generation began to dissipate. In Poland and Czechoslovakia especially it had been one of the few arguments for acquiescence to the Communist system that had genuine popular resonance. After the states of Eastern Europe extended diplomatic recognition to the FRG, it became harder and harder to invoke.

Still, Brezhnev's optimism about East-West relations seemed justified. From the Soviet point of view, the SALT process and the German treaties looked like payoffs for the gamble that a détente approach could induce U.S. recognition of Soviet political equality and West German acceptance of the postwar settlement. They in turn helped Leonid Brezhnev consolidate his personal primacy at last, in 1971. And as he consolidated power, Brezhnev also proved to be an economic optimist.

To be sure, times had changed, so Brezhnev's economic optimism was different from Khrushchev's. By about 1970 Stalinist economics were reaching the limits of their effectiveness in the Soviet Union as well as in Eastern Europe. Gone were the heady days of "We will bury you" and the prediction in the 1961 Soviet party program that the USSR would overtake the United States in economic performance by 1980. Khrushchev had seen the bright economic future purely within boundaries of socialism and the world socialist camp. The Brezhnev leadership no longer believed socialism could grow and prosper in international isolation.

But Brezhnev and his colleagues did believe that "real socialism," as it was now called, was fundamentally sound and healthy. They also thought that they were clever enough to exploit improved relations with the West to acquire the economic inputs needed for socialism to grow and prosper without systemic economic or political reform. Brezhnev's solution to the increasingly apparent limits of Stalinist economics was to steal Western technology or buy it on credit, plug it into the socialist economy, and thereby boost productivity fast enough to pay back the debts incurred. The Brezhnev leadership believed that if the proper precautions were taken, if they solidified the institutions of the socialist camp and actively prevented any political liberalization, they could use Western economic inputs to keep the system going without dangerous political spillover.

To the end of its life, the Soviet regime worked obstinately to prevent the formation of classes as such so that the economic fruits of continued development in its Brezhnevian version were not purposefully directed at the working class. The Brezhnev leadership was not *ouvrieriste*, to use the French term for pro-worker, as a matter of policy, and shortages that eroded the value of wages caused discontent among workers as among other groups. But the Brezhnev regime did keep wage differentials among employee groups narrow by any Western standard. This meant that un-skilled labor was paid better per unit of training and effort than skilled labor and intellectual work. Prices for consumer goods were massively subsidized, and even though it was unravelling for lack of funding the egalitarian social safety net was kept in place. And under Brezhnev the regime did raise the minimum wage of industrial workers more than for most other groups, just as it raised the minimum wage of farm workers more than industrial workers'. The effect (rather than the intention) was consumerism, and consumerism that disproportionately favored the Soviet working class. The economic fruits of continued development would be directed to the working class. Soviet consumerism was *ouvrieriste*. Wage differentials were kept low, which meant that unskilled labor was paid better per unit of training and effort than skilled labor and intellectual work; prices for consumer goods were massively subsidized; and even though it was unraveling due to lack of funding, the egalitarian social safety net was kept in place.

The Soviets expected this consumerism to guide Eastern Europe, for Brezhnev was as committed to Soviet primacy in the socialist camp as Khrushchev and Stalin had been. Under Stalin the Soviets had imposed their model of industrialization rather than keep Eastern Europe in classic colonial status. Khrushchev had encouraged experimentation and offered Soviet markets and raw materials in order to stabilize the system after 1956. After Czechoslovakia, the Brezhnev leadership expected the East Europeans to follow the Soviet lead in developing ties with the West in a careful and controlled fashion, in order to grow economically without fundamentally altering Stalinism.[9]

In other words, economic ties to the West were to be the alternative to systemic reform rather than its harbinger.[10] At the time, however, Westerners hoped and believed that East-West economic ties would lead to systemic reform in the East. There were those in the Soviet Union and Eastern Europe who agreed with this assessment and who resisted ties with the West for precisely that reason. The most conservative regimes, the Czechoslovaks and the Bulgarians, resisted most. Others, inside and outside the regimes, supported the expansion of Western ties precisely because they wanted liberalization in economics or politics at home. Improving economic relations with the West was popular with the populations at large. Increasingly, younger people tended to compare "real socialism" not with the even grimmer past, which they did not remember, but with Western Europe, which they could now see something of. They were likely to be modestly grateful for greater access to Western goods and Western culture, and for greater opportunities for travel to the West. But these children of socialism were restless already, and in the short run exposure to the West could be used as a favor that also served as a safety valve for their discontent.

Over the longer run, nevertheless, Western exposure endorsed by the Soviets made it harder for the regimes to summon up and sustain the old siege mentality within society. The supposed threat from the West had been a pillar of government, regularly used to justify titanic sacrifices for the building of socialism. Now that the Soviets were using East-West economic ties to avoid systemic reform, it became harder for the East European regimes to claim they were there because the world was divided between irreconcilable systems.

Given that the Soviets were willing to undermine the theory of the two camps in order to keep "real socialism" going, it would have been logical for them to accept economic reform as a means to the same end. After all, these two sources of goulash, trade and reform, were not by their nature mutually exclusive. To understand why the Soviets instead supported economic ties with the West as a means to avoid systemic reform, the record of previous reform efforts must be evaluated. Though economic reform been prescribed by both Westerners and East European liberals for well over a decade, it was always extraordinarily difficult in practice.

The attempts at economic reform can be divided into two ideal types. The first, economic decentralization, denotes the injection of true market elements such as independent price formation on the basis of supply and demand and real costs in the market. This was popular among economists in Poland, Czechoslovakia, and Hungary, and was tried in a mild way in Hungary's New Economic Mechanism introduced in 1968 and in a radical way in the Czechoslovak economic program of that same year. The second method was administrative decentralization, the devolution of economic decisionmaking out from the central authorities to the enterprises. It had been tried in Poland and Czechoslovakia in the late 1950s. Even though it had been wildly unsuccessful, it continued to appeal to conservative reformers, and was therefore tried in both the GDR and Bulgaria in the course of the 1960s. Whichever method was used, however, reform continually ran up against the limits set by the system: at the bottom, the resistance of complacent managers and workers; in the middle, the interlocking character of the system, which meant that it was hard to change one part without changing them all; at the top, the fear that such change would inevitably affect the system itself.[11]

Although in practice economic reform was never applied consistently enough to test the proposition that it would inevitably force systemic changes, the experience of the Prague Spring seemed to indicate that it would. Economic reform had been part of the general Czechoslovak reform program of 1967 and 1968, and the Soviet leadership concluded from this fact that economic reform would lead inexorably to unacceptable political reform. Even though the invasion had prevented the Czechoslovak economic program from being seriously implemented, Soviet disapproval meant that after 1968 fresh economic reform was not an option for East European regimes. Whether or not they believed in the link between economic and political reform, they knew that the Soviets did. Because the Czechoslovak program had concentrated on economic decentralization, the Soviet veto applied mainly to this method. If a country still wanted to reform, it would have to be by administrative decentralization on the East German model. After 1968 economic reform was not only very difficult, it was also politically suspect. Moreover, economic reform was gradually swept up in the general atmosphere of failure that surrounded the Stalinist system after 1968. It came to be tarred with the brush of the system it sought to ameliorate. Although Westerners continued to hold conferences and write weighty tomes about it through the 1970s, the bloom was off the rose in Eastern Europe itself, even for liberals and reformers.

Ever since Stalinism had been imposed on the area, the regimes had tried to substitute economics for politics. In the 1970s this recipe became less and less adequate for both the regimes and the populations they ruled. Both began slowly to turn their backs on economics and their faces back towards politics. Neither movement was direct. With ideology fading as a force for cohesion, the regimes experienced a diffusion of power. Central committees became conglomerates of delegates from various apparatuses in the party, in ministries, in economic and social organisms, all lobbying "government." Practically bereft of ideology, most governments sought to give a quasi-ideological expression to this diffusion by introducing changes in the legal and constitutional systems, drawing on the post-Stalinist Soviet model. This extended the system's economic and social control over society but justified it in terms appropriate to the new Brownian movement of rewards and benefits among diffuse power centers. They were more likely to appeal internationally—as "steps toward normalization"—than the old ideology. Society responded first with cynicism and then, as we shall see, with the makings of an ideology that simply omitted the system. But it too was a blend of old and new, and in its beginnings, in the 1970s, it was also much more uncertain that it had a social base.[12]

None of this adequately explains why economic reform ceased to be an attractive option in the 1970s and why the regimes were reduced to the stark choice between stagnation and going West. To complete the explanation and begin to understand where the social base for the new ideology came from, we must understand that in the Eastern Europe of the 1960s and 1970s, the cure of economic reform turned out to be almost as painful as the diseases of the Stalinist system it was intended to remedy. Ironically, the primary reason economic reform was discredited was that it threatened the post-1956 strategy of keeping the growing working class quiescent through goulash and social security. One reason the East Europeans welcomed the opening to the West was that economic reform at home was proving to be intolerable. Economic relations with the West provided not only an escape from Stalinism but an escape from the problems of reforming Stalinism.

Full employment, job security, and the considerable measure of social equality provided by socialism were genuinely appreciated by East European workers. As they compared their situation with that of workers in the West, East European workers saw that their system was less efficient, but also understood that it shielded them from unemployment, from competition in the marketplace, from the need to pay for schooling and health care, from wide gaps between rich and poor, and even from hard work. The apocryphal but famous slogan of East European and Soviet workers, "We pretend to work, and they pretend to pay us," was rooted in a hard truth.

Compared to Western economies at comparable stages of development, all the Eastern economies showed low labor productivity as well as low capital productivity. The days when such figures could be explained by pointing to the need to absorb the rural underemployed by putting them in low-technology factories had passed, for in country after country the rural labor surplus was drying up and was being replaced by labor shortages. As growth began to slow and the prospect of slowly increasing living standards began to fade, full employment, job security, and low wage differentials between the highest and lowest paid — the concrete sign of widespread social equality — became even more precious. All the evidence from Eastern Europe up to the present day shows that economic security and equality are about the only achievements of socialism that people continue to value and fear to lose.[13]

That fear became an important political factor in the 1960s and 1970s, because economic decentralization, the injection of market mechanisms into the economic system, necessarily threatens job security and social equality. The Stalinist system may have kept purchasing power low, starved consumption, and resisted technological innovation, but changing it to reward efficiency and introduce genuine competition meant that the prices of scarce goods would rise, that the industrious would be rewarded by higher incomes, and that the inefficient would be penalized. Every country that seriously tried such reforms faced resistance from its own working class. And now that resistance was no longer expressed simply as a demand for worker control of the factories, the ideal of peasant self-sufficiency translated into the cities and into socialist language that had marked the mid-1950s. At least potentially, and in the most urgent cases actually, it now involved class-conscious resistance to changes in the nationwide socialist systems of economic management.

In principle, the urgency of reform and of worker resistance to it should have been highest in the north, in the most industrialized countries, and should have declined as one proceeded southward toward Romania and Bulgaria. And in fact Stalinist industrialization was still paying large and palpable production dividends in the south in these years, so Romania and Bulgaria confined their reform efforts to tinkering.

Perhaps neighboring Yugoslavia provided them a kind of warning of the costs of reform for working-class tranquility. Yugoslav development had of course taken a substantially separate path from theirs since 1948: While still socialist, it was also radically decentralized in significant political and economic ways that were unthinkable for the more orthodox systems. Nevertheless, Yugoslavia was still socialist; it was at a comparable level of industrial development; and in the late 1960s it provided a kind of preview of the effects of economically decentralizing reform. It introduced economic decentralization in the mid-1960s, around the time Interior Minister Aleksandar

Ranković was expelled and the Yugoslav party was substantially federalized. The most famous result of these policies was the surge of nationalism that led Tito to purge the Croat and Serb parties in 1971 and 1972. Widespread worker discontent, caused by resentment of the newly wealthy, fed local nationalisms. The crackdown of 1971-72 also included a measure of recentralization that was partly designed to allay this kind of discontent.[14]

Still, Yugoslavia was scarcely a model for any other country in the area, and probably not even a warning. In the north, in the more industrially advanced economies, the potential for worker discontent was highest in principle, because there, first in Czechoslovakia and the GDR, then in Poland and Hungary, the iron ring tying these economies to the Soviets appeared and tightened first, and reform was most needed as an escape hatch out of it.

As with the de-Stalinization process, however, the way things actually worked out depended in the first instance on politics. Romania and Bulgaria did not need economic decentralization; Czechoslovakia and the GDR did, but although East German *administrative* decentralization was perhaps the most extensive in the area, the GDR avoided the economic variety like the plague, and the invasion of Czechoslovakia put a stop to implementation of either variety there. It is worth remembering, in view of what came later, that in Czechoslovakia in 1968 the free-wheeling discussion of economic decentralization that was part of the Prague Spring provoked extreme reticence among workers. This may help explain their relatively tepid support for reform until the invasion brought them massively behind their national leadership on the eve of its execution.[15] But in practice, as with de-Stalinization, it was the most and least industrialized countries whose regimes best avoided reform and the worker backlash it typically elicited, and it was in the medium-industrialized countries, Hungary and Poland, that reform had the most turbulent and serious effects.

Kádár's Hungary came first. The New Economic Mechanism (NEM) introduced in 1968 was intended to create a system that would simulate the operation of a market based on private property and competition. It allowed many prices to be determined by supply and demand, severely reduced the role of central planning and subsidies, gave enterprises some discretion in managing inputs, outputs, and wages, and allowed efficient operators to make money. Exceptions and subsidies were common, and large areas of the economy remained under central control, so the NEM really never succeeded in its objective of simulating the market. In its first years, however, it did increase wealth and consumption. By doing so, it provoked a backlash in the industrial working class. Stuck in their factories, workers had less access to the benefits of the NEM than others, and within three or four years their complaints had created a kind of workers' opposition within the party. The author of the reform, Reszö Nyers, was removed from the Politburo in 1974, and the implementation of the NEM was effectively put on hold until 1979. In Hungary, then, reform survived, but it had limits that were enforced not by the Soviets but by the Hungarian working class.[16]

The most spectacular case of worker backlash took place in Poland.[17] Using the inflated official statistics, the Polish economy grew slightly more than 1 percent a year during the 1960s, a figure one Polish economist correctly described as statistically insignificant. After nearly a decade of stagnation, Gomułka allowed himself to be convinced of the need for reform that would decentralize some decisions out to enterprises and that would make wages depend more on enterprise efficiency, and economics tsar Bolesław Jaszczuk began putting piecemeal reforms into effect in 1969.[18] On December 7, 1970, the Polish government signed an agreement with West Germany recognizing the legitimacy of the Oder-Niesse frontier. Six days later the Gomułka regime announced a sudden steep price rise. The workers in the large industrial enterprises on the Baltic Coast struck in opposition and attacked party installations. The turbulence spread to most of Poland's major factories, military and police troops were called in to suppress the it, and blood was shed.

What was not clear at the time and has been forgotten since was that the workers had risen not simply in Poland's great tradition of national insurrections, but in response to a price rise that was an integral part of a broader economic reform program that had been hurting them for over a year. The workers had no say in the reform: The workers' councils that sprang up in 1956 had been absorbed in 1958 into "conferences of workers' self-government" run by the local managers and party leaders. The reform promised to make bonuses, which constituted the bulk the Polish worker's take-home pay, depend on the performance of individual enterprises, and therefore on the effectiveness of their managers, through what was called a system of "material incentives." By February of 1970 spreading fear of unemployment was discernible even to outsiders, and by midsummer there were housewives' riots on Gierek's home turf in Silesia. By December detestation of the incentives was vocal and general. The revolt of December 1970 was overwhelming, but it was only the last step in a process that had been provoked by economic reform. The Polish workers rejected an economic reform whose designers had not consulted them and that they saw as directed against their interests.

The Soviets refused to intervene to save Gomułka. On December 20, just before the strike spread to all of Polish industry, he was replaced by Silesian party boss Edward Gierek. Gierek tried at first to keep the price rises in force, but renewed strikes by the female textile workers of Łódz in February 1971 forced him to promise a two-year price freeze. He then embarked on Eastern Europe's most enthusiastic program of goulash economics designed to secure assent to Communist rule.[19]

Once again Polish workers had risen and forced a change of leadership and program on their Communist party. Gierek's response was an ambitious program of hectic development to increase the size of the economic pie, with more for everyone, but without systemic reform. The Poland of the 1970s could not be called precisely typical, for by this time no country could stand for the region as a whole. But Stalinist development was petering out everywhere in Eastern Europe, and most of the regimes were unable to sustain economic reform. Gierek's experiment was an imaginative response to a general conundrum.

Gierek came to power as a worker who understood workers and as an economic manager who knew how to deal with workers. He had kept party rule strong in Silesia by giving them purchasing power and consumer goods to buy. From 1970 he applied this formula to the whole of Poland. The Soviets agreed with him that the problem was basically economic. When Gomułka had appealed to them to save him, their reply had been that the party had lost touch with the working class. When Gierek told them that the way to renew the party's links with the working class was consumerism, they were easily convinced. The credits Gierek attracted in the first few months of his rule were Soviet, not Western. In January 1971 the Soviets provided 2 million tons of grain and above-plan deliveries of crude oil, cement, and prefabricated housing. They added more aid after the February price freeze. All told, Gierek's Poland received $250 million in early consumer credits from Moscow, including $100 million in hard currency.[20]

This Soviet assistance was meant to be transitional. Indeed, Gierek's long-term strategy was to create and exploit a new economic relationship with the West under the umbrella of détente that the Soviets were putting in place. He proposed to create a "second Poland," fully industrialized and modern, at the cutting edge in efficient economic performance but within the basic Stalinist framework. To do so, he planned to boost purchasing power at home and import the latest Western high technology on credit. The increase in purchasing power would give workers and managers an incentive to work harder and thereby boost productivity. The imported high technology would also contribute. As productivity increased, more and more consumer goods would be available to absorb the previous increase in purchasing power. Improvements in productivity would also yield more export goods, enough to earn the hard currency needed to pay back the credits and their interest. This scheme was embodied in Gierek's first five-year-plan, which covered the years 1971 to 1975. Gross investment in fixed assets was to rise by 38.5 percent, and real wages were to increase by 17 percent. The new investment was to be concentrated in the sinews of modern industry, such as steel, shipbuilding, and petrochemicals, and in the extractive industries whose products — coal, copper, and sulfur — sold well abroad. Some new investment was even targeted to another traditional Polish hard currency earner, agriculture.[21] The position of the Polish private farmers who now had to produce more food for the workers if Gierek was to succeed was bolstered in other ways. They were now included in the national insurance network, their compulsory deliveries at prices fixed by the state were abolished, and the amount of land they could rent from the state land fund was increased.[22]

Gierek's first five-year plan was a kind of Communist New Deal, a quasi-Keynesian gamble that the economy could be restarted by restoring confidence and by borrowing to generate the investment and new production that would pay off the debt. Like the American New Deal, it was not limited to the economy. The Gierek leadership knew that it also needed to inspire new confidence in Poland both within the country and in the West, whence most of the credits would have to come. Gierek therefore embarked on a whole new program of "dialogue" with Polish society that one major analyst has aptly called "de-totalization from above." [23]

Because this new style was designed to generate the Western credits that would allow Gierek to sidestep systemic reform, dialogue was not formalized. It was nonetheless real and substantial. The Communist leadership cultivated the church, which extracted a series of concessions in church-building and religious education. The Gierek regime appealed to nationalism by initiating a campaign to rebuild the Royal Castle in Warsaw. Further, its representatives fanned out across the country to talk to representatives of major social groups. Gierek made a practice of announcing major policy steps beforehand, and even altered proposals in response to criticisms before they were passed through the parliament. After a generation of top-down command, this was heady stuff. It impressed the West, and for a time it even impressed the Poles.

Gierek complemented dialogue with institutional change. Between 1972 and 1975 the Gierek leadership introduced three stages of administrative reform that significantly altered the way the country was run. In 1973 what was called one-man leadership was introduced in both the economy and local administration. In enterprises and in local political jurisdictions, the parallel structures of party and state met in a single head, reestablishing the structure of territorial state administration that had been characteristic of interwar Poland and that had subsisted until 1950. In that same year administrative decentralization on the GDR model began to be implemented in the economy. "Large economic organizations," or WOGs in their Polish acronym, were created as an intermediate level between enterprises and ministries, and given monopolistic control over and responsibility for all organized activities connected with production and distribution of a given product. Finally, in 1975 the lowest political jurisdiction, the county, was eliminated, and the seventeen provinces, the next higher level, were reduced in size and expanded in number to forty-nine. This move allowed Gierek to replace opponents and to insure that no one after him could build up a strong local base from which to compete for power in Warsaw, as he had when he ruled Silesia as "the Polish Katanga." It also promised to increase efficiency. [24]

For the first five years Gierek's program seemed to work: The Polish economy expanded spectacularly. Annual rates of growth for both the national economy and industrial production rose by between 10 and 12 percent beginning in 1972. With management now decentralized out to the WOGs and their enterprises, investment and real wages far overshot their planned targets, as managers had no incentive not to invest and not to raise wages to attract and hold labor. Instead of the planned 38.5 percent, gross investment in fixed assets rose 69.5 percent, and new plants sprang up like mushrooms after the rain all over Poland. Instead of the planned 17percent increase, real wages rose 36 percent. Most significant for the population of a country where well-being is identified to an extraordinary degree with the availability of meat, per-capita meat consumption went up from fifty-three kilos in 1970 to seventy kilos in 1975. This meat was produced by Polish farmers with grain imported from the West on credit.[25]

Then, in the same short space of time it had taken to produce Gierek's miracle, it all went terribly sour. Growth rates started to drop in 1975 and fell below zero in 1979. National income actually decreased that year, for the first time in the history of Communist Poland and the first time in the Communist bloc since Czechoslovakia in 1962. The Gierek experiment was completely discredited, and the Poland that arose on the rubble was very different from what Gierek or anyone else had anticipated. To understand the "second Poland" Gierek actually midwifed, we must examine the reasons why he failed.[26]

East European dependence on the outside world caught up with Gierek, and with a vengeance. The dependence of his Poland was double-barreled, for his plan relied substantially on both East and West. In the West, economic recession followed the oil shock of 1973. Afterward, western countries were less willing to buy the products Poland needed to sell in order to earn the hard currency it needed to pay back its mounting debt.

Dependence on the East was already a fixture of the system Gierek was unwilling to alter. Since 1958 prices in intra-Comecon trade had been determined by the Bucharest Formula, which based them on the average of world prices over five-year periods and changed to reflect that average only every five years. As world raw materials prices were rising faster than world prices of manufactures, this formula amounted to a Soviet subsidy for the East Europeans. After 1956 the Soviets gradually accepted conditions for trade with Eastern Europe that cost them tens and perhaps hundreds of billions of dollars, compared to what they could have earned by selling on hard-currency markets. But by the 1970s the Soviets wanted to increase their own high-technology imports from the West, and paid for these imports primarily with exports of oil and gold. After international oil prices rose in 1973, the opportunity cost of selling oil to Eastern Europe at cut rates soared.

The Soviets were still selling oil to the East Europeans at late-1960s prices, which had increased by a factor of ten in the interim. The East Europeans seemed to be doing rather well, and the Soviets were still optimistic about the economic future of socialism. So in 1975 they imposed a special oil price increase, and in 1976 they designed a new formula allowing for annual adjustments in prices based on average world prices for the preceding five-year period. This still amounted to a considerable subsidy as long as world oil prices were rising, but the effect was to double the price the East Europeans paid for their oil between 1974 and 1976, and to quadruple it by 1983. The East Europeans did use Soviet raw materials very inefficiently, and the Soviets could argue that raising their cost would raise efficiency. Still, the price increases wracked the East European economies, and no country was hurt more than Poland. Poland had just directed new investment to petrochemicals and needed to send its exportable goods West to pay its debt, rather than to the Soviet Union to pay for oil.[27]

Soviet price increases hit Poland just as production began to falter. Investments had been dispersed all over the industrial landscape in plants that were not yet completed, and industry was becoming dependent on small quantities of foreign-made parts to run at all. New purchasing power and new technology were not increasing productivity as much as Gierek had expected, and new consumer goods were not coming off the production lines in sufficient number to absorb the higher wages.

After their initial agricultural reforms, the Gierek leadership soured its relations with Polish farmers. As Communists whose social point of reference was the working class, they could not resist shortchanging the private farmers who were to produce the meat so valued by Poles. The regime channeled the bulk of available credits and manufactured inputs, such as fertilizer, to the state farms rather than the private farms, and made it harder for private farmers to rent more land from the state land fund.

By the mid-1970s agricultural production stabilized, and farmers tended more and more to withhold their produce from the market.[28]

In June 1976 the regime responded to the mounting economic crisis in a way that showed it did not really understand the workers either. Aiming to soak up excess purchasing power, it announced a general retail price rise that averaged 60 percent, included a 68 percent rise in the price of meat. Just as Gomułka had done in 1970, Gierek tried to raise prices without any prior discussion. Just as they had done in 1970, Polish workers rose, and just as Gomułka had tried to do in 1970, Gierek tried to put down the strike with force. Once again blood was shed, and once again the price rise was rescinded, after the workers' ringleaders had been imprisoned. In September a workers' defense committee, KOR, was formed.[29]

At the end of 1976 the regime announced a new "economic maneuver" that amounted to cutting investments and imports. It ordered the local party authorities to reassert their control over the overheated economy. But now Gierek discovered that the party was no longer capable of running the economy. The gigantic WOGs were now too large to be controlled by the downsized party organizations in the forty-nine diminished provinces. Party bosses were no longer the equals of managers. At its Seventh Congress in 1975, the party had announced that "the construction of the developed socialist society has initiated a gradual transformation of the state of the dictatorship of the proletariat into a general national state, which, under the direction of the working class, embodies the will and interests of the entire nation." [30] But in strengthening what it called "the socialist state," the party had expected to control it. Now, as he wrestled with the economic crisis, Gierek found that the leader of the Polish government, Piotr Jaroszewicz, a man the Soviets trusted, had more authority than he did as party leader. The Polish state was threatening to slip the leash of party rule.

As the skies came down around Gierek, continued access to Western goods on credit appeared to be his only chance. Credits were still needed because Poland could not export enough to pay for imports: Between 1973 and 1979 the trade deficit with non-Communist countries ran between $1.5 and $3.5 billion a year.[31] Western banks, now gorged with Arab petrodollars, were eager to place them almost anywhere that would take them. Poland's hard currency debt, which had multiplied ten times between 1971 and 1975, from a little over $750 million to over $7 billion, now tripled again, to $21.5 billion by 1979. All the East European countries borrowed more from the West in the 1970s, but by 1979 Poland's debt made up almost half of the entire area total.[32]

During the 1970s the regime had been unwilling to crack down for fear of losing access to Western credits. The leaders of the 1976 strike were released just as Gierek arrived in Belgrade for the opening of a Committee on Security and Cooperation in Europe (CSCE) review meeting, where human rights would be in the spotlight.[33] In June 1979 he tolerated a visit home by the new Polish Pope, John Paul II, around whom the Polish nation gathered as if there was no Polish party or state.[34] In the end, Gierek's toleration ceased to help him. Even though Poland retained a liberal reputation, Western banks pulled back in 1978 and 1979 because its economic performance was so dreadful.

In desperation, the regime tried another price increase in July 1980. This time it was faced with a national uprising under a new leadership that had grown up in the shadows, a coalition of workers and intellectuals under the wing of the church, precisely the kind of coalition that every Communist regime in Eastern Europe had worked so hard to prevent after 1956.[35] A near-hysterical Gierek threw himself on Cardinal-Primate Stefan Wyszyński, begging him to save Poland from a Soviet invasion. The Cardinal refused, and Gierek suffered a mental breakdown, allowing him to be removed from office.[36] For Poland, and for all of Eastern Europe, Gierek's bankruptcy was the handwriting on the wall.

Notes

1. Quoted in Timothy Garton Ash, *The Polish Revolution: Solidarity* (New York: Scribner's, 1983), 22.

2. For those who enjoy the folklore of American politics, it was worth observing how the first suggestions from the Soviets that their economy was much smaller than ours immediately became controversial in the U.S., where the Bush Administration was struggling with how to deal with Gorbachev and change. See Robert Pear, "Soviet

Experts Say Their Economy Is Worse than U.S. Has Estimated," *New York Times*, 24 April 1990 (citing Viktor Belkin's claim that Soviet GNP is 28 percent that of the United States); William Safire (as usual quick off the mark), "Intelligence Fiasco," *New York Times*, 27 April 1990; and Michael Wines, "C.I.A. Accused of Overestimating Soviet Economy," *New York Times*, 23 July 1990.

3. On American policy in the 1960s, see Bennett Kovrig, *The Myth of Liberation. East-Central Europe in U.S. Diplomacy and Politics Since 1941* (Baltimore: Johns Hopkins University Press, 1973), 236-285; Raymond L. Garthoff, "Eastern Europe in the Context of U.S.-Soviet Relations," in Sarah Meiklejohn Terry, ed., *Soviet Policy in Eastern Europe* (New Haven: Yale University Press, 1984), 315-348, brings the story up to the turn of the 1980s.

4. For this period and for what follows I have found Gerhard Wettig's *Community and Conflict in the Socialist Camp. The Soviet Union, East Germany and the German Problem 1965-1972* (London: C. Hurst, 1975), 20-47 and passim, very specific and helpful.

5. Perhaps more precisely, J.F. Brown writes that their rule was based on "complacency bred of apparent success": *Surge to Freedom. The End of Communist Rule in Eastern Europe* (Durham, N.C. and London: Duke University Press, 1991), 30. Perhaps even more precisely, John Van Oudenaren suggests that the Brezhnev program's purpose was really to complete the Khrushchev program without its exaggerations, especially when it came to political liberalization: "The Soviet Union and Eastern Europe: New Prospects and Old Dilemmas," in William E. Griffith, ed., *Central and Eastern Europe: The Opening Curtain?* (Boulder, Col.: Westview, 1989), 108-110.

6. In a vast literature, I remain attracted by the insights of Philip Windsor, *Change in Eastern Europe* (London: Royal Institute for International Affairs, 1980), 3-11.

7. For what follows, see the good synoptic survey of *Ostpolitik* and its antecedents in Josef Joffe, "The View from Bonn: The Tacit Alliance," in Lincoln Gordon, ed., *Eroding Empire. Western Relations with Eastern Europe* (Washington, D.C.: The Brookings Institution, 1987), 129-187.

8. See J.F. Brown, *Eastern Europe and Communist Rule* (Durham: Duke University Press, 1988), 56.

9. On power diffusion beginning in the late 1960s, see Judy Batt, *East Central Europe from Reform to Transformation* (New York: Council on Foreign Relations Press, 1991), 5. On regime "constitutionalism," see Wiktor Osiatyński, "Revolutions in Eastern Europe," *The University of Chicago Law Review*, 58, no. 2 (Spring 1991), 848-850. Osiatyński argues that in the late 1950s East European Communist elites recognized (1) that socialism's economic promise was unfulfillable, (2) that without economic performance pseudo-nationalistic rhetoric could not sustain them for long, and (3) that the kind of economic reform needed to revitalize the system would threaten their power. I think that recognition came much later, and the proof is that the "constitutionalism" he himself describes as their stopgap solution was applied mainly in the 1970s. For a short summary on consumerism, see J.F. Brown, *Surge to Freedom*, 28-31. Soviet consumerist policy at home was documented through 1974 in Alastair McAuley, *Economic Welfare in the Soviet Union. Poverty, Living Standards, and Inequality* (Madison, WI.: University of Wisconsin Press, 1979), and it is now brilliantly documented and analyzed for the whole period up to April 1991 in Walter D. Connor, *The Accidental Proletariat. Workers, Politics and Crisis in Gorbachev's Russia* (Princeton, N.J.: Princeton University Press, 1991), from which the above description is

mined. For an early analysis of how the Soviets adjusted their whole foreign trade approach to permit massive grain imports from 1963 to 1965 (and thus beginning under Khrushchev), see Oleg Hoeffding, "Recent Structural Changes and Balance-of-Payments Adjustments in Soviet Foreign Trade," in Alan A. Brown and Egon Neuberger, eds., *International Trade and Central Planning* (Berkeley: University of California Press, 1968), 312-337. When we come to Eastern Europe, recent studies present evidence that by the 1970s income dispersion was being reduced in Hungary but widened in Poland: Henryk Frakierski, *Economic Reform and Income Distribution. A Case Study of Hungary and Poland* (Armonk, N.Y.: M.E. Sharpe, 1986), and Maria Hirszowicz, *Coercion and Control in Communist Society: The Visible Hand in a Command Economy* (New York: St. Martin's, 1986), 86-126. Typically, György Konrád and Ivan Szélényi see consumerism mainly as conscious political strategy: "The Elite's Counteroffensive," in *The Intellectuals on the Road to Class Power* (New York: Harcourt Brace Jovanovich, 1979) 215-219.

10. For a treatment of the 1970s that makes just this point, see "New Substitutes for Economic Reform" in Paul M. Johnson, *Redesigning the Communist Economy: The Politics of Economic Reform in Eastern Europe* (New York: Columbia University Press, 1989), 205-211.

11. For a useful survey of the reform experience as of the early 1970s, see Morris Bornstein's introduction to the collection of essays he edited as *Plan and Market. Economic Reform in Eastern Europe* (New Haven: Yale University Press, 1973), 1-22. Bornstein is also the author of the distinction between "economic" and "administrative" decentralization: "Economic Reform in Eastern Europe," in *East European Economies Post-Helsinki: A Compendium of Papers submitted to the Joint Economic Committee, Congress of the United States* (Washington, D.C.: Government Printing Office, 1977), 102-134.

12. For a good summary of why reform failed in just such a volume, see Hans-Hermann Höhmann, "Economic Reform in the 1970s — Policy with No Alternative," in Alec Nove, H.-H. Höhmann and Gertraud Seidenstecker, ed., *The East European Economies in the 1970s* (London: Butterworth, 1982), 1-16. For a more magisterial treatment, see Włodzimierz Brus, "Institutional Change within a Planned Economy," in Michael Kaser, ed., *The Economic History of Eastern Europe, 1919-1975,* vol. III (Oxford: Clarendon Press, 1986), ch. 23-26. And for a tongue-in-cheek account of the muddle into which reform had slipped by the end, see János Mátyás Kovács, "Reform Economics: The Classification Gap," *Daedalus,* 119, no. 1 (Winter 1990): 215-247. Judy Batt indeed judges that "(i)n fact, economic reform was adopted as a form of substitute politics; purposes that were properly those of politics were thrust onto the economy": *East Central Europe,* 5.

13. See Walter D. Connor, *Socialism, Politics and Equality: Hierarchy and Change in Eastern Europe* (New York: Columbia University Press, 1979), and Jerry F. Hough's comments on the philosophical and social issues involved in economic reform, in *Soviet Leadership in Transition* (Washington, D.C.: The Brookings Institution, 1980), 131-138.

14. On the 1969 to 1972 Yugoslav crisis in general, see Steven L. Burg, "The 'Yugoslav Crisis': National, Economic, and Ideological Conflict and the Breakdown of Elite Cooperation," in his *Conflict and Cohesion in Socialist Yugoslavia* (Princeton: Princeton University Press, 1983), 83-187. On the social differentiation aspects of the crisis, see Bogdan Denis Denitch, *The Legitimation of a Revolution. The Yugoslav Case* (New Haven: Yale University Press, 1976), 172-184, and Fred Singleton, *Twentieth-*

Century Yugoslavia (New York: Columbia University Press, 1976), 159-164. Konrád and Szélényi, *Intellectuals on the Road*, suggest that in Yugoslavia the intellectuals' disdain for cooperation with the workers left them stranded and helpless when the regime cracked down on them in 1971: 71-72.

15. On significant Czechoslovak worker resistance to economic reform, which conservatives exploited, see H. Gordon Skilling, *Czechoslovakia's Interrupted Revolution* (Princeton: Princeton University Press, 1976), 579-585, which suggests that support for reform among workers began hesitantly and, though it picked up, never encompassed a majority. For concrete examples showing the crucial effect of the invasion in firming up workers' support for reform, see Peter Hruby, *Fools and Heroes. The Changing Role of Communist Intellectuals in Czechoslovakia* (Oxford: Pergamon, 1980), 100-108.

16. On egalitarian workers' backlash and the slowdown of the NEM in Hungary while both were still fresh, see Walter D. Connor, "Social Consequences of Economic Reforms in Eastern Europe," in Zbigniew M. Fallenbuchl, ed., *Economic Development in the Soviet Union and Eastern Europe, vol. I* (New York: Praeger, 1975), 65-99. For a more recent account, see Judy Batt, "The Political Limits of Economic Reform in Hungary, 1968-1978," in her *Economic Reform and Political Change in Eastern Europe* (New York: St. Martin's, 1988), 233-278. On the backlash in both Hungary and Czechoslovakia, see Paul M. Johnson, *Redesigning the Communist Economy*, 139-202. In her more recent work (*East Central Europe*, 4) Batt introduces a political /economic typology for Poland, Hungary, and Czechoslovakia. She argues that Poland and Hungary embarked on economic reform to shore up Communist power, backed away from radical reform (the only kind that could have brought the intended results) because it would undermine that power, and therefore introduced reforms so half-hearted that they were worse than none at all. By contrast, the Czechoslovak regime did not reform at all for precisely these reasons, but, beyond economic stability, the result was stagnant living standards which gravely weakened it when it was faced with the challenge of Gorbachev's *perestroika*.

17. For informed meditation on the general problem of worker unrest that focuses on the December 1970 events in Poland, see J.M. Montias, "Economic Conditions and Political Instability in Communist Countries: Observations on Strikes, Riots and Other Disturbances," *Studies in Comparative Communism*, 13, no. 4 (Winter 1980), 283-299.

18. The estimate is from Włodzimierz Brus, cited in Garton Ash, *Polish Revolution*, 11, and Keith John Lepak, *Prelude to Solidarity: Poland and the Politics of the Gierek Regime* (New York: Columbia University Press, 1988), 138. See also Stanisław Gomułka, "The Polish Crisis: Will It Spread and What Will Be the Outcome," in Jan Drewnowski, ed., *Crisis in the East European Economy. The Spread of Polish Disease* (London: Croom Helm, 1982), 65-71, with citations. There are brief descriptions of the Jaszczuk reform in Janusz G. Zieliński, *Economic Reforms in Polish Industry* (London: Oxford University Press, 1973), 17-21; in Zbigniew Landau and Jerzy Tomaszewski, *The Polish Economy in the Twentieth Century* (New York: St. Martin's, 1985), 249-250; and best of all Pelczynski in R.F. Leslie, ed., *The History of Poland Since 1863* (Cambridge: Cambridge University Press, 1980), 400-403.

19. The following account draws heavily on the introduction to Garton Ash's *Polish Revolution*, and on Lepak, *Prelude to Solidarity*. But as we plow through it, we should also remember the more piercing judgment of Poland's greatest contemporary novelist: "When (Gierek) revoked price increases the first time and his rotten premier (Jaros-

zewicz) appeared on television whining in a tearful voice about the historic advances made by the government and the Party, when I saw that scandalous spectacle on television, I realized that the great empire of invincible Russia had just cracked in two. . . . Tanks should have advanced and leveled those unruly cities and villages, and only then would the good Tsar, meaning the First Secretary, repeal some part of his inhuman ukase on the sly. Meanwhile, Gierek had revoked the unfortunate decree at the first sign of human dissatisfaction on the party of society. Just as in France or Norway. For the first time a foolish little smile appeared on the monster's face. A smile we spotted immediately. And we immediately sensed that this smile was the beginning of the final agony, which could last another half century or end in death tomorrow at daybreak": Tadeusz Konwicki, *Moonrise, Moonset* ([1982] New York: Farrar, Straus and Giroux, 1987), 36-37.

20. Lepak, *Prelude to Solidarity*, 79.
21. For a good account of Gierek's economic policies, written after the crisis broke, see Włodzimierz Brus, "Aims, Methods and Political Determinants of the Economic Policy of Poland 1970-1980," in Nove, Höhmann, and Seidenstecker, eds., *East European Economies*, 91-138; the figures are at 92.
22. On agriculture, see Andrzej Korbonski, "Victim or Villain: Polish Agriculture since 1970," in Maurice D. Simon and Roger E. Kanet, eds., *Background to Crisis: Policy and Politics in Gierek's Poland* (Boulder: Westview, 1981), 271-298, and a more recent survey of developments since 1970 by a CIA analyst, "Polish Agriculture: Policy and Prospects," in *East European Economies: Slow Growth in the 1980s, Vol. 3: Country Studies on Eastern Europe and Yugoslavia, Selected Papers Submitted to the Joint Economic Committee, Congress of the United States* (Washington, D.C.: Government Printing Office, 1986), 450-464.
23. Staniszkis, *Poland's Self-Limiting Revolution* (Princeton: Princeton University Press, 1984), 150-188. For comparison and contrast, see Hirszowicz, *Coercion and Control*, "Poland's Recurring Crises: Theory and History," 23-54, and "Command Economy Without Coercion?" 55-85.
24. On the administrative changes in the political and economic areas respectively, see Lepak, *Prelude to Solidarity*, 76-103 and 135-164.
25. The figures are from Garton Ash, *Polish Revolution*, 15-16.
26. For good economic analysis of why Gierek failed: Domenico Mari Nuti, "The Polish Crisis: Economic Factors and Constraints," in Drewnowski, ed., *Crisis in the East European Economy*, 18-64, which treats both exogenous and endogenous factors; Stanisław Gomułka, "Specific and Systemic Causes of the Polish Crisis, 1980-1982," in his *Growth, Innovation and Reform in Eastern Europe* (Madison: University of Wisconsin Press, 1986), 227-250; and Kazimierz Poznanski, "Economic Adjustment and Political Forces: Poland since 1970," in Ellen Comisso and Laura Tyson, eds., *Power, Purpose, and Collective Choice: Economic Strategy in the Socialist States* (Ithaca, N.Y.: Cornell University Press, 1986), 63-110.
27. For useful summaries of the subsidization argument, see Brown, *Eastern Europe*, 123-130; Michael Marrese and Jan Vanous, "The Content and Controversy of Soviet Trade Relations with Eastern Europe, 1970-1984," in Josef C. Brada, Ed A. Hewett and Thomas A. Wolf, eds., *Economic Adjustment and Reform in Eastern Europe. Essays in Honor of Franklyn D. Holzman* (Durham: Duke University Press, 1988), 185-222; and Charles Gati, *The Bloc that Failed* (Bloomington: Indiana University Press, 1990), 112-124. For special attention to East European energy dependency on

the Soviets in these years, see John P. Hardt, "Soviet Energy Policy in Eastern Europe," in Terry, ed., *Soviet Policy in Eastern Europe*, 189-220.

28. For a fresh account of how the agricultural policy worked in a single village, see C.M. Hann, *A Village Without Solidarity. Polish Peasants in Years of Crisis* (New Haven: Yale Univerisity Press, 1985), 44-56.

29. The best history, by a participant, is in Jan Józef Lipski, *KOR. A History of the Workers' Defense Committee in Poland* (Berkeley: University of California Press, 1984), 30-61, but the day-to-day account of the 1976 crisis in George Blazynski, *Flashpoint Poland* (New York: Pergamon, 1979), 255-292, retains its immediacy.

30. Cited in Lepak, *Prelude to Solidarity*, 70.

31. See Zbigniew A. Fallenbuchl, "The Economic Crisis in Poland and Prospects for Recovery," in *East European Economies Post-Helsinki*, 359-398, and especially 369.

32. See Allen E. Clapp and Harvey Shapiro, "Financial Crisis in Eastern Europe," in *ibid.*, 242-262, and especially 243.

33. See Lepak, *Prelude to Solidarity*, 182.

34. See Garton Ash's unforgettable short account of this "miracle" in *Polish Revolution*, 28-30.

35. For a cautious but prescient examination of the possibilities for a new worker-intellectual coalition across the area, written before Solidarity, see Walter D. Connor, "Dissent in Eastern Europe: A New Coalition?," *Problems of Communism*, 29, no. 1 (January-February 1980): 1-17.

36. See Lepak, *Prelude to Solidarity*, 205.

EIGHT

THE RETURN TO POLITICS, 1980-1987

After World War I, the new states of Eastern Europe could not be said to contain modern nations in the sense then understood in the West. In a way, the interwar leaders were an ideological vanguard for nations that did not yet exist. Before they could exist, the peasant majorities had to be given a stake in them, had to identify with them, had to believe in them. Nationalism, with its intellectual roots in the West and an uncertain record in liberating the region, had to become real and persuasive to millions rather than just to thousands, through land reform, through economic transformation, through education. Interregional strife, capital shortage, depression, and then war pushed the nation-building process forward even as these same forces set limits to it, and the experience of foreign domination during World War II carried it further still.

After that war the Stalinists, bearers of another imported ideology, tried to drive the process to conclusion by changing its class content. They considered themselves the vanguard of a class that did not yet exist, and they embarked more seriously than had the interwar elites upon the economic transformation that would create it. Economies were revamped, the peasants were driven into the cities to become workers, and true national societies were created. Yet they were still different from Western national societies, and not just because they were new and raw, but in their structure. They were ruled by self-selecting political elites, a phenomenon not new to Eastern Europe but also not peculiar to there; more peculiar in Western terms was the absence of property-based middle classes.

Under Stalinism the elites and those elements of the intelligentsia they managed to co-opt and integrate into the power structure as the decades went by fulfilled some of the same social and political functions as Western middle classes. For instance, they controlled and disposed of a great deal of each nation's wealth, as if it were their property. But it was not: It belonged to the socialist state, acting in the name of "the people." Not only in principle but also in practice they continued to function as officials rather than as a middle class. As a result they proved incapable of providing impersonal mechanisms for upward and downward social mobility that enjoyed general respect and assent, because the criteria for social advance and decline remained resolutely political and personal. The "We versus They" psychology of their origins remained basically intact; the political elite was exclusionary in its essence. In particular, while the elite co-opted much of the expanded intelligentsia into the power structure, it was relentless in its efforts to keep the intelligentsia as such separated from the working class, and it was ruthless toward those intellectuals it could not co-opt. As politics returned to Eastern Europe in the 1980s, Stalinist regimes limped along as before, sustaining themselves by doling out goods and co-opting traditional nationalism as best as they could. But intellectuals who did not have a piece of power, those who most resembled and most admired and emulated their predecessors in the traditional intelligentsias of the area, began to seek and then to find an alternative ideology that would unite them with the masses and then with power.

The Polish crisis had demonstrated that consumerism was a very weak reed, and the search for other ways to govern constituted much of the politics of the 1980s. But the most important investigation of alternatives took place outside the confines of the party and the state.[1] Speaking before the U.S. Congress in February 1990, Czechoslovakia's new President Václav Havel declared that "Consciousness precedes being."[2] What he meant was that it had been changes in ideas that had preceded and produced the changes in society and politics that had brought him to Prague Castle and to Washington. Havel's assessment contains an exceptionally important truth, for a particular set of ideas was important in bringing change to the region. These ideas, shaped and promulgated by men such as Havel, will be examined later in this chapter. It must be said now, however, that societies must be prepared for ideas, must find them useful, and must prefer them to others. The convergence of the ideas of a few and the will of many, of the intelligentsia and the working class, is the most important domestic political development in the Eastern Europe of the 1980s.

The East European working classes were by now no longer gray seas of peasants fresh from the countryside. In the Poland of the 1980s two of three workers had now been born in the city.[3] In the early postwar years, simply moving out of rural misery had been seen as an absolute social gain, for the family if not for the individual. This kind of status advancement was precious in these status-oriented societies. For those who experienced it, it remained so whether or not it meant rising living standards. Then, after a while, living standards had risen and had generally, in most places, kept rising. Moreover, in the early days of communism the regimes could promise more than just this one-time advancement. Both workers and peasants had access to higher education, the ticket to further advancement into the ranks of the intelligentsia.

The possibility of peasant and worker advancement created an atmosphere of dynamism and a feeling that anyone could improve his lot. This dream of opportunity dissipated as Stalinist economic development exhausted itself, economic growth slowed, and classes restratified. Higher education ceased to expand and the standard of living stopped improving as economic growth sputtered beginning in the 1960s. The much-enlarged working class now started to congeal: Skilled workers could no longer hope to escape it, unskilled workers could no longer hope to take their places, and there were no more underemployed peasants to put pressure on them all from underneath. Working-class status became hereditary.

As the objective availability of status positions leveled off, their subjective value declined. In the first years of Communist rule, as the number of workers and intellectuals grew, the categories "worker" and "intellectual" retained a traditional status rank for East Europeans. Though not in unison, the countries of Eastern Europe gradually moved from being peasant to postpeasant societies, and the traditional honor categories mutated. Communism of course glorified workers, but that alone could not secure their loyalty, as 1956 demonstrated. Moreover, status is inherently relative, depending on other benchmarks for its value. As time passed, the point of reference for East Europeans changed from their own peasant prewar era to present-day Western Europe.[4]

The situation of the intelligentsia was also changing, in a distinct way.[5] Like the working class, it had been vastly expanded. Since 1956 educated people had been given a piece of power and had been invited to compete for and share some of the perquisites of high position in these societies, provided they did not contest the system of self-selected party rule. Most of the intelligentsia were now technicians employed by the state to run the economy. As the regimes had intended, these technocrats had grown until they vastly outnumbered the humanistic intellectuals who were the traditional standard-bearers of traditional national values. The humanists now felt socially threatened by the technocrats and by the impersonal, efficiency-oriented values they claimed to represent. In absolute terms, education had also increased considerably the number of humanists, and they now rediscovered both the traditional moral values that had made their intelligentsia forebears great and their traditional national roles.

More and more technocrats were also dissatisfied with the system. Much of the stuff of Communist politics in these countries involved competition between bureaucracies staffed by these technically trained intellectuals. If constant deadlock is not to produce stagnation, political elites must arbitrate these bureaucratic battles. This truism of political science was particularly evident in the tight hierarchical systems of Eastern Europe, which claimed to rule in the name of ideas. By the 1970s and 1980s the party elites that had to decide among bureaucratic preferences had been discredited without and partially demoralized within, and they were increasingly unable to exercise that function efficiently. Unable to take the judgments of their political superiors seriously, technocrats could no longer do their jobs to their own satisfaction, and became increasingly frustrated with their position.[6]

Gierek's failure not only illustrated the general disaffection of intellectuals and workers, it also marked their alienation from party rule in particular. During the crisis of 1980-81 the Polish party shrank to under 3 million members, of which a quarter joined Solidarity. The party was unable to keep up with events, let alone direct them. The Gdańsk agreement signed between Lech Wałęsa and the Polish government in August 1980 allowed for wage increases, price decreases, state broadcast of

Catholic mass, freedom for some political prisoners of 1970 and 1976, and the formation of a legal independent trade union. But the Soviets, Poland's other Warsaw Pact allies, and a large portion of the Polish party could not accept the agreement's political concessions. For three months in the spring of 1981 Solidarity held its fire and kept its troops in line to give the party a last chance to reform itself, at its Ninth Extraordinary Congress in July. There, party reformers tried to democratize a party in which 75 percent of the Central Committee were party officials and economic managers, groups that constituted 5 percent of the party membership. The reform effort failed, and *apparatchiks* and managers remained in control. Without democratization, control of the party was increasingly irrelevant to control of Poland. As the political process degenerated that fall, the party and its new leader, Stanisław Kania, were palpably incapable of taking charge.[7] General Wojciech Jaruzelski assumed the party leadership in October. In December martial law was implemented, not by the party but by the element of the Polish state that controlled the most physical force, the army.

The area's regimes sensed that the increasing disaffection of workers and intellectuals created a hospitable environment for a resurgence of nationalism. Workers could no longer hope for economic or status advancement. The number of humanistic intellectuals had increased, as had their attachment to the national values they had traditionally represented. The technocrats were adrift, and their efficiency values seemed futile. With the parties discredited, workers, humanists, and technocrats were ripe for alternative ideologies. If parties somehow missed these signs, the behavior of their own members alerted them to the nationalist danger to their rule. For example, among those trying to reform the Polish party in the spring of 1981 were a new breed of neo-Stalinist populists. They spoke the language of economic and social equality for the working class, rather than the language of efficiency dear to the technocrats. They failed, but their program could have accommodated nationalism.[8]

The regimes responded by adding a kind of nationalism to their repertoire of governance. Four of the regimes tried to co-opt symbols of the national past. The Poles had been doing so from the mid-1950s. Since the mid-1960s Ceauşescu had turned the celebration of the national past into a veritable engine of rule in Romania. Official Romanian history culminated in him. In the 1980s others followed more tentatively down the same path. Honecker's GDR tried to harness the ghosts of both Martin Luther and Frederick the Great. In Bulgaria, Todor Zhivkov's daughter Lyudmila threw her Politburo rank behind a new program celebrating the national culture.[9]

In Hungary, Kádár's economically oriented regime felt obliged to respond to the intellectuals' campaign over the situation of the Hungarian minority in Romania.[10] Even under the one area regime that did not assert a nationalist claim, in Czechoslovakia, Hungarians were also persecuted. Slovaks, who had extracted a measure of working federalism from the shambles of reform following the Soviet invasion, used their new autonomy to tighten up on their own Hungarian minority.[11]

In the Balkans, ethnic homogenization was an extension of state-sponsored nationalism. There, the region's least developed countries happened to have Europe's largest minorities. Ceaușescu's increasing repressiveness fell most heavily on Romania's 2 million or so Hungarians. In Bulgaria the Zhivkov regime embarked in 1984 and 1985 on a campaign to assimilate the country's Turkish minority by forcing them to adopt Bulgarian names and the Bulgarian language. When politics returned to Yugoslavia after Tito's death in 1980, one of the forms it took was a Serbian effort to eliminate the autonomy of the Serbia's two constituent provinces, the Kosovo, with its Albanian majority, and the Voivodina, with its large Hungarian minority.[12]

Bureaucratic nationalism did succeed in producing a reawakening of national political cultures throughout the area in the late 1970s and early 1980s. As a result, regimes found themselves contending not only with increasingly aroused populations but also with international controversy. In addition to minority concerns, issues such as the Transylvanian dispute between Hungary and Romania, the "blank spots" in Polish-Russian history, and even the maritime boundary between East Germany and Poland now began to float up to the surface of East European intrastate relations. Still, these regional conflicts were not as troublesome to the regimes as the the domestic implications of nationalism. For whether they played it repressively or nostalgically, harshly or gently, nationalism was not a game the regimes could win. Their own antinational pasts and their need to respect Soviet sensitivities stacked the cards against them. Like consumerism, it could keep them going for a while, but it threatened constantly to turn against them.[13]

Despite the Gierek experience, the regimes continued to practice consumerism actively, having no other alternative and no other inspiration from the Soviets. The Soviets diagnosed the Polish disease as economic; as in 1970, they told themselves that the Polish party had lost touch with the working class on such issues as wages, prices, and the availability of goods. During and after the crisis of 1980-81, the Soviets gave the Poles $5 billion in economic assistance. The rest of the East European economies weathered the 1970s and 1980s not well but not disastrously. The least developed countries, Romania and Bulgaria, were able to sustain the benefits of Stalinist development into the early 1970s. After Polish negative growth pulled the growth rate of the entire region below zero in 1981, a gradual recovery began. By the mid-1980s most of the countries were running modest trade surpluses with hard-currency trading partners.

Still, the long-run prognosis was bleak. In the nineteenth century Eastern Europe had essentially missed the industrial revolution that swept the West. These basically agricultural economies depended on export markets, as the depression and the German advance proved. Stalinism transformed the regions' economies, industrializing them and changing their dependence on export markets for agricultural goods into a need for raw materials and markets for machinery, which they found in the Soviet Union. By the 1980s it was becoming increasingly clear that the Soviet Union and Eastern Europe were missing what has been called the second industrial revolution, in which growth depends on rapid assimilation of information technology. Brezhnev had turned the Soviet Union and Eastern Europe toward the West, but his strategy of inserting Western technology into centrally planned economies was by now condemning them to permanent second-rate economic status.

The limits of consumerism based on expanding trade with the West displayed the full extent of Eastern Europe's dependence. For external economic and political reasons, Western trade did not bolster consumerism as much as East European regimes had expected. Economically, Western demand had been reduced by the effects of the oil shocks of 1973 and 1979. The agonizing demise of détente made it clear that politics would dam the remaining trickle of exchange with the West. The United States tarred Eastern Europe with the Soviet brush as it tried to punish the Soviet Union economically for invading Afghanistan and other offensive international behavior. The graph of East-West economic ties turned sharply downward, especially after martial law was declared in Poland in December 1981.[14]

The disaffection of workers and intellectuals, the weakness of the parties, the nationalist efforts of the regimes, and the limits of consumerism combined to make the return of nationalism more likely. Traditional nationalism, however, was only one of several options for Eastern Europe, and by no means its necessary future. For their part, East Europeans were certainly looking at other choices. By the 1970s the development of these societies under communism had produced a potential workers' opposition in search of an ideology. On the eve of the Gdańsk workers' negotiations with the government, two Warsaw intellectuals arrived to present Lech Wałęsa with a petition of support. Wałęsa told them: "We are only workers. The government negotiators are educated men. We need your help." [15] The help they wanted, and the help they received during the 1980s, extended far beyond traditional nationalism.

Just as workers were no longer peasants in factories, intellectuals were no longer noble or bourgeois sword-bearers of the one unadulterated national tradition. In the first years of Stalinism, the intelligentsia welcomed their inclusion into politics. Whether for or against communism, they spoke the language of power. By 1980 those who had supported communism had the guilt of collaboration to overcome; the technical intelligentsia had been disappointed by its taste of power; and those who had always rejected communism still worried perpetually about how to be effective. The year 1968 underscored these problems by demonstrating the unreality of reforming communism and revealing the brute international facts that made removing it impossible. The region's intelligentsias were now syncretic, drawn from across the social spectrum and drawing on various intellectual traditions. They included revisionist and dogmatist Communists, ex-Communists, nationalists, and adherents of the area's various religious traditions.

The first response was to trump the Stalinist abolition of politics by going it one further: The alternative ideology that marginalized humanists began to develop in the 1970s resolved the dilemmas of the intelligentsia by advocating what came to be called antipolitics. Instead of seeking to overthrow the system from without or to change it from within, intellectuals began to act and think outside the system, to live, as Adam Michnik put it, as if they were free. Instead of the language of power, they began to speak the language of rights: national rights, social rights, sometimes minority rights, but above all individual rights. Aside from the moral strength that the proclamation of these rights lent to members of a repressed minority, the purpose of advocating them was to create the habits of civil society, of unfettered human interaction. People should sidestep the system in order to live a truthful personal life, to act without violence, but to act. By avoiding the compromises of politics, individuals could try to light candles in the darkness of the society of the lie. The core of this ideology was ethics; its criteria were the good and the evil, honor and dishonor, truth and falsehood. Lech Wałęsa said, "We need truth as much as coal," and the Pope told the Poles to "call good and evil by name." [16] Though ostensibly nonpolitical, this idea of society as a realm existing between freely interacting moral agents and the state constituted a fundamental challenge to systems that claimed totalistic authority on the basis of universally valid ideas.

In Poland this ideology was conditioned and mediated by the Catholic church. The Polish church had always had a national role, and it had fought successfully to remain an active, living organism outside the Communist regime. By the 1970s it was no longer the peasant-based, national church of yore. Under the auspices of Vatican II and led by its two cardinals, the Primate Stefan Wyszyński and Karol Wojtyła of Kraków, the Polish church broadened the scope of its earthly role. It extended its traditional language of rights beyond the community of believers to the national community, and most specifically to workers. When Wojtyła returned to Poland as Pope John Paul II, Poles stood together by the millions, in perfect discipline and living solidarity. The Polish party and state simply fell out of consciousness. That feeling found expression a year later in the organization Solidarity, and was sustained under martial law. The Polish working class received its new ideology not directly from the intelligentsia but through the Polish church, and it was this factor that made it the ideology of a mass movement. The expansive Catholic advocacy of human rights dovetailed with the emerging ideology of Polish intellectuals. The alternative to the regime was thus indeed nationalism, but a nationalism that spoke the language of human rights for all.[17]

The social role of the Polish church is unique in Eastern Europe. Outside Poland, intellectuals and workers remained isolated from each other. This was particularly the case in Romania and Bulgaria, with their new, country-born working classes, the weak separatist traditions of their intelligentsias, and their strong traditions of state control of Orthodox religious establishments. In Romania and Bulgaria the old Stalinist formulas were coming under strain, but they continued at least for the time being to produce results. Compared to Poland, however, everywhere in Eastern Europe there were fewer opposition intellectuals, and they struggled under harsher and more repressive conditions toward a new ideology appropriate to their societies. But even without a mediating institution such as the Polish church, the struggling intellectual oppositions of the other countries also fastened on the question of rights.[18]

This was partially a function of the emphasis that Western governments and Western elites began to put on human rights in the 1970s. As Westerners became interested in human rights in the East, they were also gaining leverage in the region as a result of détente and the Soviet model of consumerism via trade with the West. Every East European regime had followed the Soviet lead in 1975 and signed the Helsinki Final Act, with its recognition of the universal validity of human rights and its concrete commitments to respect them and expand human contacts across the East-West divide. The regimes could downplay and qualify that recognition, and they could harass the intellectuals who insisted on implementation of the Final Act, but they could not deny their own signatures or their commitments in principle.[19]

Easier to overlook than Helsinki was a second stimulus for an ideology legitimizing moral rights within a free society: its increasing plausibility. Eastern Europe was still governed by authoritarian regimes, but terror and political imprisonment were now rare. Less fearful than the generation before them and more influenced by the West, young men and women found it not just more attractive but also more feasible than before to establish private "life styles" that ignored the system in place as much as possible. The highest aspiration of many was to become successful businessmen within the shadow economy. Though repressed, single-issue political groups demanding new policies on such issues as the environment and minority rights were able to survive. As a small measure of dissent became possible, pluralism in principle became thinkable.

All across the region, the alternative ideology that emerged in the 1970s dealt not with power but with rights. Much of this ideology recalled the peasant origins of these now-urban societies and their workers and intellectuals. The East European peasantries had also left governance to others and had understood politics as morality, as a question of good and bad men rather than effective or ineffective programs. It was also consistent with the traditional self-definition of intellectuals as bearers of the national soul, as governors of the spirit set off against the vulgar administrators of matter. At its most isolated, in the case of the loose grouping of opposition intellectuals called Charter 77 and especially its playwright member Václav Havel in Czechoslovakia, the emerging ideology was most fiercely attached to this ancient definition of politics as a question of salvation through suffering and virtue. Before communism arrived, that definition had appealed most to the poorest peasants, the sharecroppers and landless laborers whose lot was lifelong back-breaking labor without hope of earthly improvement. Communism had succeeded in implanting this old credo among the very best of its subjects. For some of the finest of the new opposition at least, the very notion of politics as a rational social endeavor, which had distinguished the Western world since the Enlightenment, had now been discredited along with its Communist false prophets.[20]

Even Solidarity was strongly marked by the concept of politics as Manichean drama. Major political issues of 1980-81 included such moral concerns as the truth about the past and the punishment of the guilty. This political moralism was particularly evident during the last three months before the crackdown of December 1981. The economy spiraled downward, and Solidarity's turbulent working-class base spun increasingly out of its leadership's control. Workers refused to think politically and insisted on total victory. They were understandably confident that they had defeated the Polish party but they were overconfident that the Polish state, and especially the army, could not resist them either. As Michnik later recalled, these three months witnessed the rise of populism and nationalism richly decorated with religious symbols. Moral authoritarianism, arising from the very bosom of Solidarity, became one of its main ideological weapons. As Michnik put it, this dark exclusionary face of the new ideology made Solidarity's goal of building a self-governing republic, rather than seizing power, all the more important if Poland was to avoid guillotines down the road.[21]

The old political culture was alive. At its best, though, the Solidarity idea made not only for moralistic politics but also for effective politics. For fifteen months an independent movement in a Communist country defined issues, formulated programs, deployed its troops, and negotiated as an equal with the authorities. It was not always successful, but that too is part of politics. In the end it was simply crushed by force. Nevertheless, Solidarity unforgettably demonstrated that the working class and the intelligentsia could unite and compete effectively for the leadership of a nation.[22]

What is more, Polish Solidarity told the whole Communist world that it was doomed to politics. Solidarity had insisted that if the working class was to make the sacrifices that economic reform would require, workers would have to participate in policy formulation through a democratic process. Even after Solidarity was defeated by the Polish state and driven underground, it managed to keep intact its structure, its Western support, its ideology, and its democratic approach to politics. Solidarity's message that political reform was a necessary precondition of successful economic reform was clear to every country of the Communist world.[23]

The regimes of Eastern Europe could ignore the message, but to do so was to deny the emerging reality. They did just that, because the lesson of Solidarity was too painful to accept. After the movement was crushed, they continued to insist to themselves, the Soviets, and the West that every issue was essentially economic. They contended that stability could be guaranteed by consumerism, more economic ties with the West, and perhaps some modest economic reform. Political reform was too certain to bring instability in its wake, and human rights advocacy remained illegitimate interference in their internal affairs. With characteristic boldness, Ceaușescu turned to neo-Stalinist repression in order to pay off Romania's foreign debt and reestablish its independence, at the price of turning his country into a pariah for both West and East. The other regimes counted on inertia, Soviet support, and Western economic recovery to keep them going. Eastern Europe remained as dependent on the outside world as ever, albeit in new ways that communism had itself invented.[24]

Soviet attention was directed away from the region as the 1980s began.[25] Brezhnev, who had long been ill, died in November 1982. As after Stalin's death and Khrushchev's ouster, the Soviets were distracted from Eastern Europe by a succession struggle. They had been relieved when martial law was imposed in Poland and convinced at first that the problem was solved. Poland's crisis had regional implications, for the GDR and Hungary now sought to move into Poland's traditional position as the Soviet Union's most important ally in the area. The GDR developed its relationship with West Germany, and Hungary tried to supplant Poland as the West's favorite regional bridge to the East. Both of them began to support a European détente for the Europeans and to argue publicly that within limits small countries were responsible for preserving peace in Europe even if superpower relations were bad. Coming from Hungary, a country far from Soviet lines of communication to the Germanies and highly dependent on Western trade to keep growth going, such arguments raised no serious objections. But when the East Germans began to speak of significantly improved relations with *West Germany*, and of a special responsibility of Germans to keep war from breaking out ever again on their soil, they finally attracted Soviet attention. In 1984, the Soviets reined them in, first by cultivating the newly reelected government of Helmut Kohl in West Germany and then by forcing both Honecker and Bulgaria's Todor Zhivkov to postpone planned visits to Bonn.[26] Because Eastern European regimes, concerned about their own power, could not fully exploit the nationalisms of their populations as they asserted themselves internationally, it took very little to keep the international system in place.

As we have seen, a hollow bureaucratic nationalism and a consumerism bereft of Western support were more and more the only remaining sources of domestic support for East European regimes. Once again Poland under martial law demonstrated how little support they provided. The military crackdown did not solve the problem as the Soviets had assumed it would. Nationalism was of little avail to the Polish state. Driven underground, Solidarity remained intact and faithful to the values it had learned before it was repressed. These values were national, but also religious and democratic, and they were proof against the Jaruzelski regime's most earnest efforts to co-opt them. Moreover, it also proved impossible to refloat the economy. Western trade, already dwindling, essentially stopped after military repression began. That left economic reform as the only possible path to a more effective consumerism. But, while the regime floated an economic reform program that had been worked out with Solidarity before martial law was imposed, underground Solidarity continued to insist that economic reform required the support of workers, gained through a democratic political process. Without such a process the authorities felt too uncertain of support to use martial law to impose reform. They tried to keep consumption levels up in order to make repression easier, but in an economy without Western ties and without a reform option, that decision placed an intolerable burden on the already-exhausted Stalinist management system. Any hope of digging out of the crisis by Stalinist means alone, even slowly and patiently, gradually died away.[27]

Despite the dramatic events in Poland, by itself the degeneration of the Communist regimes did not suffice to revive the issue of the status of Eastern Europe within international politics. In principle, the West denied that Stalinism was Eastern Europe's destiny, as it always had; in practice, it continued to accept that destiny for Eastern Europe, as it had since 1956. For the Soviets and the West to turn their attention toward Eastern Europe, they would have to see a connection between the developments in the region and the issues they defined as critical to their interests. In the early 1980s these issues were military security and arms control.

For decades now, the Soviet Union and the West had tacitly agreed that the issues that divided them were essentially military. Soviet influence in Eastern Europe was accepted, and Western countries generally dealt with the countries of the region bilaterally and as a function of their relations with the Soviet Union. Beginning in 1972 the Conference on Security and Cooperation in Europe emerged as a new framework for multilateral negotiation on some of the systemic differences that lay behind the military security problem. The Helsinki Final Act that it produced in August 1975 represented a tradeoff between Western recognition of postwar territorial and security arrangements and Eastern recognition of the validity of human rights and the importance of contacts between societies as well as between governments.[28] We have already touched on its impact in East

European domestic politics. But although the CSCE process was precious to the East Europeans inside and outside of government (if for different reasons), it was of secondary importance to the West. Western governments regarded CSCE as a lever to get other things, such as a Berlin settlement and the beginning of conventional arms talks (called talks on Mutual and Balanced Force Reductions, or MBFR) that could defuse Vietnam-era political pressure to return troops to the United States. The human rights provisions had been seen mainly as sops to domestic political interest groups, not as fundamental elements in a new international order. In other words, for the West CSCE was not really about the division of Europe. Throughout the 1970s Western policy toward Eastern Europe relied on the cultivation of bilateral ties with individual Eastern countries. The West hoped that economic, cultural, scientific, and political relations would alleviate the consequences of the division of Europe by small steps, but it did not directly challenge that division in the short term.

As the 1980s began, therefore, the West still conceived the East-West divide primarily in military terms. Western attention was riveted not on the weakening of the East European system but on the degeneration of arms control. Still, the death of détente brought the status of East Europe slowly back into focus as an important East-West issue, not through the front door but through a series of service entrances. The first was opened by the tensions within the Western Alliance that détente's end produced. The administration of U.S. President Ronald Reagan had a comprehensive and ideological view of the East-West competition and tended to lump all Communist countries together with the Soviets. By the same token, it tended to see East-West ties in Europe primarily as vehicles to punish the enemy through sanctions, without intrinsic merit. America's allies resisted this conception, and NATO was divided.

The Polish crisis of 1981 brought this disagreement to the fore and spurred its resolution. The United States wanted to impose sanctions on both the Poles and their Soviet patrons, but the Reagan administration was also determined to lead the West from the beginning, in order to avoid the disarray the Soviet invasion of Afghanistan had provoked in NATO two years earlier. The first priority of the West Europeans, on the other hand, was to avoid irreparable damage to East-West relations in Europe. The issue was joined in urgent NATO consultations in January 1982, and the result was a compromise. The West Europeans agreed to both political and economic sanctions, on the condition that these sanctions could be reversed if the Polish regime ended martial law, released political prisoners, and initiated a genuine dialogue with the church and Solidarity.[29] These requirements looked like pie in the sky at the time, but conditional reversibility allowed for at least the possibility of renewed relations between the West and Eastern Europe.

Meanwhile, the U.S. desire to assert leadership in NATO rather than act unilaterally also led the Americans to discover the Helsinki Final Act. In order to persuade the West Europeans, the United States needed some broader rationale — beyond immediate outrage — for punishing the Soviets and East Europeans. East and West had committed themselves to the Helsinki Final Act, and CSCE was chosen to justify the Western sanctions.

Because CSCE included security as well as systemic aspects, it already had active appeal to Europeans, East and West, in conditions of deteriorating superpower relations. For the East European regimes (as well as for the Soviets), CSCE legitimized a status quo to which they were attached. The West Europeans saw CSCE as a way to assert their special regional interest in the military security and arms control issues that the two superpowers commonly negotiated bilaterally. Since 1978 the West Europeans had been trying to strengthen the security side of CSCE, but their efforts had yielded only a set of negotiations on certain confidence-building measures, such as notification of troop maneuvers. Talks on actual reductions in conventional forces had remained in MBFR, as they had since 1973. In the early 1980s the West Europeans redoubled these efforts. Because they had less confidence that the superpowers would protect their security interests, they seized even more tightly upon CSCE as a way to voice their concerns and advocate independent approaches.[30]

West Europeans of course had a voice in the political struggle over American deployment of new intermediate-range nuclear forces (INF). During the mid-1970s the Soviets had deployed powerful SS-20 missiles targeted only at NATO Europe. In order to assuage fears that this would reduce the U.S. commitment to defend Western Europe by exposing the United States to strategic attack, NATO had decided in 1979 that new U.S. INF would be deployed in 1983 if negotiations with the Soviets to limit or eliminate INF did not succeed by then. Deployments began on schedule in late 1983, and the Soviets walked out of all arms control negotiations and refused to set new dates for either INF or the ongoing strategic arms reduction talks (now rebaptized START to distinguish them from the SALT negotiations of the 1970s) until the United States backed down on INF.

In Western Europe and in the United States, the nuclear debate continued even after the decisions of 1983. Gradually Western public opinion began to recall why nuclear weapons had been deployed in Europe in the first place: to provide an inexpensive deterrent to Soviet conventional military power that would allow the West to recover and then prosper economically. It followed that raising the nuclear threshold — the point at which Soviet conventional advantage in a war might force NATO to use nuclear weapons — required that Soviet conventional power be reduced, or that Western conventional power be increased. The latter option would be tremendously expensive, and no one wanted to pay. In short, the first economically plausible step toward reducing the risk of nuclear war was to reduce the imbalance of conventional forces. So while the main political focus stayed on nuclear weapons, the conventional part of the military problem began to receive some serious attention for the first time in a generation. Westerners began to consider once again why the Soviet Union had put so many soldiers and so much hardware on the Elbe River line: Soviet forces served two purposes in Eastern Europe, to counter NATO and keep the Communist system in place.

The Soviets, however, remained transfixed by the nuclear issue. There was as yet no reason for them or the Eastern Europeans to reflect on the systemic reasons for Soviet conventional superiority. It took a whole series of foreign and domestic policy developments to remind the Soviets of the connection and force them to make some hard choices.

This progression began in mid-1984. Yuriy Andropov had died in February and was succeeded as party general secretary by Leonid Brezhnev's crony Konstantin Chernenko. Chernenko was obviously ailing, and by midyear an interim power-sharing agreement was worked out between him and the youngest Politburo member, Mikhail Sergeievich Gorbachev, a man who had inherited much of Andropov's elite support. Soviet foreign policy began to move, but not in a way that had any immediate significance for Eastern Europe. Superpower relations were tentatively unblocked that summer and fall. After Reagan's landslide reelection in November, agreement was quickly reached with the United States to resume nuclear arms negotiations. The trend toward engaging the United States continued when Chernenko died and Gorbachev succeeded him in March 1985.[31]

During his first year or so in power, Gorbachev stuck very much to traditional ways: personnel changes and minor economic tinkering at home, superpower relations and arms control abroad. Neither domestic political change nor the systemic roots of the division of Europe was on his agenda. But as the new leadership learned how hard it would be to move the immense Stalinist bureaucracy in any direction, it began to generate the visionary foreign policy programs that Soviet leaders had to develop to demonstrate their fitness. Nuclear arms control was the natural first focus for such efforts. In January 1986 Gorbachev proposed complete nuclear disarmament by the year 2000. Once he was on this visionary track, the next logical issue was conventional armaments in Europe. In April 1986 in East Berlin he proposed substantial, equal reductions in NATO and Warsaw Pact forces from the Atlantic to the Urals. The only short-term result of Soviet energy was rapid success in the CSCE confidence-building measures talks going on in Stockholm. They ended in September with ground-breaking new agreements on "challenge inspections," inspections of troops at the discretion of the opposing alliance.[32] But the new program and the Stockholm agreement did raise the military security of divided Europe higher on the international agenda and assured the smaller allies that they would be involved in negotiations on the problem.

Still, the overwhelming emphasis in U.S.-Soviet relations remained on nuclear issues, at the November 1985 Geneva summit and then at the surprise Reykjavik meeting of October 1986. Buried in the high drama of near success and final failure over strategic and space arms at Reykjavik was a breakthrough on INF. The superpowers agreed that each side would have at most one hundred long-range INF warheads, all outside Europe.[33] Although the Soviets immediately relinked actual signing of this agreement to conclusion of agreements on START and space, the "zero option" — the removal of all INF from Europe that President Reagan had proposed in November 1981 — was now within reach. The possibility of removing every intermediate-range nuclear missile from Europe posed the political question of the next step — which had to be on the conventional side — in the sharpest possible terms.

It was very easy for the Soviets to keep pushing their denuclearization campaign: It was in their January 1986 program, it kept the nuclear issue front and center, and it helped divide the West. But the longer it continued, the more the West Europeans were reminded that nuclear weapons were a relatively cheap way of deterring the Soviet conventional military threat. After an INF agreement was reached in December 1987, even more attention turned to conventional force reductions. The political logic of their campaign thus brought the Soviets face to face with the issue of why they needed so much force in Europe. To argue credibly for denuclearization, they needed to do something about their conventional force superiority. They were thereby led back to the systemic differences between East and West and obliged to look again at the weak and fragile Stalinist dictatorships that their forces had been put in place to defend.

The first Soviet steps toward a new policy approach to Eastern Europe were very tentative. As speeches by Gorbachev in Prague and by the then "second secretary," Yegor Ligachev, in Budapest in April 1987 demonstrated, their dilemma led them in contradictory directions. Some of the announced approach was new, but most of it was old. The most notable point of Gorbachev's speech was about nuclear arms control: It was in Prague that he proposed the so-called second nuclear zero, the elimination of "tactical" nuclear missiles, weapons in the range between battlefield weapons and those to be renounced in an INF agreement. When he and Ligachev did address Eastern Europe, they called on the regimes there to improve the quality of the goods they produced for the Soviet market, but left it to the individual countries to decide what economic and political mechanisms were required to do so. This was indeed a license for more diversity, but it was also quite Khrushchevian. The Soviets were gambling on the old "iron ring," gambling that East Europeans would continue to need access to Soviet markets and raw materials whatever their relationship with the West and whatever reforms they introduced at home.[34]

It was certainly an intelligent gamble. The iron ring was now tightening even on the less industrialized East European states.[35] For most of the postwar period, Romania had been able to sell hard goods, oil, and agricultural goods for hard currency. That was one reason why Romania could afford its relative independence of the Soviets. Now even Romania was no longer self-sufficient in oil. Ceaușescu had cultivated the Shah of Iran during the 1970s not just because he liked his style but also to barter machinery for oil. After the Shah fell in 1978, Romania was driven back onto the Soviet market for oil, joining the rest of the region.[36] After the crises of 1956 Khrushchev had reinforced the socialist camp's economic base to prevent new ones that would be laid at his door. From 1987, Gorbachev was soldering the iron ring before any new crisis broke out. If and when the crisis came, the Soviets clearly hoped, the finger of blame would point squarely at the East European regimes and not at Moscow.

So although they increased Soviet attention to the region, foreign policy dynamics were not enough to generate a new Soviet approach to Eastern Europe. In the end it was Soviet domestic politics that unlocked the last service entrance. The crucial year in this regard was 1987, the year it became apparent that economic reform was politically stymied in the Soviet Union. Gorbachev had a Central Committee he could count on to prevent the kind of ouster that struck the antiparty group in 1957 and Khrushchev in 1964, but not one he could count on for support on particulars. Though economic reform had general support, Gorbachev could not push through any specific program. The huge state-party economic management apparatus that constituted the core of the Soviet elite was blocking economic reform on the ground and talking it to death in the Central Committee. In 1987, therefore, Gorbachev turned to politics to mobilize mass support for reform and to lay the groundwork for getting the political support that it needed.

This turn from economic to political reform was unprecedented, and it catalyzed political tension throughout society, including even the Politburo. Ligachev emerged as a closet spokesman for Soviet conservatives in the year 1987.[37] Despite the tension, however, or because of it, the whole leadership decided, as a matter of principle and policy, that economic reform was not going to be feasible unless it was accompanied and underpinned by major political reform. In other words, domestic political dynamics had driven the Soviets to the conclusion Solidarity had reached in Poland seven years before: *no economics without politics.*

The Gorbachev leadership's objective was to save socialism by making it work, and its conclusion that saving socialism required the reintroduction of politics had important implications for Eastern Europe. The deeper implication came to the surface only in 1989: If socialism was to be saved, the Soviet Union, where it had originated and where its support was strongest, would have to be its bastion. If the more fragile post-Stalinist regimes had to be sacrificed in order to insulate the Soviet Union, so be it. A second implication surfaced almost immediately. Beginning in 1987 the Soviets licensed adoption of their new formula — *politique d'abord*, no economics without politics — throughout Eastern Europe. To be sure, they were determined not to impose it directly, if only to avoid the onus of blame for explosions. And at about the same time, they announced that military force was of no use in the nuclear age when it came to resolving political problems. But as both shifts took place under the general ideological cloak of "new political thinking," their implications for Eastern Europe specifically were left unclear. Like the Soviets themselves, though, East European Communists still regarded the Soviet Union as the leader of the socialist camp. The legitimization of politics at the expense of economics and force therefore had potentially dramatic consequences for the rest of the empire.

The new Soviet line set the Stalinist orthodoxy adrift in each East European country. If the Soviet Union was still the model, it was becoming a model for the political reform needed to make economic reform work, for *glasnost*, for democratization, for legitimate public roles for intellectuals and hitherto repressed groups.[38] Thus, if the East European Communist old guard continued to follow the Soviet model, they were committed to political reform. Yet abandoning the Soviet line would also put these men in a terribly difficult position. If the Soviet Union was no longer the model, then the inefficiencies and tyrannies of East European Stalinism became all the harder to justify and would have to be legitimized increasingly on grounds of national specifics. In two short years, this dilemma collapsed the shell that still kept Stalinism in place.

Notes

1. On the areawide implications of the Polish crisis, see Georges Schöpflin, "Poland and Eastern Europe: The Impact of the Crisis," in Jean Woodall, ed., *Policy and Politics in Contemporary Poland* (New York: St. Martin's, 1982), 23-32.

2. "Excerpts from Czech Chief's Address to Congress," *New York Times*, 22 February 1990.

3. By contrast, Romanian census data for 1966 showed that 50 percent of the Romanian urban population had been born in the countryside, according to sociologist Henri Stahl, cited in Olga A. Narkiewicz, *Eastern Europe 1968-1984* (Totowa, N.J.: Barnes and Noble, 1986), 50. On the political effects in Romania, see "The Village and the Larger Village. Peasants and Workers in Ceauşescu's Romania," in Michael Shafir, *Romania. Politics, Economics and Society. Political Stagnation and Simulated Change* (Boulder: Lynne Rienner, 1985), 139-144.

4. Walter D. Connor has been both the historian of these changes and the prophet of their consequences. Writing (before Polish Solidarity) in his *Socialism, Politics and Equality: Hierarchy and Change in Eastern Europe* (New York: Columbia University Press, 1979) he pointed out (pp. 330-331) how intellectuals in Poland and Hungary had survived from the predemocratic past into the nondemocratic present as "buffers to central power" precisely *because* equality of condition had not proceeded as far in those countries as elsewhere; and he warned (p. 344) that "There is a risk here that frustrated aspirations will lead to . . . class politics . . . a politics of the working class, particularly: the class that has been formed by socialism. Such a politics could be explosive." He brought the East European story up to the mid-1980s in his "Class, Politics and Economic Stress: Eastern Europe after 1984," in Jeffrey Simon and Trond Gilberg, eds., *Security Implications of Nationalism in Eastern Europe* (Boulder, CO.: Westview, 1986), 49-68. And he has now brilliantly documented, up to April 1991, the same trends in the Soviet Union, where they usually take hold a decade or two later than in Eastern Europe: *The Accidental Proletariat. Workers, Politics, and Crisis in Gorbachev's Russia* (Princeton, N.J.: Princeton University Press, 1991), especially "A New Working Class? Hereditization and Education under Khrushchev and Brezhnev," 48-72. Joseph R. Fiszman, "Education and Social Mobility in People's Poland," in Bernard Lewis Faber, ed., *The Social Structure of Eastern Europe* (New York: Praeger, 1986) documents the shutdown of access to education in the 1960s, and the eight Polish studies published in Kazimierz Slomczynski and Tadeusz Krauss, *Social Stratification in Poland* (Armonk, N.Y.: M.E. Sharpe, 1986) are rich in data on the slowdown in upward mobility and increasing tensions in perceptions, and especially the rise of working-class resentment. There is an argument that although KOR and the church helped in Poland, the revolt of 1980 had its strongest and most authentic roots in working class experience, especially that of 1970: see Roman Laba, "Workers Roots of Solidarity," *Problems of Communism*, 35, no. 4 (July-August 1986): 47-67, and Lawrence Goodwyn, *Breaking the Barrier: The Rise of Solidarity in Poland* (Oxford: Oxford University Press, 1991).

5. In addition to Zygmunt Bauman, "Intellectuals in East Central Europe: Continuity and Change," *Eastern European Politics and Societies* 1, no. 2 (Spring, 1987): 162-186;

György Konrád and Ivan Szélényi, *The Intellectuals on the Road to Class Power*(New York: Harcourt Brace Jovanovich, 1979); and Ferenc Fehér, Agnes Heller, and György Markus, *Dictatorship Over Needs* (New York: St. Martin's, 1983), see also Maria Hirszowicz, "Intelligentsia Versus Bureaucracy — The Revival of a Myth," in her *The Bureaucratic Leviathan* (New York: New York University Press, 1980), 171-202.

6. On how far the political elite managed to co-opt the expanding corps of experts, see Jack Bielasiak, "Lateral and Vertical Elite Differentiation in European Communist States," *Studies in Comparative Communism*, 11, nos. 1 and 2 (Spring/Summer 1978): 121-141, and, on Poland, Michael Kennedy, *Professional Power in Poland*(Cambridge: Cambridge University Press, 1991).

7. These data are drawn from Timothy Garton Ash, *The Polish Revolution: Solidarity* (New York: Scribner's, 1983), 98 and 171-181. For an extended account of the whole struggle within the party in 1981, albeit without much consideration of ideological issues, see Werner G. Hahn, *Democracy in a Communist Party. Poland's Experience since 1980* (New York: Columbia University Press, 1987). The rash of CPSU CC Politburo minutes now breaking out of ex-Soviet archives vividly demonstrates how frustrated and indecisive (as well as nasty) the Brezhnev leadership was when it came to grappling with Poland in 1980-81: *Gazeta Wyborcza*(Warsaw), no. 261 (5 November 1992), 1; *Rzeczpospolita* (Warsaw), no. 292 (12-13 December 1992), 1; *Gazeta Wyborcza*, no. 292 (12-13 December 1992), 10-11.

8. On this hard-line renewalism, see also Norman Davies, "Echoes: The Past in Poland's Present," in his *Heart of Europe. A Short History of Poland*(Oxford: Clarendon, 1984), 402-404, and Adam Michnik's contemporary judgments in "Darkness on the Horizon (August 1981)" and "A Year Has Passed (August 1981)," reprinted in his *Letters from Prison and Other Essays* (Berkeley: University of California Press, 1985), 117-123 and 127-129. More recently, Elemér Hankiss has pointed out that the idea of workers' self-management has now popped up in conservative "leftwing" groups and militant workers' groups in Hungary: "In Search of a Paradigm," *Daedalus*, 116, no. 1 (Winter 1990): Note 44 at 213.

9. On Ceauşescu and his regime after 1965, see Mary Ellen Fischer, *Nicolae Ceauşescu. A Study in Political Leadership* (Boulder: Lynne Reiner, 1989), 160ff. On the GDR, see J.F. Brown, Eastern Europe and Communist Rule (Durham: Duke University Press, 1988), 258-261, and Dan Beck, "The Luther Revival: Aspects of National Abgrenzung and Confessional Gemeinschaft in the German Democratic Republic," in Pedro Ramet, ed., *Religion and Nationalism in Soviet and East European Politics* (Durham: Duke University Press, 1989), 223-240. On Bulgaria (both Lyudmila Zhivkova and the Turkish minority), see J.F. Brown, "Conservatism and Nationalism in the Balkans," in William E. Griffith, ed., *Central and Eastern Europe: The Opening Curtain?*(Boulder: Westview, 1989), 283-313. For a good summary of the whole range of nationalist impulses throughout the area as of the mid-1980s, see Woodrow J. Kuhns, "Political Nationalism in Contemporary Eastern Europe," in Simon and Gilberg, eds., *Security Implications of Nationalism*, 81-108.

10. The development of Romanian-Hungarian tensions over Transylvania has now been thoroughly documented in Raphael Vago, *The Grandchildren of Trianon. Hungary and the Hungarian Minority in the Communist States* (New York: Columbia University Press, 1989), 201-260.

11. See Milan J. Reban, "Czechoslovakia: The New Federation," in George Klein and Milan J. Reban, eds., *The Politics of Ethnicity in Eastern Europe* (New York: Columbia University Press, 1981), 215-246. One of the new Havel government's early acts was to sign an agreement on mutual respect for minority rights with Hungary: Henry Kamm, "Leaders of 3 East European Nations Seek to Improve Ties with West," *New York Times,* 10 April 1990. But nearly three years later the problem had not only not gone away but, with Slovakia independent, was getting worse: Stephen Engelberg (with Judith Ingram), "Now Hungary Adds its Voice to the Ethnic Tumult," *New York Times* (25 January 1993).

12. For a convenient brief summary of the Bulgarian assimilation campaign against the Turkish minority, see Philip Shashko's review article "The Past in Bulgaria's Future," *Problems of Communism,* 39, no. 5 (September - October, 1990), 75-83. For thoughtful comments on ethnic homogenization and the phenomenon of bureaucratic nationalism in general, albeit heaviest on Yugoslavia, see Ivo Banac, "Political Change and National Diversity," *Daedalus,* 116, no. 1 (Winter 1990): 141-159 but especially 147-157.

13. For a careful reconstruction of a delicate process, see Thomas S. Szajna, "Addressing 'Blank Spots' Polish-Soviet Relations," *Problems of Communism,* 37, no. 6 (November-December 1988): 37-61. Leszek Kołokowski has pointed out that nationalist passions had been asserting themselves in parallel with regime enfeeblement for thirty years before 1989, so that it "was not an explosion blowing up a sound, well-settled building; rather, it was like the breaking up of an egg, from inside the shell, in which an embryo chicken had been maturing for some time... Still, the chicken was frail at the beginning": "Amidst Moving Ruins," *Daedalus,* 121, no. 2 (Spring 1992): 51. I would add only that the passions that were growing went beyond nationalism.

14. See Keith Crane's fine survey of Soviet-East European economic relations and dilemmas to 1987: "Soviet Economic Policy toward Eastern Europe," in Mario Carnavale and William E. Porter, eds., *Continuity and Change in Soviet-East European Relations. Implications for the West* (Boulder, CO.: Westview, 1989), 75-134; at greater length, Franklyn A. Holzman, *The Economics of Soviet Bloc Trade and Finance* (Santa Monica, CA.: RAND, 1991), 145-172; and, for Eastern Europe's economic relations with the West in the 1980s, John Pinder, *The European Community and Eastern Europe* (London: Royal Institute of International Affairs, 1991).

15. Ivan Szélényi in Rudolph L. Tökés, ed., *Opposition in Eastern Europe* (Baltimore: Johns Hopkins University Press, 1979), 188. At more length, see "Some Notes on the Relationship Between the Working Class and the Intellectual Class," in Konrád and Szélényi, *Intellectuals on the Road to Class Power,* 220-233. Wałęsa's response to the arriving intellectuals is cited in Garton Ash, *Polish Revolution,* 51.

16. Wałęsa is cited in Garton Ash, *Polish Revolution,* 281, the Pope in Timothy Garton Ash, *The Uses of Adversity* (New York: Random House, 1989), 47-51 ("The Pope in Poland [1983]").

17. See also Christopher Cviic, "The Church," in Abraham Brumberg, ed., *Poland. Genesis of a Revolution* (New York: Random House, 1983), 92-10, and Vincent C. Chrypinski's essay on Poland in Pedro Ramet, ed., *Catholicism and Politics in Communist Societies* (Durham: Duke University, 1990). The importance of the church in and for the Polish movement aroused tension with Western intellectuals, who were usually leftist. Garton Ash, *Polish Revolution,* 304-41 and especially 308-312 ("Embarrassment on the Left") is a good introduction, but see also Ferenc Fehér and Agnes Heller, *Eastern Left, Western Left: Totalitarianism, Freedom and Democracy* (Atlantic Highlands, N.J.:

Humanities Press International, 1987), and Tony Judt, "The Rediscovery of Central Europe," *Daedalus*, 116, no. 1 (Winter 1990): 23-54.

18. In the vast literature on the development of intellectual oppositions in the 1970s and 1980s, I have been most enlightened by Tony Judt's "The Dilemmas of Dissidence: The Politics of Opposition in Eastern Europe," *Eastern European Politics and Societies*, 2, no. 2 (Spring 1988): 185-240. But see also the two surveys by Vladimir Tismaneanu, the first from before the fall, *The Crisis of Marxist Ideology in Eastern Europe: The Poverty of Utopia* (London: Routledge, 1988), and the other bringing the story through and past 1989, *Reinventing Politics—Eastern Europe from Stalin to Havel* (New York: Free Press, 1992). On Poland itself, in addition to Josef Lipski, *KOR. A History of the Workers' Defense Committee in Poland* (Berkeley: University of California Press, 1984), see David Ost, *Solidarity and the Politics of Anti-Politics. Opposition and Reform in Poland Since 1968* (Philadelphia: Temple University Press, 1990), 55-148.

19. Gorbachev, Helsinki, Tocqueville, as Timothy Garton Ash put it in his first summing-up on the causes of the revolutions of 1989: "The Year of Truth," reprinted in his *The Magic Lantern* (New York: Random House, 1990), 140-141.

20. On this aspect of Havel's thought, see Judt, "Dilemmas of Dissidence," 233-238; on the parallel with the wretched of the earth under the old regime, see Schöpflin, "The Political Traditions of Eastern Europe," *Daedalus*, 116, no. 1 (Winter 1990): 78-79. And since 1989, Havel in power has continued to worry the problem of relations between politics and morality like a terrier. As examples, see "Paradise Lost," *New York Review of Books* (9 April 1992), 6-8, reprinting an address he gave at New York University in October 1991, and "My Dream for Czechoslovakia," *New York Review of Books* (25 June 1992), 8-13.

21. Adam Michnik, "Letter from the Gdańsk Prison (1985)," reprinted in his *Letters from Prison*, 89-90. On the roots in (postpeasant) working-class experience, see "The Legacy of Polish Society," in Jadwiga Staniszkis, *Poland's Self-Limiting Revolution* (Princeton: Princeton University Press, 1984), 34-37.

22. The best overall accounts of 1980-81 in Poland remain Garton Ash, *Polish Revolution*, and Neal Ascherson, *The Polish August: The Self-Limiting Revolution* (New York: Viking, 1982), but see also the analysis of a diplomatic eyewitness: Nicholas G. Andrews, *Poland, 1980-81: Solidarity Versus the Party* (Washington, D.C.: National Defense University Press, 1985). On what a huge surprise the worker-intellectual alliance was to an intellectual participant, see Wiktor Osiatyński, "Revolutions in Eastern Europe," *University of Chicago Law Review*, 58, no. 2 (Spring 1991), 832-837.

23. On Solidarity under martial law, see Ost, *Solidarity and the Politics of Anti-Politics*, 149ff. On the areawide implications, see "Reform or Revolution?" in Garton Ash, *Uses of Adversity*, 288; Brus, "The Political Economy of Reform," in Paul Marer and Włodzimierz Śliwiński, eds., *Creditworthiness and Reform in Poland* (Bloomington: Indiana University Press, 1988), 77; and Stanisław Gomułka, "The Polish Crisis," in Jan Drewnowski, ed., *Crisis in the East European Economy. The Spread of the Polish Disease* (London: Croom Helm, 1982), 65-71. As Gomułka put it, "The Polish crisis suggests that the pressure is probably building up either to broaden the narrow political base of present governments, so that their decisions concerning prices and wages, as well as other matters, may be seen by individual workers to command legitimacy or, alternatively, to replace command central planning by a competitive market mechanism so that the responsibility for price and wage reforms is defused": 70.

24. For an anatomy of the Romanian economic bind, see Marvin R. Jackson, "Romania's Debt Crisis: Its Causes and Consequences," in *East European Economies Post-Helsinki*, 489-542. Judy Batt provides the best short account of the regimes' political/economic dilemmas in the 1980s—clear, knowledgeable, and analytical: *East Central Europe from Reform to Transformation* (New York: Council on Foreign Relations Press, 1991), 3-21. But it can be usefully supplemented by the "Special Issue on Economic Reform" edited by John R. Lampe for *Eastern European Politics and Societies*, 2, no. 3 (Fall 1988) and the inconclusive discussion of "leadership drift" in the special issue of *Studies in Comparative Communism*, 22, no. 1 (Spring 1989), both written before the collapse, and the updated country-by-country surveys, which have the advantage of including Yugoslavia and Albania as well, in J.F. Brown, *Surge to Freedom. The End of Communist Rule in Eastern Europe* (Durham, N.C. and London: Duke University Press, 1991), 70-245, written afterwards.

25. What follows draws heavily on the somewhat longer account in my *The End of the Cold War?* (New York: St. Martin's, 1990), 133-156.

26. For a useful brief survey with citations to the literature, see William E. Griffith, "The German Democratic Republic," in Griffith, ed., *Central and Eastern Europe*, 319-321.

27. See Fallenbuchl, "Economic Crisis in Poland," in Fallenbuchl, ed., *Economic Development*, 359-398, and P. Lewis, *The Long Goodbye: Party Rule and Political Change in Poland since Martial Law. Political Authority and Party Secretaries in Poland* (Cambridge: Cambridge University Press, 1989). CPSU CC Politburo minutes from the mid-1980s testify to continuing Soviet leadership frustration in dealing with the Jaruzelski regime: *Gazeta Wyborcza* (Warsaw), no. 293 (14 December 1992), 6.

28. For a fine account of the origins by a U.S. participant, see John J. Maresca, *To Helsinki. The Conference on Security and Cooperation in Europe 1973-1975*, new ed., (Durham: Duke University Press, 1987). The story is carried forward, if less analytically, in Nils Andrén and Karl E. Birnbaum, *Belgrade and Beyond: The CSCE Process in Perspective* (Alphen aan den Rijn: Sijthoff & Noordhoff, 1980) and Jan Sizoo and Rudolf Th. Jurrjens, *CSCE Decision-Making: The Madrid Experience* (The Hague: Martinus Nijhoff, 1984).

29. See the text of the Special Declaration issued in Brussels by the North Atlantic Council January 11, 1982, in *American Foreign Policy. Current Documents 1982* (Washington, D.C.: Department of State, 1985), 459-461, and Lincoln Gordon, "The View from Washington," in Gordon, ed., *Eroding Empires*, 116-118.

30. For a convenient summary of these developments, see Jonathan Dean, *Watershed in Europe. Dismantling the East-West Military Confrontation* (Lexington, Mass.: Lexington Books, 1987), 185-190.

31. On the "Chernenko interlude" and the Gorbachev succession, see Dusko Doder, *Shadows and Whispers. Power Politics Inside the Kremlin* (London: Harrap, 1987), 206-289, and Christian Schmidt-Häuer, *Gorbachev. The Path to Power* (Topsfield, Mass.: Salem House, 1986), 96-111.

32. On the mix of old and new in Soviet policy until 1987, as well as the changes that began then, see the careful reconstruction, carried through the summer of 1989, in Mark Kramer, "Beyond the Brezhnev Doctrine: A New Era in Soviet-East European Relations," in *International Security*, 14, no. 3 (Winter 1989/90): 25-67. In *Surge to Freedom*, 53, J.F. Brown suggests that the Soviet shift on Eastern Europe had been decided in a series of high-level Soviet and alliance leadership meetings in the fall of 1986, for implementation the next year, following Gorbachev's unveiling of domestic

"radical reform" at the January 1987 CPSU CC Plenum. For intelligent retrospective discussion of Gorbachev and Eastern Europe (and how hard it was to tell what was happening), see Judy Batt, *East Central Europe*, 22-27. For longer contemporary treatments, see Karen Dawisha, *Eastern Europe, Gorbachev, and Reform: The Great Challenge* (Cambridge: Cambridge University Press, 1988) and Nicholas N. Kittrie and Ivan Völgyes, eds., *The Uncertain Future: Gorbachev's Eastern Bloc* (New York: Paragon House, 1988). Stephen E. Hanson stresses just what a crucial turning point 1987 was from the perspective of the Gorbachev leadership's first four years: "Gorbachev: The Last Leninist True Believer?" in Daniel Chirot, ed., *The Crisis of Leninism and the Decline of the Left. The Revolutions of 1989* (Seattle and London: University of Washington Press, 1991), 33-59. And for the full flavor of the Gorbachev tragedy when it was almost over, see David Remnick's review article "Dead Souls," *New York Review of Books* (19 December, 1991): 72-81. On Stockholm, see the text of the Document of the Stockholm Conference on Confidence- and Security-Building Measures and Disarmament in Europe issued there on 22 September 1986, in *American Foreign Policy. Current Documents 1986* (Washington, D.C.: Department of State, 1987): 256-267.

33. See Shultz's press conference in Reykjavik 12 October 1986, and in Brussels 13 October 1986 in *ibid.*, 81-82 and 87.

34. For discussion of the two speeches and the references, see the version of a talk I gave on 21 May 1987, reprinted as "Strategy and Tactics in U.S. Foreign Policy toward Eastern Europe," in Marer and Sliwinski, eds., *Creditworthiness and Reform in Poland*, 305-314 and 313n.

35. For a convenient summary through middecade of the area's economic problems and the tightening of the iron ring, see Roger Kanet, "East European Trade in the 1980s: Reorientation in International Economic Relations," in Philip Joseph, ed., *The Economies of Eastern Europe and Their Foreign Economic Relations* (Brussels: NATO, 1986), 291-310.

36. Alan Smith estimates that the Shah's fall cost Romania $1 billion in hard currency in the end: "Is There a Romanian Economic Crisis? The Problem of Energy and Indebtedness," in Drewnowski, ed., *Crisis in the East European Economy*, 103-130. In addition to Smith and Marvin R. Jackson, *East European Economies Post-Helsinki*, see M.R. Jackson, "Perspectives on Romania's Economic Development in the 1980s," in Daniel N. Nelson, *Romania in the 1980s* (Boulder: Westview, 1981), 254-305, and another of John Michael Montias's relentless predictions that unless Romania developed its agriculture, it would be driven back onto the Soviet market: "Romania's Foreign Trade between East and West," in Paul Marer and John Michael Montias, eds., *East European Integration and East-West Trade* (Bloomington: Indiana University Press, 1980), 321-344.

37. To his credit, Moshe Lewin discerned and analyzed the first fruits of that change the same year: see "The New Course" in Moshe Lewin, *The Gorbachev Phenomenon. A Historical Interpretation* (Berkeley: University of California Press, 1988), 83-153. On the foreign policy side, see Yevgeniy Primakov, "New Philosophy of Foreign Policy," *Pravda*, 9 July 1987, cited in *Foreign Broadcast Information Service Daily Report: Soviet Union*, 14 July 1987.

38. As I pointed out in a talk entitled "Approaching Relations with Eastern Europe in the late 1980s" at the Wilson Center in Washington, 30 October 1987, reprinted as *Occasional Paper No. 12* of the East European Program of the Center's European Institute (Washington, D.C., mimeo., April 1988). Alfred Evans, Jr. points out that in the Soviet Union itself, letting the genie of civil society out of the bottle in 1987 without having legitimate conflict resolution mechanisms in place contributed mightily to the dissolution evident by 1991: "Gorbachev's Unfinished Revolution," *Problems of Communism*, 40, no. 1-2 (January-April 1991), 18-41.

NINE

THE ROAD TO 1989

Stalinism had tried to atomize society, to force each individual to face the state alone. In the same way, Stalin had separated the states of Eastern Europe, discouraging intraregional cooperation and forcing the Soviet policy line upon each country. Though much had changed in the meantime, the understanding that Soviet policy was to serve as a model for Eastern Europe and the backup threat of Soviet intervention remained in force well into the 1980s. As the Romanian joke went, the Moscow phone number for fraternal assistance was 56-68-80. In 1987 Gorbachev had acknowledged the value of free political choice for individuals, if only to facilitate economic reform. It was at first unclear whether this endorsement of pluralism extended to international socialist relations. The Soviet model now called for political reform, but the Soviets were also saying that their example was no longer obligatory for other socialists. As he traveled around Eastern Europe, Gorbachev was at pains to describe Soviet reform plans and the new political reform line, but also not to impose it. Still, the Soviets continued to speak of the superior interests of socialism and refused to take the steps, such as explicitly renouncing the Brezhnev Doctrine, that would have helped convince the world that they had really given up their claims to hegemony.

By comparison, the Western policy approach was a model of clarity, and this was modestly helpful in Eastern Europe in a peculiar way. The Western position was clear not because the Western countries were particularly smart or caring; Western attitudes toward Eastern Europe were byproducts of other concerns. Ironically, the tensions that the end of détente helped produce within the West were now exacerbated by the prospect of its revival. Absorbed in their own disagreements, the Western countries had little additional energy for Eastern Europe. They had struggled through to a clear Eastern Europe policy, reversible sanctions, in 1982, after Jaruzelski declared martial law in Poland. In practice, the concept had been generalized to apply to all of Eastern Europe during the 1980s.

The modest exception was West Germany. Economic recovery allowed the West Germans to return to their practice of paying the GDR for human rights improvements, such as some new toleration of religious practice, a major expansion of visits from East to West, and more dissident releases. West German money, and the minor reforms that it brought, amounted to a safety valve that helped keep the old GDR regime in place without fundamental change. The FRG also extended a billion dollar loan to Hungary in return for better treatment of that country's German minority. But the generalization and continuation of reversible sanctions ended the hopes of most East European conservatives that Western economic recovery would automatically refloat East-West economic relations and thereby allow them to avoid reform.[1] Elsewhere, West Germany and the other Western countries generally held to the line that they were not going to repeat the experience of the 1970s and pour resources into unreformed East European systems. The converse was also true. They were willing to help those states that introduced political reform sufficient to compensate for the austerity that would be needed for economic reform that was deep enough to use Western resources well. The 1982 line seemed to fit the East European situation, and changing it would have meant adding Eastern Europe to an already full Western political plate.

East European conservatives were doubly stranded, for both the West and the Soviet Union, each for its own reasons, were arriving at the same conclusions. In order to develop profitable relations with either, the East European regimes were now called on to introduce a significant degree of reform. When asked in 1987 about the difference between *perestroika* and Dubček's Prague Spring, Gorbachev's foreign policy spokesman Gennadiy Gerasimov replied "nineteen years." After crushing the Czechoslovak uprising, the Soviets had disallowed economic decentralization for every Eastern European country except Hungary, on the logic that it leads to political reform: neither of which was desirable. Now Gorbachev's

Soviet Union was affirming the link between economic and political reform in positive terms: Both were desirable. By 1988 the Soviets had implemented administrative decentralization (the Law on State Enterprise) and even some economic decentralization (via laws on cooperatives and joint ventures). *Glasnost* was allowing Soviet leaders and thinkers to advocate even more radically market-oriented reforms. Because the outside world had for so long been conditioned to think that a policy position publicly advocated in the Soviet Union must have the support of someone in power, East European reformers had to believe that somebody up there liked them, that radical economic reform was now politically legitimate.

Meanwhile, reformers outside the system, such as those in Solidarity and Charter 77, found a fresh appeal in the dual prescription of democracy and the free market. It was attractive as a license, for Soviet support of human rights and *glasnost* made it harder for local conservatives to justify repression. But as outside reformers worked through the issues of how to build civil societies for ethical purposes, they discovered deeper, severely practical reasons for promoting democracy and free markets in their societies. Hard practical experience had taught them that while the regimes could be forced to concede rights on paper, they habitually forbade their exercise. Outside reformers began to see that the exercise of rights could be durably guaranteed only by inhibiting the regimes from revoking them long enough for them to enter into the political culture. In addition to giving populations a recourse against their rulers, democracy would encourage the day-to-day political activity that would build such a political culture. The free market could also help. One reason the regimes found it so easy to prevent the exercise of rights was that those trying to assert their rights had no independent economic base. Because the state was the universal employer, the *nomenklatura*, the self-selecting political elite, had the whip hand over everyone else. The free market was attractive to outside reformers because it would give the men and women who were able to survive in it new economic possibilities for resisting the political elite when it tried to renege on its concessions.[2]

Outside reformers thus joined a growing, though not general, agreement in favor of some measure of reform. Most Communist reformers were not interested in political reform as such, but they were increasingly interested in the free market. In the conservative regimes of Bulgaria and Czechoslovakia, the Kádár model of goulash communism through economic reform without political reform was starting to glow. In the more liberal regimes, Communist moderates began to cast about for new opportunities for themselves and their children, and began to see those opportunities in the free market. If some political relaxation was needed to begin economic reform, they were willing to support it. Of course, the extent and character of the support for reform, and the way it worked out in practice, varied from country to country.

Poland was the one country in the region that badly needed rapid access to Western economic resources. It was also the one country where the party was now thoroughly discredited as a vehicle for efficient government. Even before 1987 Poland's military regime had shown itself willing to test the sliding scale between political reform and Western economic ties that the West had put in place in 1982. It had done so carefully, in a back-and-forth pattern of liberalization and repression delicately calibrated to the winds from Moscow. As Gorbachev consolidated power, the scope of Polish liberalization widened, and the West responded by expanding trade and contacts. This process culminated when Poland released all its political prisoners in September 1986, and the United States responded by lifting its remaining sanctions in February 1987. In mid-1987, as Moscow's new line was emerging, Deputy Prime Minister Mieczysław Rakowski gave Jaruzelski a secret paper that stated frankly that the Soviets could no longer be counted on to save party rule in Poland. To save itself, Rakowski argued, the Polish party had to change its very nature and reequip itself to compete successfully in a democratic political system. It would have to master persuasion and leave behind the "administrative means" it had always used to stay in power.[3]

Meanwhile, the Solidarity miracle was starting to fray at the edges. Solidarity was smaller, it was worn down by repression, and the working class was filling up with young people who had experienced only repression and not the great days of 1980-81. As repression eased, the organization was starting to fissure, just as the military regime hoped it would. So both the regime and Solidarity were frightened by the great wave of strikes that broke out in April and May 1988, driven by radical young workers who took orders from no one. "No Freedom Without Solidarity" was still their watchword, but they were less and less willing to follow Solidarity's leadership. Wałęsa barely managed barely to control them, at the price of joining them. As inflation skyrocketed from 64 percent in 1988 to 640 percent in 1989, both the regime and Solidarity began to move toward negotiations. Polish Communists resisted compromise, however, and in response Jaruzelski put Rakowski in charge of the government in September. For Rakowski as for Gorbachev, the argument for devolving power was "Comrades, there is no other choice." Still, it took four months, and the threat of Jaruzelski's resignation, before even this hangdog, discredited party would agree to begin round-table negotiations with Solidarity. They opened on February 6, 1989.[4]

As in 1956, Hungary's situation resembled Poland's in significant ways. It also felt dependent on the West. Abstracting the GDR and its special circumstances, Hungary was the socialist country most dependent on Western trade. It had the highest per-capita hard-currency debt in the world, $19 billion for a country of 10 million people. And the economic reform that was to produce the export surpluses to pay it off, that had been put on hold in the mid-1970s and then picked up again toward the end of the decade, was now running out of steam: growth rates were tipping toward the negative. So the westward urge in Hungary was strong on economic grounds alone.

The political impulse was perhaps even more important. Part of it was domestically driven and specific. Beginning in 1982 Ceaușescu decided to pay off Romania's foreign debts and hunker down on the regime's Stalinist basics, and thenceforth Hungary had been quietly cultivating Western support on the issue of the embattled Hungarian minority in Romanian Transylvania. This was a unity issue in Hungarian politics. It helped the regime by deflecting nationalism away from the Soviet Union, appealing to both nationalist conservatives and reformers who valued human rights, and striking a nationalist chord in the populations. Because nationalism was involved, the Soviets stayed carefully clear of the issue, which meant that the Hungarians had to look West for international sympathy and action.

Much of the political urge toward the West was more general, however, a function of a national mood swing set off by economic downturn but issuing into a feeling of national political crisis. During most of Kádár's rule, the Hungarians had been proud of their uniqueness and optimistic about their future. Now, as they encountered difficulties that threatened to resubmerge them in the gray East European pack, they swung toward bleak pessimism about the future and convinced themselves of the need for radical change.

Here, however, the similarities with Poland ended and indeed switched into reverse. In 1956, Poland had weathered the crisis partly because its party kept together; the bill, in the form of party factionalism had come only later, in the 1960s. The Hungarian party, however, had disintegrated, precipitating a national catastrophe, and Kádár had had to build what amounted to a new one over the better part of a decade. Now, in the late 1980s, the Polish party was discredited and faced a strong opposition, while the Hungarian party was still in charge and had before it only bits and pieces of embryonic opposition floating in the amorphous society that it had created and was no longer sure how to manage. It was this contrast more than any other that determined the quite distinct courses the two countries took toward the events of 1989. As a last gift of party rule, this contrast also reproduced the odd Polish-Hungarian leapfrogging motion that had been a feature of the 1956 crisis too, but once again with different results.[5]

For the Hungarian party believed it could manage the process of change. With no experience resembling Solidarity, not only would the process take place without substantial input from the working class but there was a strong reformist element within the party of just the kind that had been crushed by the *apparat* at the Polish party's Ninth Extraordinary Congress in the summer of 1981. Much of the Hungarian process therefore turned on the interaction of party bureaucrats and intellectuals both inside and outside the party, but with the party itself as the main vehicle and objective.

The process began with a palace coup in May 1988. In the middle of the new Polish strike wave, the various factions in the Hungarian party came together to kick Kádár upstairs to a new presidency and to replace most of his people, thereby clearing the decks for change. The new regime of Károly Grósz initiated a broad national discussion of change, as Gierek had done in Poland fifteen years before. But hesitant officials still constituted the center of gravity in the party, and much of the national discussion focussed on historical issues—the character of the 1956 crisis and national rehabilitation for Imre Nagy—as is natural when the winds of change begin to blow in polities where history is an instrument of rule. The shadow of 1956 in turn cast a specter of blood over the whole process, and polarized it. Beginning in the fall of 1988, party conservatives embarked on a campaign of low-level but broad-scale attrition *against* the opposition even as they began, during the winter, to organize a roundtable *with* the opposition. The idea of the roundtable was contemporary Polish, but the hope was for a divided, complaisant opposition, very unlike Solidarity: it was reminiscent, in fact, of 1945 in Hungary, when the Soviets and their Hungarian clients had scoured the countryside to create political parties that could join the Communists in coalition.

The opposition also remembered 1948, when the Communists had destroyed them piecemeal. In April 1989, two weeks after the successful conclusion of the Polish roundtable talks, they proclaimed their united insistence on negotiating together and without power-sharing as a pre-agreed objective. Meanwhile, frightened by the memories of 1956 that the national discussion evoked, party officials all over the country had been joining the ranks of the party reformers. Since they too were confident of their capacity to lead the process if only they could gain control of the party, the reformers swung behind the concept of free political competition, without power-sharing and with the winners legitimated by free parliamentary elections. Given the weakness of the opposition, they were sure of winning in such a competition, and when the Hungarian round table finally met in June 1989, following the first semi-free Polish elections and the triumphal reburial of Imre Nagy's ashes in Budapest, the Hungarian party was already willing to concede more democratic political pluralism than Solidarity had dared to ask for earlier in the year.[6]

With all these differences, however, both Poland and Hungary were similar in that they followed the Gorbachev leadership's new line that political democratization was needed if economic reform was ever to work. Two other regimes, in Bulgaria and Czechoslovakia, gave their formal approval to the Soviet prescription, but really hoped to use economic reform to avoid political reform. Bulgarian lip service could go pretty far: In the summer of 1987 that old fox Todor Zhivkov announced that he was taking the Bulgarian party completely out of government, just as Gorbachev wanted. When the Soviets urged a more measured pace, he returned to Sofia with the message that he had tried, but that Moscow had turned him down. Bulgarian politics proceeded as before.[7]

The more dour and recently "normalized" Czechoslovaks were no longer capable of such liveliness: Hag-ridden by the ghost of 1968, theirs was lip service pure and simple. While Zhivkov at least tinkered with economic reform, the Czechoslovaks did no more than talk about it. Gustav Husák had combined the presidency and party leadership, in the best Stalinist tradition. In December 1987 he gave the party post to a man who was younger but even grayer than he was, Miloš Jakeš, the bureaucrat who had managed the expulsion of half a million members from the party after the Prague Spring was crushed. Still, both the Bulgarians and Czechoslovaks slightly expanded their tolerance for dissidents, intellectual and religious. Dissidents were few and unorganized in Bulgaria, but in Czechoslovakia Charter 77 had gathered such people since 1977. By 1988, for the first time in forty years, the regime felt obliged to imitate unofficial celebrations of national holidays as well as repress them. By Polish and Hungarian standards, this was a pittance.[8]

The two remaining regimes denied the need for any reform at all. Honecker's GDR and Ceaușescu's Romania insisted that they had already done what Gorbachev was now attempting in the Soviet Union. They repressed most dissent and exported the remainder to the West. In these two countries the separation of working class and intelligentsia remained practically complete. There were major differences between them, however. The GDR was comparatively rich and had a special relationship with the FRG. Honecker's regime felt it could afford to take some steps to preempt opposition and bolster its liberal image to the West. It allowed the kinds of things — more visits, more emigration, more church activities — that the Federal Republic needed to justify economic support.[9]

Romania, by contrast, was poor, and an international pariah. Both of these conditions were magnified after 1982, as Ceaușescu tried to restore the nation's independence by cutting imports and starving consumption in order to pay off foreign debt. His formula for maintaining power was Stalinist. He relied on the police (the *Securitate*) rather than on the party to secure his rule. When workers rose in the Transylvanian city of Brașov in late 1987, their leaders were shipped away en masse. And when retired old-guard Communist grandees complained on behalf of the workers and urged reform on Ceauşescu, they were put under house arrest outside the reach of the Western embassies in Bucharest. In February 1988 Ceauşescu renounced U.S. most-favored-nation tariff treatment, before the U.S. Congress withdrew it as punishment for his human rights violations. Romania sank ever farther into the miserable isolation his brand of independence had wrought.[10]

Romania was as isolated from the Soviet Union as it was from the West. In general, as Western and Soviet definitions of interest began to coincide, they began to prioritize their relations with the countries of Eastern Europe in the same way. For both the Soviets and the West, Poland and Hungary, the political reformers, were now moving to the top. In the middle were Bulgaria, Czechoslovakia, and, because of West German patronage and its own concessions, the GDR. At the bottom, or off the scale entirely, was Romania.[11]

This convergence was still not enough to bring Eastern Europe to the top of the East-West agenda, however. That required another push from the international system. As the Western nuclear debate continued to bubble and froth, Gorbachev kept up the Soviet denuclearization campaign by proposing the "second zero," a ban on nuclear weapons with ranges between those of battlefield weapons and INF. NATO could hardly refuse, for it had no such weapons. It bought on to the proposal in June 1987, and it was incorporated in the INF treaty signed in Washington that December.

But Western conservatives were sickened by the pace of denuclearization. They reacted in two different ways. First, particularly in West Germany, many of them fled forward and joined the left in pressing for the "third zero," the elimination of battlefield nuclear weapons. Second, particularly in the United States, conservatives began to rediscover the virtues of nuclear deterrence and oppose further arms control. As long as Ronald Reagan was in the White House, they could not push too hard. Both types of conservatives could be reassured somewhat by a compromise formula adopted by NATO ministers in the same June 1987 meeting where they accepted the second zero. It allowed for the possibility of negotiations on the third zero, but only on the condition that agreements were reached first on conventional and chemical arms.[12]

The Soviets needed to take the lead in pressing for conventional arms reductions if they were maintain their push for nuclear arms control. Simultaneously, the Gorbachev leadership was recognizing that the Soviet economy was going to need a boost as structural economic reform was implemented. The special budgetary and ideological place of military forces, one of the particular concerns of the Soviet thinkers whose efforts in the early 1980s provided the sinews of "new political thinking" in Soviet foreign policy, was now called into question by the terrible performance of the Soviet economy. Gorbachev began to endorse a philosophy of "reasonable sufficiency" as the guide for Soviet military spending. Reasonable sufficiency accepted that cuts in military spending could increase national security by strengthening the economy and that force postures should be defensive, and it was consistent with the proposition that political problems should be solved by political, not military, means.

Reasonable sufficiency for Soviet security also signaled a larger change in Soviet international thinking: It meant that Gorbachev had abandoned the optimism of Khrushchev and Brezhnev. Stalin had metaphorized Marx's class struggle into a model for international politics, by dividing the world into two camps, socialist and imperialist. Marx had written that with a little help from its friends the forces of history would give the working class an inevitable victory over the bourgeoisie; on the strength of apparent victories in the Third World in the 1960s and the acceptance by the United States of détente in the 1970s, Khrushchev and Brezhnev had believed that the international dominance of the Soviet Union was well on the way to becoming reality. By Gorbachev's time, faith in socialism's ineluctable progress was hard to sustain. Defeats in the Third World during the 1970s, the bloody struggle in Afghanistan, and the unmistakable failure of Brezhnev's strategy of keeping pace with the West economically by borrowing Western technology: These had all taken their toll. In 1988 Gorbachev explicitly rejected the class struggle as a model for international relations; "all-human values" now took primacy. And he began to look to the Soviet military for help in fashioning a stopgap solution to domestic economic woes.[13]

Gorbachev was thus responding to both domestic and international imperatives in his December 1988 address to the UN General Assembly. Reiterating his support of universal human values and reasonable sufficiency, he announced a Soviet decision to unilaterally remove half a million troops from Europe and Asia.[14] This gave the first real impetus to "conversion," the use of military resources for civilian purposes within the Soviet Union. But in practical terms the only way Gorbachev could gain international assent and ratification for his new approach was via agreement to a new round of conventional arms control under the authority of CSCE. In the CSCE review conference underway in Vienna, the West was as usual demanding new human rights commitments in return, and in January 1989 the original CSCE purpose of addressing the systemic roots of security problems was revived as the price of getting new conventional arms talks on track. The CSCE countries committed themselves to major human rights improvements and to attend a 1991 human rights conference in Moscow. They also agreed to begin two new negotiations on conventional arms in Europe, one on confidence- and security-building measures (CSBMs), one on force reductions (Conventional Forces in Europe, or CFE).[15] Accordingly, negotiations on conventional arms, which began in March 1989, now moved to the center of the East-West relationship.

But the West Germans were still not satisfied, and kept pushing for negotiations on the third zero, for battlefield nuclear weapons. In April 1989 Chancellor Kohl called for immediate superpower talks on the issue. As East-West tension abated, West-West tension continued to rise, creating two major political problems. One problem could only be solved by the incoming Bush administration, for it had to do with American leadership: How to stay ahead of Gorbachev? The other problem concerned the entire Western Alliance: If the military confrontation in Europe was fading, what was NATO's *raison d'être*? If the elaborate structure of deterrence that NATO had built up over forty years was to be kept in place, if political support was to be maintained for the necessary defense expenditures, NATO's essential purpose had to be redefined.

Soviet and Polish domestic politics helped condition the West's answers. At the Soviet party conference of June 1988, Gorbachev had not convinced the party to reform itself to compete in an open political system along the lines proposed by Rakowski, but he had convinced it to establish such a system, with a president and a new, freely elected legislature. In March 1989 partly free elections to the new Congress of Peoples' Deputies brought in a substantial opposition. In April the round-table negotiations in Poland ended with a historic compromise. The party would keep the presidency, and together with its client parties representing peasants and shopkeepers it was guaranteed a majority in the main body of parliament (or so everyone thought). A new Senate with lesser powers would be established on the basis of wholly free elections. Solidarity, now legal, was expected to control it. This compromise was a trauma for everyone concerned, including Solidarity, which had been born to sidestep power and had always resisted sharing it.[16]

The Soviet elections and the Polish compromise reassured the West about Soviet intentions. In May 1989 the Bush administration arrived at a single answer to both the question of how to stay ahead of Gorbachev and the question of how to redefine NATO's purpose. On his first trip to Europe as president, Bush proposed U.S. troop cuts in Europe and made a pacesetting offer to the Soviets on CFE. In broader terms, he urged that NATO rededicate itself to the task of ending the division of Europe. NATO's first priority should be to negotiate a new conventional balance that would eliminate the asymmetries that had favored the Soviet Union for two generations and which the Soviets had built up in order to protect the Stalinist regimes they had imposed in Eastern Europe. But the alliance's larger goal was now to be political, to bring divided Europe back together, "whole and free." Relieved to see an intelligent American proposal that met everybody's needs for the time being, the European allies agreed. NATO also managed to reach a compromise on battlefield nuclear weapons, agreeing to seek partial reductions.

Bush then affirmed his patronage of a united Europe by visiting Poland and Hungary, the political reformers, in July. From there he went to the Bastille to join the French celebration of the bicentennial of their revolution and to mobilize the support of the six other leading industrial countries of the Group of Seven for this approach. Just before Bush arrived, Gorbachev announced in Paris that he too believed East and West should now focus their energies on ending the division of Europe. The other leading industrial democracies climbed on board, their decision eased by a letter from Gorbachev suggesting that a reforming Soviet Union now deserved to join their international economic system.[17] The United States, Western Europe, and the Soviet Union had agreed that the time had come for Poland, Hungary, Czechoslovakia, Bulgaria, Romania, and the German Democratic Republic to rejoin Europe.

Specifically, they agreed that the Poles and the Hungarians deserved support. From Gorbachev's point of view, those two peoples were following his lead. They were bullying their parties into transmogrifying themselves into "parties of a new type," Gorbachevian rather than Leninist, parties that could compete effectively in open democratic political systems rather than ruling by command. Even before the renewal of parties was complete, the new political systems had to be put in place, and they had to be equipped with new socioeconomic bases created by introducing market elements into the economy. Gorbachev and his Polish and Hungarian homologues were gambling that the market would produce local equivalents of middle-class democrats who would support their reformed parties out of gratitude and self-interest.[18]

When they took over in the late 1940s, the East European Communists had defined the problem in a parallel way: They had looked to industrialization to create a working class that did not yet exist and to refashion the intelligentsia, confident that both would be grateful and support them. Now Gorbachev and the Polish and Hungarian party reformers sensed that the workers and intellectuals would leave them unless they used the market to create a new middle class of people who were more oriented toward impersonal norms and values than workers and intellectuals were, and unless they renewed themselves to appeal to such people. The reformers were not sure it could be done, and they saw the new state structures they were putting in place to parallel party rule as fallback structures of governance in case it could not be done as well as prods to party renewal. But simply to put those alternative structures in place they still needed the party. Because the Poles and Hungarians were trying to do what Gorbachev was trying to do at home, he felt he had a stake in what was happening in Poland and Hungary, and that they deserved Soviet support.

The Western perspective was much simpler. The West liked Poland and Hungary because they were doing what the West had said Eastern Europe should be doing for over forty years, democratizing their politics and trying to marketize their economies. But, whether the reasons were simple or complex, the Soviets and the West now agreed for the first time since the late 1940s, or since 1956 at the very latest, that what happened in Eastern Europe really mattered to them. For the first time in more than a generation, the East Europeans had chance to influence their neighbors' policies significantly, in addition to being influenced by them.

The new consensus among the Soviets and the West was tested first in Poland. Poland's partly free elections of June 4 had resulted in a resounding victory for Solidarity. Solidarity won 92 of the 100 seats of the freely elected new Senate, which was no surprise. The remaining 8 were unfilled, as no candidate received the required 50 percent of cast ballots. In the Sejm, Solidarity won 160 of the 161 seats it was allowed to contest. The remaining 299 had been allotted to the Communists and their allies. But they actually won only 5, because voters routinely crossed Communists and their allies off the ballot, often drawing a large "X" upon an entire page of candidates, and thus prevented official candidates from winning the necessary 50 percent.

Jaruzelski then called on Solidarity to join in a coalition government with the Communist party. Solidarity refused, and in the runoff elections to fill the empty seats it took every one it could contest except a Senate seat taken by an independent. But because the runoffs did not require 50 percent support for election, the Communists and their allies were able to claim the remaining 297 Sejm seats. In July Solidarity followed the roundtable agreement and duly allowed Jaruzelski to be elected President, and Jaruzelski turned over his party post to Rakowski. But when the time came to form a Communist-led government, Poland plunged into uncertain wrangling. Kiszczak was named as prime minister on August 2 but was unable gain agreement for his cabinet.

Solidarity had always shied away from sharing power: It had risen and survived as a trade union movement whose task was to build civil society while leaving government to others. It was politically irresponsible on principle. That purity set it apart from the corrupt Communists and constituted a large part of its attraction to the Poles. By freely voting for it, the Poles had challenged Solidarity to enter politics, in very harsh circumstances. Solidarity would have to take political coresponsibility for an economic reform program that would inevitably impose massive austerity on its working-class base.

On August 14 Kiszczak announced that he could not form a government. Lech Wałęsa decided for coresponsibility, and for power. On August 16, in a dramatic midnight visit to the Sejm, he pried the peasant and shopkeepers' parties out of their traditional junior partnership with the Communists and into a coalition for a Solidarity prime minister. The Communists had maintained these parties after 1948 as symbols of their triumph over the old East European social order, and now that order took symbolic revenge on them. Jaruzelski supported Wałęsa's opposition government in principle, and Kisczak resigned on August 17. But as the party was called on to give up real power, it threatened to halt the entire process, just as it had in late 1988 before the round-table discussions began. This time it took a phone call from Gorbachev to Rakowski to swing it into line. On August 19 Jaruzelski designated Tadeusz Mazowiecki, one of the Warsaw intellectuals who had brought their petition of support to the striking shipyard workers in Gdańsk almost exactly nine years before and whom Wałęsa had drafted to help the workers negotiate with the government ("we are only workers, we need your help"), as Eastern Europe's first non-Communist head of government since the late 1940s.[19] Mazowiecki, a Catholic believer, represented both the first successful unification of workers and intellectuals since 1956 and the postpeasant ideology that has helped bring them together.

The new Bush Administration in Washington had led the Western response to East European change. The Polish roundtable had concluded successfully on April 6, and on April 17, in Hamtramck, Michigan, President Bush had welcomed the result and announced a modest assistance offer. It included Hungary as well as Poland, even though the Hungarians were still struggling over the shape of their roundtable.[20] That struggle remained drenched in history and morals: for two more months the main issue in Hungarian politics was who would capture credit for the reburial of Imre Nagy's ashes. It was a new, emerging, and practical brand of politics involving interests and programs and compromise that had quickly broken through the corroding system throughout the area, and the Hungarians simply had less experience with it than did the Poles.[21] The reburial took place June 16, and only after that did the Hungarian roundtable get underway. But the Hungarians were learning practical politics fast. The two sides, the party reformers and the opposition, shared sponsorship and credit for the impressive Nagy ceremonies, and the roundtable talks quickly focussed on the practical details of a new, pluralistic constitutional system. On his way to the Group of Seven meeting in Paris in early July, therefore, President Bush visited both Poland and Hungary to urge them forward and validate his Paris appeal to the leaders of the other industrialized states to make ending the division of Europe a major international priority.

Now, however, Western support (and the desire for more) caught up with the Hungarians. For some years they had been quietly directing Western attention to the problems of the Hungarian minority in Transylvania. In their symbolic mode, as a gesture to the West and their own population, the Hungarians had dismantled part of their physical border with Austria in May 1989. As Western media cameras rolled, Hungarian leaders cheerfully cut through the barbed wire that had defined Hungary for much of the West ever since 1956. But now East German tourists began to flee West through Hungary, across this open border. And the next month, in June, the Hungarians began to accept as refugees substantial numbers of Romanian Magyars who had been trying to slip across their border though they lacked the resources to support the newcomers. These two gestures together created a new and powerful practical dilemma for Hungary.[22]

On the one hand, in order to receive assistance from the United Nations High Commission for Refugees (UNHCR) to support Romanian Magyars, Hungary needed to sign the UN Convention on Refugees, which requires signatories to accept refugees who may face persecution in their own countries. On the other hand, like all East European states, Hungary and the GDR had an international agreement committing each to prevent the other's tourists from going West. Tourism between socialist countries was important to all the regimes because it did not involve hard currency, but it was particularly important to the hard-line regimes because for them it was a safety valve that allowed the rest of the system to remain in place. It was particularly important to the GDR, which could not easily use nationalism to appeal to its people and had little else to offer. The GDR had not previously felt threatened by allowing travel, trusting the others to honor their agreements and to send its tourists home. But now its tourists were leaving by the thousands for Austria through Hungary.

When the Hungarians enforced an exit permission requirement, East Germans began to pile up in Budapest. By September 1 there were 3,000 waiting there and perhaps 100,000 elsewhere in the country. Hungary could only secure UNHCR aid and maintain its liberalizing Western image by accepting them and allowing them free passage, and thereby violating its solemn commitment to the GDR.

At the July 7-8 meeting of the Warsaw Pact leaders in Bucharest, Gorbachev had called for "independent solutions to national problems," and after months of wrestling with their dilemma, on September 10 the Hungarians chose their commitment to human rights over their commitment to the GDR and took down the rest of the physical border. Gorbachev's foreign policy spokesman Gennadiy Gerasimov said that the development "did not directly affect" the Soviet Union. The GDR promptly closed down travel to Hungary, which only served to direct the flow to Czechoslovakia and Poland, where thousands of East Germans had gathered in beleaguered West German embassies by the end of September.

The East German crisis was beginning: the Hungarian transformation shifted gears, moving into the practicalities of democratic politics. The Hungarian roundtable concluded September 18 with an agreement for fully free elections for both a new President and a new parliament. Party reformers were confident that their candidate, Imre Pozsgay, could win early presidential elections, but a large section of the opposition generated a referendum in favor of parliamentary elections first, which narrowly carried in November. That killed Pozsgay's chances, and when general elections were held in March 1990 it was already a new Hungary and a new Eastern Europe.[23]

The East Germans who left were certainly not hunger refugees — as someone put it, they were voting not with their feet but with their cars — and they were not precisely political refugees either. They were mainly skilled workers and their families. When asked why they were leaving, they merely said that they were seeking a better life in the West. Poland had taught that the essential element in successful domestic resistance to communism in Eastern Europe was a coalition of workers and intellectuals, united by a renewed nationalism. Such a coalition did not exist in East Germany. Like the Honecker regime, the East German opposition believed that socialism should continue in East Germany. It therefore remained within the terms of traditional ideological debate, arguing about building democratic socialism, a prospect that had seemed nonsensical in the rest of Eastern Europe since at least 1968. Maintaining socialism implied a continued subservience to the Soviet Union and strict limits on German nationalism, so while nationalism was modified elsewhere by intellectuals in order to include moral rights and responsibilities, the East German opposition had to avoid it. The comparatively high living standards the GDR achieved with West German help allowed intellectuals and rulers to continue to believe that the working class could support socialism.

By September events had progressed far enough elsewhere to allow workers to make their preference known without ideological assistance. Meanwhile, the East German regime had scheduled a major celebration of its fortieth anniversary, with all the Communist leaders including Gorbachev in attendance, for early October. To save face, the regime negotiated a one-shot departure for the East Germans camping in Prague and Warsaw and tried to put off the problem of how to staunch the flow until after Gorbachev had left.

On October 7 the Hungarian Communist party voted to reject Marxism and become a democratic socialist party, but by now all eyes were fastened on East Berlin. At the anniversary celebration, it became clear that neither the East German population nor Gorbachev was going to give the regime the luxury of postponing decisions. In private and in public, Gorbachev made it delicately but unmistakably clear to the East German leadership that real change was required if communism was to survive, and the regime was obliged to use force to suppress the crowds chanting "Gorby! Gorby!" After Gorbachev left, huge demonstrations continued and spread throughout the country. In fact they were bigger in the provincial cities, away from television cameras, than in East Berlin.

The moment of truth came on October 9. Honecker gave the police the shoot-to-kill order, but the local authorities in Leipzig refused to apply it, and they were then supported by much of the rest of the leadership. On October 10 the police stood by as protests began, and the demonstrations grew day by day after that. They were sponsored by the intellectual opposition, still largely reform Communist with an admixture of religious leaders and environmentalists, but their own demands were politically inchoate. They simply wanted change. On October 18 Honecker was retired and replaced by the much younger Egon Krenz, but the East Germans continued to leave, and demonstrations continued to grow: 300,000 in Leipzig on October 23, 500,000 to a million in East Berlin on November 4. Meanwhile, Gorbachev had boldly labeled neutral, social democratic Finland one possible model for Eastern Europe and had publicly reiterated the Soviet Union's determination not to intervene in the political processes underway. On November 7, the anniversary of the Bolshevik revolution, the East German cabinet resigned. On November 9, after a week in which 50,000 people fled the country, East Germany's national borders were opened everywhere, including at the Berlin Wall, the seal and symbol of the division of Europe since 1961. A few days later, as the passion to name and punish the guilty waxed to a hurricane, the eighty-one year old minister of state security, Erich Mielke, a lifelong Communist, stood before the parliament and declared pathetically: "But I love you all . . . Ich liebe Euch doch alle . . ." It was probably true; but the days of communism as personalism and police force were ending.[24]

During that second week of November Gorbachev seems to have privately sent the leaderships in Bulgaria and Czechoslovakia the same message he had delivered publicly in East Berlin and Helsinki the month before: We will not save you, and if you are to save yourselves, you must change.[25] These were the two countries that had had relatively strong parties in the 1940s and that had hoped to get through the 1980s with a bit of economic reform and some lip service to political reform, on the model of Kádár's Hungary. Just as Zhivkov had been more agile at that game than Husák and Jakeš, so his Bulgarian colleagues were quicker to respond to Gorbachev's message than the muscle-headed Czechoslovaks. The Bulgarian party got rid of Zhivkov on November 10. They then updated their imitation of Hungary, eschewing simple Kádárism and trying to create an opposition. The little groups of dissidents that were just beginning to coalesce under Zhivkov were now invited to organize themselves for dialogue with the party. The party also embarked on a series of symbolic measures, including reversal of the forced assimilation campaign against Bulgarian Turks, designed to prove that it had been washed clean by Zhivkov's removal.

The response to Gorbachev was different in Czechoslovakia because both the party and the opposition were different. In describing what 50 million unnatural deaths over half a century had meant for the quality of the Russian elite by the time of Khrushchev's ouster in 1964, George Kennan once used the word "stupidization." [26] Although both the cause and the effect were milder in Czechoslovakia, the word is apt in describing the Czechoslovak party after 1968. The party had removed its quality people and was therefore completely discredited among the intelligentsia.[27] The party's standing within the large, strong, and traditionally Communist Czech working class was less certain, for workers had not really been asked for twenty years. For its part, the minority of the intelligentsia that had tried to remain politically active had used the grim years after 1968 to work through the issues and arrive at the point where Polish intellectuals had been a decade earlier, before Solidarity. They had developed an ideology of building civil society by active personal witness, without overtly challenging Communist power. As might be expected given the Czech intelligentsia's long collusion with communism, that ideology was heavily focused on the moral and ethical issues of guilt and reconciliation. It confronted the regime of Gustav Husák, the man whom Czechoslovaks aptly called "the President of Forgetting," [28] with memory and salvation. But this opposition had been very isolated, and it remained to be seen whether its ideology would appeal to the working class and the population at large if and when the call for radical change sounded.

On November 17, some 50,000 people attended a rally called by students to commemorate the Nazi shooting of one of their predecessors. Although the rally had a permit, it quickly became a protest against the regime, and the police moved in. One hundred students were arrested, and at least thirteen were hospitalized. With serial revolution seizing the rest of the area, the effect was not intimidation but revulsion, which issued in a wave of demonstrations. The opposition, including Charter 77 and Václav Havel, organized itself as the Civic Forum on November 19 and began to lead. It threw its weight behind the general strike called by students for November 27. On the twenty-fourth the party leadership resigned, but Prague demonstrations of 500,000 and then 800,000 people rejected the new leadership, which was appealing to the workers to ignore the strike. On the twenty-seventh the strike was completely observed throughout Czechoslovakia, demonstrating conclusively that the opposition and its new ideology of reconciliation and expiation had the support of the working class and the rest of the country. "Betrayed" by the workers, the Communists, disciplined to the last, unanimously turned power over to Václav Havel.[29] Because Havel is a superb politician as well as a wonderful artist, he took the message of salvation through suffering and confession and turned it back to the whole Czechoslovak people. Havel insisted that all Czechoslovaks were guilty and that there was a place in the new and better order for everyone who repented. By the end of the year he was president of Czechoslovakia, and spent his first day in the presidential offices in Prague Castle in black denims and a lavender shirt.[30]

That left Ceaușescu. He had grown great on anti-Sovietism, and he had long ago rooted out all, or almost all, Soviet assets from Romania. As a result, Gorbachev had only a vague influence on a terrorized elite and an atomized population: Whatever he had done in Bulgaria and Czechoslovakia could not work in Romania. Ceaușescu was certainly not one for repentence. On the contrary, the course of events elsewhere in the socialist world convinced him that he had been right all along. He believed that Gorbachev and his ilk were reaping the harvest of the seeds of feudal and bourgeois decadence that they had planted and tended. He had quashed the intelligentsia and prevented any possibility that an opposition could form and work its way through intellectual issues. Above all, he had kept the intelligentsia from infecting what he saw as the healthy masses of workers and peasants. As he told an American deputy secretary of state, he was tremendously popular; everywhere he went, every speech he made, people cheered him — and Romania continued to build socialism, still poor, but richer every day, and above all on the right path. The occasional disturbances down below were unimportant, provoked by enemies of socialism.

So Ceaușescu believed, and to enforce his Stalinist understanding of history, he relied on Stalinist methods. As Romania developed, he knew, the party would be increasingly composed of intellectuals, which meant it was going to be increasingly unreliable. So Ceaușescu had kept the party in a state of Brownian movement by constantly shifting people around. With his wife and family he had run the party, the army, and the rest of the country using a single state institution, the *Securitate*. Like Stalin at the end of his rule, Ceauşescu ruled personally through the police, or parts of it personally loyal to him and his family.

When revolution came to Romania it caught almost everyone in the country completely unprepared. The Ceauşescus and the *Securitate* were of course ready for isolated revolts and were certain that they could suppress them and prevent them from spreading. When revolt broke out on December 16 in Timişoara after the *Securitate* tried to arrest a priest who had protested the regime's treatment of ethnic Hungarians, Ceauşescu was confident enough to leave on a state visit to Iran. Upon his return, he called a demonstration of support in Bucharest for December 21. To his surprise (which registered across Romania via television), elements of the crowd protested. The next day he declared a state of emergency and fled Bucharest with his wife Elena.

The opposition had no program beyond expulsion of the Ceauşescu and had very little leadership. Their leaders realized that Ceauşescu had forever discredited communism, but they had no ideology of their own. There had been some talks among retired Communist leaders and second- and third-level Communists whom cadre rotation had consigned to menial jobs. When the Ceauşescus fled and protesters took over the Central Committee building and the television station, these people moved in, gathered whatever likely looking representatives of various social groups happened to be present into a new National Salvation Front, proclaimed themselves the government, and sought alliances with the forces of order.

The Front's first priority was to survive against elements of the *Securitate* still fighting for Ceauşescu. Some of them had killed Ceauşescu's defense minister after he had refused to enforce the emergency, and they were shooting protesters in defense of their absent chief. Other parts of the *Securitate* and the remaining army leadership, which had been as tyrannized by Ceauşescu as everyone else, defended the Front. As long as the Ceauşescus were at large, however, fighting continued, and during the three days following their flight the outcome was by no means certain. So personal had Romanian politics become that in order simply to survive, the Front had to kill the Ceauşescus on Christmas Day in a mock trial in the worst Stalinist tradition. The bloody outcome had to be shown again and again on national television before their defenders gradually stopped fighting. Ceauşescu was unrepentant to the end, waiting for supporters to rescue him and insisting that he answered only to the people. He never expected to go.

Romania was now a political desert, parched but for the fresh blood of the innocent and the guilty offered in December. That blood had purchased some freedom of choice for Romanians, but they lacked institutions and coherent ideologies from which to choose. They were left by Ceauşescu's death to pick through the bits and pieces of their national experience to see what could be used to construct a new political culture. In Romania, more than elsewhere, the past has rushed back in to fill the void, even if not forever.[31]

Notes

1. On "Deutschmark Diplomacy and Its Limits," see Josef Joffe, "The View from Bonn," in William E. Griffith, ed., *Central and Eastern Europe: The Opening Curtain?* (Boulder: Westview, 1989), 154-159, and Hanns-Dieter Jacobsen, "The Foreign Trade and Payments of the GDR in a Changing World Economy," in Ian Jeffries and Manfred Melzer, *The East German Economy* (London: Croom Helm, 1987), 235-260. On prisoner buyouts, see Craig R. Whitney, "East Germans Tell How Bonn Paid for Prisoners," *New York Times*, 1 August 1990: 33,000 between 1964 and 1989, with prices rising from the equivalent of $10,000 to $60,000 per head. On Hungary's debt crisis and entry into the IMF in 1982 (without Western objection but also without Western sacrifice of principle, if it is accepted that Hungary was already relatively very liberal), see Paul Marer, "Hungary's Balance of Payments Crisis and Response, 1978-1984," in *East European Economies: Slow Growth in the 1980s, Vol. 3: Country Studies on Eastern Europe and Yugoslavia, Selected Papers Submitted to the Joint Economic Committee, Congress of the United States* (Washington, D.C.: Government Printing Office, 1986), 298-321.
2. As Polish and Czechoslovak opposition leaders made clear in private conversation during these years.
3. Rakowski's memo is cited and used extensively in Timothy Garton Ash, *The Uses of Adversity* (New York: Random House, 1989), 264ff. The background was the degenerating social and political atmosphere in Poland during these years. Something of the flavor of the lived experience can be tasted in Michael T. Kaufman, *Mad Dreams, Saving Graces: Poland—a Nation in Conspiracy* (New York: Random House, 1989).
4. See Timothy Garton Ash, *The Magic Lantern* (New York: Random House, 1990), 16-17 and 42, and, on the impact of the strikes of April-May 1988 and the beginning and course of the round-table talks, David Ost, *Solidarity and the Politics of Anti-*

Politics. Opposition and Reform in Poland Since 1968 (Philadelphia: Temple University, 1990), 182ff.

5. This leapfrogging effect is clearest in the fine account of 1989 developments in the two countries in Ronald D. Asmus, J.F. Brown, Keith Crane, *Soviet Foreign Policy and the Revolutions of 1989 in Eastern Europe* (Santa Monica, Calif.: RAND, 1991), "Poland and Hungary," 32-84.

6. The basic accounts are Georges Schöpflin, Rudolf Tökés and Ivan Völgyes, "Leadership Change and Crisis in Hungary," *Problems of Communism*, 37, no. 5 (September-October 1988) (through May 1988, based on insider evidence) and László Bruszt and David Stark, "Remaking the Political Field in Hungary: From the Politics of Confrontation to the Politics of Competition," in Ivo Banac, ed., *Eastern Europe in Revolution* (Ithaca, N.Y. and London: Cornell University Press, 1992), 13-55 (from mid-1988 through late 1989). For a vivid evocation of the mood leading to the crisis, written in 1985, see Garton Ash, *Uses of Adversity*, 143-156. On how Kádár's "hybrid society" (and economy) degenerated into crisis, see Elemér Hankiss, "In Search of a Paradigm," *Daedalus*, 116, no. 1 (Winter 1990), 183-214. Hope for a reformed socialist paradigm was very hardy: see Ivan Szélényi, "Eastern Europe in an Epoch of Transition: Toward a Socialist Mixed Economy," in Victor Nee and David Stark, eds., *Remaking the Economic Institutions of Socialism: China and Eastern Europe* (Stanford, CA.: Stanford University Press, 1989), 208-232. On one culmination of the crisis, see Garton Ash, "Budapest: The Last Funeral," in his *Magic Lantern*, 47-60.

7. See Henry Kamm, "Bulgarian Rejects Political Opening" and "Bulgaria Reins in Its Enthusiasm for Change," in *New York Times*, 30 January and 3 February 1988. Zhivkov presented his radical restructuring plan to a hastily called Central Committee session on July 28; the party conference in the last week of January 1988 failed to provide details. J.F. Brown judiciously weighs the evidence as to whether Zhivkov's "July concept" was a clever preemptive strike, as I suggest here, or flatfooted imitative overkill that the Soviets had to rein in: *Surge to Freedom. The End of Communist Rule in Eastern Europe* (Durham, N.C. and London: Duke University Press, 1991), 186ff. But we agree that the Bulgarian regime began to totter thereafter.

8. "Police Attack Protesters at Prague Demonstration," *New York Times*, 29 October 1988. For figures on the extent of the post-1969 purges, see Peter Hruby, *Fools and Heroes. The Changing Role of Communist Intellectuals in Czechoslovakia* (Oxford: Pergamon, 1980), 146-149.

9. On the evolution of GDR trade, visits, and contacts in the 1980s, see David Childs, "The SED Faces the Challenges of Ostpolitik and glasnost," in David Childs, Thomas A. Baylis, and Marilyn Rueschmeyer, eds., *East Germany in Comparative Perspective* (London: Routledge, 1989), 3-10.

10. For this phase of the Ceauşescu regime, which turned out to be the last, see J.F. Brown, "Conservatism and Nationalism in the Balkans," in Griffith, ed., *Central and Eastern Europe*, 293-300, Daniel N. Nelson, *Romanian Politics in the Ceauşescu Era* (New York: Gordon and Beach, 1988), and Trond Gilberg, *Nationalism and Communism in Romania. The Rise and Fall of Ceauşescu's Personal Dictatorship* (Boulder: Westview, 1990).

11. Charles Gati, *The Bloc that Failed* (Bloomington: Indiana University Press, 1990), gives a useful country-by-country summary in almost reverse order. See also J.F. Brown's remarks on what he calls the "laissez-faire," or Mark II, period in the Gorbachev leadership's approach to Eastern Europe, from 1989, in *Surge to Freedom*, 60-70.

12. See the statement issued by the North Atlantic Council in Reykjavik, 12 June 1987, in *American Foreign Policy. Current Documents 1987* (Washington, D.C.: Department of State, 1988), 262-264.

13. See Gorbachev's report to the 19th All-Union Party Conference in *Pravda*, 26 July 1988, p. 4, as translated in Gordon Livermore, *Soviet Foreign Policy Today* (Columbus, Ohio: Current Digest of the Soviet Press, 1989).

14. See the complete text of Gorbachev's UNGA address in *Pravda*, 8 December 1988, as translated in Livermore, *Soviet Foreign Policy Today*.

15. *CSCE. Vienna Follow-Up Meeting. A Framework for Europe's Future. Selected Documents No. 35* (Washington, D.C.: Department of State, January 1989).

16. See Bernard Gwertzman and Michael T. Kaufman, eds., *The Collapse of Communism* (New York: Times Books, 1990), 25-30, 33-36. See also Jan T. Gross's analytic retrospective, "Poland: From Civil Society to Political Nation," in Ivo Banac, ed., *Eastern Europe in Revolution*, 56-71. Brown gives an extremely useful chronology of 1989 events in the area as a whole, with added sections on Yugoslavia and Albania, in *Surge to Freedom*, 271-302.

17. See Stephen Greenhouse, "Gorbachev Urges Economic Accords," *New York Times*, 16 July 1989.

18. Post-Communist rulers of course feel even more strongly about the need to use the market to create a "class basis" for democracy. In presenting himself and his government to the Polish lower house in January 1991, President Lech Wałęsa's first prime minister, Jan Krzysztof Biclecki, made clear that "I consider a tested system of a market economy as a foundation of liberty ... This [policy] promises the quickest market results and creates the foundation for developing a middle class . . . We shall support [development of the market] not only for the sake of the country, but because we are very much interested in the kinds of social changes that consolidate democracy." From Warsaw Domestic Radio Service in Polish, 4-5 January 1990 (translated by *Foreign Broadcast Information Service*). See also Lawrence Weschler, "Shock," *The New Yorker* (10 December 1990), 120.

19. Beyond the works cited in notes 5 and 16 above, there is accessible material on these events in Garton Ash, *The Magic Lantern*, 25-46 ("Warsaw: The First Election"), and Maya Latynski, "Poland," in Larry Garber and Eric Bjornlund, eds., *The New Democratic Frontier. A Country-by-Country Report on Elections in Central and Eastern Europe* (Washington, D.C.: The National Democratic Institute for International Affairs, 1992), 98-104.

20. The small package promised at Hamtramck grew as liberation proceeded and other Western countries followed suit. For the United States, Congress authorized a total of $942.2 million in assistance to Poland and Hungary for fiscal years 1990-1992, with $813.2 million for Poland, $60 million for Hungary, and $69 million for both. On the process, see Robert Pear, "Congress Approves Aid of $852 for Poland," *New York Times*, 19 November 1989; Alan Riding, "Aid to Poland and Hungary Pledged by Western Nations," *New York Times*, 14 December 1989, with figures, and Peter Truell, "Poland Signs $710 Million IMF Accord," *Wall Street Journal*, 26 December 1989.

21. I suggested that this brand of politics was likely to emerge in an evening discussion at the Wilson Center in Washington on December 12, 1988. A version of those remarks has been reprinted as "Eastern Europe: Back to the Future?" *Occasional Paper No. 22*,

East European Program of the Center's European Institute (Washington, D.C.: mimeo, October 1989).

22. The shape and content of this Hungarian dilemma are identified by Jon Elster, "Constitutionalism in Eastern Europe: An Introduction," *The University of Chicago Law Review*, 58, no. 2 (Spring 1991), 454-455, and later in the same issue by Wiktor Osiatyński, "Revolutions in Eastern Europe," 838-839.

23. This relies on the account by Bruszt and Stark, "Remaking the Political Field in Hungary."

24. On the antecedents of the East German revolution, see Vladimir Tismaneanu, "Nascent Civil Society in the German Democratic Republic," *Problems of Communism*, 38, nos. 2 and 3 (March-June 1989), 90-111, and on emigration as political dissent, Norman M. Naimark, "'Ich will hier raus': Emigration and the Collapse of the German Democratic Republic," in Ivo Banac, ed., *Eastern Europe in Revolution*, 72-95. There is a convenient record of the revolution itself in Elizabeth Pond, *After the Wall. American Policy toward Germany* (New York: Priority Press Publications, 1990), 7-19, and an exciting insider's account is evidently in press: G. Jonathan Greenwald, *Berlin Witness: An American Diplomat's Chronicle of East Germany's Revolution* (Penn State Press, forthcoming).

25. J.F. Brown weighs the evidence for direct Soviet connivance in the East European revolutions of 1989, including the theory that Gorbachev pushed change next door to discredit his domestic opponents, in *Surge to Freedom*, 57-60. On Bulgaria, he carefully reconstructs the chain of events leading up to Zhivkov's ouster, noting that Mladenov, who replaced him, was "credibly reported" to have stopped in Moscow the day before on his way back from China: 191-197. Gati usefully documents the warning signs of change in the Soviet attitude toward the Czechoslovak leadership in the summer and fall of 1989 in *The Bloc that Failed*, 178-179. On Gorbachev's Helsinki speech, see Bill Keller, "Gorbachev in Finland, Disavows Any Right to Regional Intervention," an October 25 *New York Times* article reprinted in Gwertzman and Kaufman, eds., *The Collapse of Communism*, 163-166, which also contains a contemporary report on Soviet messages to both the Czechoslovaks and Bulgarians: R.W. Apple, Jr., "Unease in Prague; A Soviet Warning on Foot-Dragging Is Given to Prague (November 15)," 204-206. How much weight the Soviets actually threw around is a political issue in the post-Communist era: see John Tagliabue, "Honecker Suggests that Moscow Schemed to Undermine Eastern Bloc," *New York Times*, 3 November 1990.

26. During his 1976 visit to Moscow, when I was his U.S. Embassy Control Officer.

27. For chilling commentary on the process by one of its Slovak victims, see Milan Šimečka, *The Restoration of Order. The Normalization of Czechoslovakia 1969-1976* (London: Verso, 1984).

28. Garton Ash, *Uses of Adversity*, 61.

29. Recounting the Federal Assembly's November 29 vote without dissent to delete the leading role of the party from the Constitution and remove Marxism-Leninsm as the basis of education, Garton Ash was inspired to recall George Orwell: Once a whore, always a whore: *Magic Lantern*, 111.

30. Garton Ash's gripping eyewitness account and personal commentary, "Prague: Inside the Magic Lantern," in his *Magic Lantern*, 78-130, remains indispensable, but we now also have Tony R. Judt's fine "Metamorphosis: The Democratic Revolution in Czechoslovakia," in Ivo Banac, ed., *Revolution in Eastern Europe*, 96-116, which begins the story earlier and takes it through mid-1990, and Theodore Draper's

retrospective on the whole period from the Velvet Revolution until just before the breakup of the Czechoslovak state in January 1993: "A New History of the Velvet Revolution," *New York Review of Books*, 14 January 1993, 14-20, and 20-26. Draper is somewhat embittered, and seems to feel that had the revolution been less velvet, the state might not have broken up; but the citations to the latest literature are valuable. Havel's presidential attire on the first day is described in Craig Whitney, "Havel Traces Passage from Jail to the Castle," *New York Times*, 12 January 1990. It later became more presidential: Timothy Garton Ash, "Eastern Europe: Après Le Déluge, Nous," *New York Review of Books*, 16 August 1990, 51.

31. Mrs. Ceauşescu asked her guards not to hurt her on the grounds that she had been a mother to them all: Celestine Bohlen, "Interim Romanian Leaders Named as Fighting Subsides," *New York Times*, 17 December 1989. The best early account of the Romanian revolution (before and after) is Robert Cullen, "Report from Romania: Down with the Tyrant," *The New Yorker*, 2 April 1990, 94-112. Afterward, even the exact circumstances of the Ceauşescus' deaths remained ambiguous and became controversial: "Last Exits in Romania," *Time*, 4 June 1990, 21, and Mary Battiata, "Romanian Revolution: Truth Still a Casualty," *International Herald Tribune*, 27 December 1990. In fact, the conspiracy thinking natural to Romanian political culture marked the events themselves and positively impregnates all Romanian accounts of what actually happened in and after December 1989 to the point where even the most careful and sober reconstructions by foreigners are (and perhaps always will be) unable to extricate fact from plot stories. The two best I have seen are Katherine Verdery and Gail Kligman, "Romania after Ceauşescu: Post-Communist Communism," in Ivo Banac, ed., *Eastern Europe in Revolution*, 117-147, and István Déak, "Survivors," *New York Review of Books*, 5 March 1992, 43-51, which casts the revolution and its aftermath against a very fair summary background of modern Romanian history and cites the most recent literature.

AFTERWORD

POST-COMMUNIST
EASTERN EUROPE IN
HISTORICAL PERSPECTIVE

WHY SHOULD WE CARE?

Looking back over Eastern Europe's experience during the three years since the revolutions of 1989, the first question to ask is why anyone would still wish to read a history of the region's Communist era?

Eastern Europe under communism was rich in moral drama, and there is a readership for history as moral drama in the West, but it is small. Those who have moved from the West to the area since 1989, and who may find its recent history instructive, are not numerous either. It is true that the ranks of Western diplomats, businessmen, teachers, and advisors resident in Eastern Europe have filled out. The more farsighted of the diplomats among them may be drawn by the area's return to what Vojtech Mastny has sardonically termed "the proper business of diplomacy: the management of conflicts arising from such normal development as the formation and liquidation of states, the drawing and redrawing of boundaries, and the plight of people caught in all these changes."[1] But having lived in the area again since the fall of 1990, I can testify that new Western residents number in the thousands rather than the tens of thousands and that they are all drawn primarily by the excitement of the area's transformation, by its turbulent present and its open-ended future. They are less likely to be interested in its Communist pre-history.

By contrast, Western publics are having their noses rubbed in the area's Communist and pre-Communist pre-history almost every day. Writing this afterword two years ago, after its year of freedom and following its 1989 moment in the sun, I saw Eastern Europe slipping back into its familiar nether world of Western inattention. Nothing of the kind has happened. Instead, there have been waves of attention, with shoals and shallows and eddies in-between.

1990 was by and large a year of hope, as country after country embarked on its version of liberation and new direction. By and large they all grasped the banner the West had held before them over four long Communist decades: liberal democracy and the free market. We knew and were told there would be difficulties and intricacies, but overall the mood was cheerful, even complacent.

The mood soured badly in 1991. The liberation process continued, down to the least of the East European regimes, in Albania. But now it was accompanied by the breakup or beginning death throes of the federal states that Communism had inherited and re-created from the post-World War I settlement—Yugoslavia, Czechoslovakia, and the Soviet Union itself. In August, the world was shaken by the near-miss coup attempt against the Soviet leadership that had triggered the whole liberation process. It was all the more frightening because it was generated in-house, from within that leadership. The end of the year brought the disintegration of the Soviet federal state the Bolsheviks had created almost seventy years before.[2] With disintegration came bloodshed. In what had been Yugoslavia and the Soviet Union, there were armed conflicts on a scale that Europe and the world had forgotten for two generations. The conflicts abruptly recalled two World Wars; they sowed dragon's teeth for the future.

Meanwhile, country after post-Communist country ploughed into what Ralf Dahrendorf has described as the necessary "economic vale of tears."[3] An old question began to reemerge through the tears as they eroded the initial consensus for democracy and the market. The question was whether democracy and the market were in fact compatible—at least in today's post-Communist world. Coming after the high hopes of 1989-90, this question was disillusioning, disturbing, even shocking. By year's end, most

Western commentary was at most only wanly hopeful. In general, it was bleakly pessimistic.[4]

I think it likely that both East and West were coming to grips with the magnitude of the revolutions underway since 1989, and they did not like what they saw. Describing the American Civil War's combatants, Lincoln, in his second Inaugural Address, said, "Each looked for an easier triumph, and a result less fundamental and astounding."[5] That was certainly true for the participants in what I hope will be the last act, in the 1980s, of this century's global civil war. But it was also true after that act's 1989 dénouement. And some of the actors rushing onto the new stage of the post-Communist era looked and sounded for all the world as if they had stepped out of the century's second decade, when the global civil war began in Europe. That just made things worse.

The situation did not stabilize in 1992, either in the post-Communist world itself or in Western opinion. But there was a certain polarization. In the wake of liberation, diversification has set in. Countries and nations have begun to go their separate ways, some of them "fundamental and astounding" indeed.

The area continued to pump out bad tidings. War on former Yugoslav territory spread to Bosnia-Hercegovina, became even deeper and bloodier than in Slovenia and Croatia, and threatened to move southward and spill across old Yugoslav international borders. By year's end, the Czech and Slovak Federal Republic had separated into two new states, although in contrast to Yugoslavia the split was as peaceable as the 1989 "Velvet Revolution" that set it in train.[6] Armed conflict—and of course huge turmoil—continued in the countries of the former Soviet Union. Because of the Soviet imperial legacy and the continued existence of thousands of nuclear weapons, conflict and turmoil in these lands not only kept Western opinion mobilized but cast a pall over the whole reform effort in Eastern Europe. Lithuanians, in the fall elections, voted out the movement that had led their liberation struggle and gave a parliamentary plurality to the local post-Communist party. And at the other end of the half-continent, in Romania, elections kept in power a heavily post-Communist wing of the National Salvation Front, which had inherited leadership from the shambles left by the Ceauşescu regime.

But there was also good news. Within Eastern Europe itself, the old and new countries north and east of former Yugoslavia (including Lithuania and Romania) tried to pursue, or take the first steps toward, market-oriented economic reform and liberal-democratic political arrangements. In the process they came up with differing solutions, in differing sequences, and with different degrees of progress. Countries preoccupied with national and ethnic issues tended to defer economic reform. Nevertheless, there were signs of progress and even signs of incipient "success" in the sense of recessions bottoming out before radical political margins ate significantly into pro-reform centers.[7] Meanwhile, the international community led by the West kept at work building a "new European architecture" capable of offering its new Eastern members an honorable place and a minimal sense of security.[8] In contrast to 1991, when the news was usually bad, or at least shocking, 1992 brought some good tidings too.

To the extent that the polarization of Western opinion in 1992 reflects diversification on the ground, it is a natural development. It can become unhealthy if it prompts Western opinion to pick good guys and bad guys prematurely, since that could force Western governments to distribute their scarce political and economic resources unwisely. Definitive results are not yet in, and it would be a serious mistake to lock in policy judgments in early 1993 in ways that would draw new lines in Europe. At the same time, it is healthy to recognize the "crawling diversification" taking place in the region so long as Western conditions for cooperation with *any* post-Communist country—determined movement toward liberal democracy, respect for human rights, and market-oriented economic arrangements—remain firmly in place. Compared to the hopes for a quick and easy transition that dominated much of Western thinking in 1990 and were followed by the disillusionment of 1991, such realism is the beginning of policy wisdom.

Still, not even the advent of realism in judging the post-Communist world will guarantee readership for a book on its Communist history. Each wave of Western opinion has after all been predicated on the perception that what we were watching and grappling with—good and bad—has resulted from the *disappearance* of communism in the area—radical, final, "fundamental and astounding." In other words, most Westerners are convinced that the hectic developments underway stem from

Communism's collapse, from what Ken Jowitt has now named "the Leninist extinction."[9] So the questions stand: "Why try to understand the area's experience *under* communism? Is it not already ancient history?"

My answer is that "the Communist era" in Eastern Europe's history was in fact a complicated epoch in the life of the peoples of the region, who brought a specific set of characteristic features to it; that these features were essential to the ways in which they worked their way through the challenges of those decades; and that these features have survived—in some ways transmogrified almost out of recognition, but alive—into the new post-Communist era they are now creating. Dependence, nationalism, the heritage of peasant society: these were features common to them all. The forms these features took and the ways they interacted with each other in the last decades of Communist rule were not only characteristic but also important for the role they played in bringing that rule to an end. They also define the tools these peoples have in their struggle to move forward, with help from their friends, into a new and better era.

THE NEW SHAPE OF THEIR DEPENDENCIES

Eastern Europe's historic dependence on outside forces was never more striking than in the moment of its liberation from Soviet rule.

The West played an important role in that liberation. Throughout the long, hard Cold War years, the West held high the banner of freedom, democracy, and prosperity through the market. Towards the end, human rights were inscribed on the banner too. More importantly, the West made its ideology work at home. Western Europe stayed free and largely democratic and became prosperous. So, over time, the West came to provide an example for the East, an alternative working model, as well as an inspiring set of slogans. Meanwhile, beginning in the late 1960s, Communist ideology began to lose its political potency in the East, and a new generation of Stalinist rulers were driven back, more and more, to use economic performance to justify their rule. They came to see economic and political interaction with the West not just as a threat but also as a help to themselves and finally even as a crutch for their crumbling system of governance.

In the 1980s, as the rot accelerated and the East European rulers became more and more desperate, the Western policy they had to deal with, if they were to engage the West, was both peculiarly restrained and peculiarly firm. It was restrained in the sense that it said the West, following the Polish crisis of 1980-81, was still willing to reengage with the East economically and in other ways. It did not announce a new Western offensive to exploit the weakening of the Stalinist system. But it was firm in demanding a political quid pro quo. There would be reengagement *only* if the system changed politically and *only* in return for significant political liberalization. The approach did not carry enough of a threat to be rejected out of hand, but it was firm enough to goad some Soviets and some East Europeans into further steps along the road to reform. They felt they could afford to gamble that through reform they could keep, rather than lose, power. The approach had the effect of being wise, for it created an effective Western option for the East.

Nevertheless, this Western option was a bridesmaid. The bride of the revolution appeared on the *eastern* rim of the area's historic dependence. It was the lifting of the Soviet hand, beginning in 1987 with Moscow's renunciation of the use of force to maintain Soviet hegemony over Eastern Europe, that allowed the revolutions of 1989 to take place at all. The Soviet leadership under Gorbachev was driven primarily by its own domestic imperatives. But these included keeping the Soviet Union a world power, and here the Western option was indeed a factor, for this leadership was cognizant at last of how much *the Soviet Union* depended on the outside world. It wanted a breathing space in international affairs that would permit it to refurbish the country for global competition.

To get that breathing space, the leadership sought to change the Western perception of the Soviet Union as an aggressive, expansive, militarized great power. The intermittent spectacle and constant threat of Soviet tanks rolling through East European capitals had been at the core of that image. To eliminate it, the Soviets under Gorbachev were willing to gamble that they could preserve the essentials of Soviet influence in Eastern Europe without the threat or use of tanks. They hoped they could count on Eastern Europe's deep economic dependence on Soviet raw materials and markets and on political reforms that would force the area's ruling parties to become competitive in open and more legitimate political systems, just like the Soviet party. At critical moments the Soviets were even willing to connive, to exert direct pressure, to push Eastern Europe in the approved direction.

We can now look back and see that, of course, the gamble failed at both the political and economic ends of the stick.[10] The creator and "last resort" of Soviet power in Eastern Europe, the Soviet armed forces (or what is left of them) are pulling out. They have left Hungary and former Czechoslovakia, and they are due out of the ex-GDR and Poland by 1994. The residue still provokes fears, but these are increasingly fears of public disorder and arms and materiel trafficking by rogue elements. The main brake on their departure seems increasingly to be the inadequacy of resettlement quarters at home. At the very least, ex-Soviet forces are no longer capable of projecting power to Eastern Europe.

Potential indirect means of asserting dominion or even influence have also fallen away. During the Gorbachev years, efforts to create new and more open political systems for reformed parties to compete in often foundered on the parties' obdurate refusal to reform. There was reform, but it often took place without them or against them, and when they themselves participated it was often too late. In the free, or even the semi-free, elections that marked the transition from party rule, the parties—unreformed, reformed, or in the process of reforming—were then most often swept out of power. Post-Communist parties under Social Democratic labels have succeeded throughout most of the area in keeping only between a tenth and a sixth of the electorate. They have retained or regained power or a piece of power in "Yugoslavia," the former republics of Serbia and Montenegro, in Macedonia, in Romania, and in Lithuania; in Bulgaria they are the largest opposition party.[11] In most places they appeal mainly to the remnants of the old party/state apparatus and their families. Nowhere are they any longer Leninist in any recognizable sense, except perhaps in Serbia and Montenegro, and even there the party has changed more than just its name. And of course in the meantime, the Soviet power centers, which used such parties to assert dominion, have disintegrated along with the Soviet Union. Those that have risen in their place are embattled, preoccupied with their own survival. But even new power centers that wished to use party ties to assert dominion from the East would find they no longer had adequate partners in the area.

At the economic end, any Soviet hopes of exploiting Eastern Europe's structural dependence on Soviet raw materials and Soviet markets were also blasted beyond hope of recall first by the galloping degeneration of the Soviet economy and then by the breakup of the Soviet Union itself. The East Europeans needed to keep alive as much trade as possible with the Soviets and their successors. That has perhaps made them even more tactful and constructive in their dealings with the sick colossus and follow-on colossi than they would have been otherwise. Certainly the decline in "Soviet" trade, of between one-third and two-thirds, that they have all registered has seriously aggravated (and made it more difficult for them to escape) the "reform recession" they are all undergoing. All are busy trying to reactivate and expand trade and business ties, usually on a barter basis because of the collapse of the ruble and the Soviet and post-Soviet hard currency penury. But most have had significant and even surprising success in shifting exports, even those from creaking state firms, to the much more demanding Western markets. Nowhere in Eastern Europe can Russia or other successor states realistically hope to use trade and business to generate decisive political influence against the will of the area countries themselves.

With the lifting of first the dominion and then the threat of the East, the shape of Eastern Europe's dependence on the outside world has changed fundamentally and for years to come. But that means neither that the area has become totally independent nor that dependence has simply shifted from East to West. It may be that no country can be totally independent in today's world. It is certain that the West has been neither able nor willing to step into the East European power position vacated by the Soviet Union. Indeed, the West's refusal to become deeply and directly involved may be one cause of the ex-Yugoslav crisis. Elsewhere, this general diffidence has been more benign and sometimes even helpful. The Eastern threat has evaporated, but Western tutelage has not replaced it.

This is not to say that Western engagement in the East European transformation has not been substantial. Political support has been steady. Economic assistance in all its various forms has amounted to tens of billions of dollars. There has been plenty of advice, and there have been plenty of advisors. Western businessmen are not only making money but are helping their local partners learn how to make money in market conditions. At certain moments in many countries, Western support has played a critical role in getting and keeping things moving. The $1 billion fund to help stabilize złoty convertibility in December 1989 helped make Polish "shock therapy" possible; the 50 percent reduction in Poland's official debt agreed to by the Paris Club in March 1991 helped Poland keep going. But, looking at the area as a whole over these three years, what is important to remember is that except in eastern Germany East European reform has been primarily a bootstrap operation, self-generated and self-supported as far as it has come.

The mainspring of reform has therefore been domestic. Just as domestic imperatives generated the revolutions of 1989 once external circumstances permitted them to operate, so too, after four decades of Communist rule artificially imposed and maintained by the East, the deep and broad domestic political consensus for joining (or rejoining) Europe has been the driving force behind reform. To a greater or lesser degree, that consensus marks every East European polity and determines both the goals they set for themselves in the post-Communist era and the instruments they have for achieving them. More than what Western Europe and the rest of the West have *done*, it is what Western Europe and the rest of the West *are* that fuels and directs the East European transformation.

For the Europe that Eastern Europe wishes to become is the Europe of liberal democracy and economic prosperity, based on the market that the West advertised since the beginning of the Cold War and made a reality as the decades rolled on. The widespread East European aspiration to join that Europe is not always a stabilizing factor. In ex-Yugoslavia, for instance, this aspiration promotes division between the "Northwest" (Slovenia and Croatia) and the Serbs. But for those who reject joining or rejoining Europe—the Serbs, the Russian right, integral nationalists of every stripe— their rejection has had the effect of marginalizing them politically.[12] Generally, this hunger and thirst to become European, or become European "again," is strong, and it helps stabilize turbulent processes, because it provides a centrist core of belief and a program that resists the encroachment of the radicalisms proliferating at the margins of East European politics.

THEIR NATIONALISMS OLD AND NEW

The best known of these East European radicalisms is nationalism. At its worst, it is also the most vigorous. The horrors of the wars in Croatia and Bosnia remind us after all these years of how strong and brutal nationalism can be. The scale of the killing and raping is sufficient proof that nationalism is alive and awful in this part of the world. It is also the most publicized of the radicalisms that have emerged or reemerged. Scholars and journalists, scrambling (and sometimes scampering) to keep up with events they did not predict, have kept East European nationalism continuously before the eyes of Western publics and elites[13] to the point where it overshadows every other characteristic of the region's experience.

This fixation, which is understandable given the natural outrage at nationalism's resurrection and the bloodshed it is causing, extends beyond explication to interpretation. Scholars and journalists are struggling to make sense of the nationalist phenomenon. So, too, are diplomats and policymakers (as the inertial attachments of Western governments to the disintegrating Eastern federal states showed). And very often they resort to "history," and thus take the easy way back to the theory of "inherent" East European nationalism and its corollary—that the area has simply reverted to the conditions of its first liberation after World War I.

There may be something to that theory. But, as this book has tried to show, the history (and thus the present moment) is in fact more complex. For nationalism, like dependence, has had its own "long march" through the experience of Eastern Europe and its peoples. It has never been a "given." It is always a contingent and specific phenomenon like all the rest, changing its form, its weight, and its impact over time, and depending on circumstance.[14]

Even nationalism's march through the Communist period was tortuous. At the outset, together with agrarianism, it was the great ideological alternative to Communist rule in the area. The East European societies had only recently been consolidated on a national basis, first by the state-building efforts of the interwar period, then by wartime oppression, finally by fear of communism itself. The first Communist rulers ruthlessly suppressed its human carriers. But, once it had been decided to keep national boundaries and much of the traditional state structure intact in

Eastern Europe, the Stalinists were forced to steal their nationalist opponents' clothes.

From the beginning, every regime proclaimed itself the embodiment of all that was best in the local *national* tradition, while trying to define that tradition to its (Marxist) advantage. Even after unwanted elements had been excluded by definition, the national issue slipped into the heart of Communist politics via the service entrance as "National Communism"— the question of legitimate separate national paths to the agreed common goal. For the first decade of Communist rule, nationalism was the ghost in the machine, the dominant issue in a system where "everything is political, except politics."[15] The partial legitimation of separate paths after 1956 partially defused it, and the subsequent decades (until the 1980s) were marked by small accommodations, small tolerances, and small differentiations among the regimes.

But the framework remained resolutely Marxist in its insistence that nationalism was basically a class ideology within the previous system, a remnant condemned to disappear. Only one regime, in Romania, made a semi-serious attempt to reconcile national and international interests as an issue of Marxist doctrine.[16] But the Ceauşescu regime was such a peculiar hybrid that the result was mere wooden words, which could not inject sap into a tree that was dying anyway. All the regimes were singularly ill-equipped to deal with the challenge of the 1980s, when new opposition groups simply side-stepped the whole Marxist framework and invented a new ideology of rights.

This new ideology had a place for national, ethnic and minority rights, but at least in "mainstream dissidence," it also went far beyond them by seeking to integrate them into an overarching framework of universal validity. The regimes were fearful of being outflanked by new coalitions that might include portions of the party/state apparatus, to whom rights and nationalism also appealed. They proved inept at dealing with an ideology that virtually ignored their *raison d'être*, and they tried to manage the challenge with a panoply of instruments based on power. They repressed, they isolated and insulated, they tried somewhat to buy off and coopt nationalism with their propaganda and their policies. Neither very successful nor unsuccessful, the bulky regimes and the slender oppositions thus spent the 1980s moving crab-wise toward the exit of Communist power without realizing that it was in front of them. Communism's end in 1989 left the oppositions alone, blinking in the sunshine of freedom, with nationalism one of the tools that they brought in their kitbags for the power struggles ahead.

In the three years since, nationalism has been a political force everywhere. These were, after all, revolutions buoyed forward by the thirst for national independence from foreign domination. Many of the East European intellectuals who led them and gave them their ideology were historically minded and therefore acutely conscious of the present power of their nation's past. Many of these polities are now nations in fact as well as in theory, and the new electorates are sensitive to national issues. "Who owns the national past?" is a live one. Some are demonstrably ready not just to vote but also to kill and die for their side's claim. East European nationalism is alive, and it is often desolating in its consequences.

But, given its history, what is equally striking to me is how *little* nationalism has conquered area-wide. Traditional nationalists—integral, exclusivist, maximalist—were a minority element in the victorious revolutionary coalitions. Since the revolutions they have proved strongest only in the area's two post-1918 federal states, Yugoslavia and Czechoslovakia, where the blanket of Communist rule prevented the articulation and then the working through of national and ethnic issues in political terms. Nationalists, indeed, helped bring these states down.

Their homologues in the former Soviet Union did the same there, and in spades. Indeed, the surge of traditional nationalism that many expected throughout Eastern Europe got underway in the Soviet territories with the first Armenian-Azerbaijani outbreak in February 1988. It has continued to roll forward ever since, taking the Union with it along the way.

But even in the former Soviet Union, it is worth pointing out, much of the surge has been anti-centralist rather than classically nationalist. As Martin Malia recently argued, the surge has been against Moscow the center of the party, not against Moscow the capital of Russia. It comes from local elites, many of them created and fostered by the Soviet state, struggling for local control over local economic, political, and cultural resources. Many do not yet represent nations in any East European sense. Since Communist federations were actually systems of highly ramified and thoroughly articulated central control, even that kind of localism can require dismantling the whole federation.[17]

Furthermore, even where nationalists have taken power they have usually done so in coalition with other forces, and they have always done so in specific circumstances. It has always happened in the course of contingent processes of cause and effect, rather than as a gift of East European history. Good historical accounts of such processes, say in Yugoslavia, are always useful antidotes to hysterical commentary (even from historians) arguing that today's tragedies are significantly rooted in events of the 6th century A.D.[18] Now that the federal states are gone it is worth registering the fact that they were the only polities in which old-fashioned nationalism gained a real purchase on power. Elsewhere in Eastern Europe, traditional nationalists and their parties have not done very well in the free political competitions (and especially the free elections) that have followed 1989. In most places, and in their crystalline form, they are marginal.

It is worth speculating briefly as to why this should be so. I suspect that one reason that nationalism has been so weak in most of Eastern Europe compared to the Soviet and post-Soviet varieties is that conditions in the East now resemble those in Eastern Europe itself before the war, when nationalism was in its heyday. I suspect Eastern Europe has now gone beyond them. Years of Communist oppression may have cut nationalism down to size, but the main reasons are structural. The minorities on which it traditionally battened have been much reduced, first by wartime destruction and postwar migration, then by emigration. Even under communism, societies became more and better articulated. Even under communism, national state structures were in the end consolidated.[19] The conditions—economic, social, political—that made nationalism the region's great political ideology before communism are simply no longer there.

Or perhaps it is only that changes in internal and external conditions have transformed most East European nationalism into something different, even though it keeps its basic attributes of generating self-definition, self-esteem, and a measure of security in a hostile world. That "something different" would be what Victor Zaslavsky has called "a new nationalist myth." It is a myth shared by the Slavic and Baltic republics of the former Soviet Union as well as post-Communist Eastern Europe. "It is the myth of belonging to European culture, the myth of return to real or imaginary European roots, the myth of normal development brutally interrupted by the Bolshevik experiment or the Russian aggression or both."[20]

It is this new myth that underpins the widespread political consensus for joining or rejoining Europe which dominates most of Europe's eastern half today. Careful readers of this book will have some basis for judging how much or how little the myth corresponds to reality. But that it is a myth they will have no doubt. It impels East Europeans toward liberal democracy and free market economics, because that is what Western Europe has come to represent; toward cooperation, devolution of sovereignty, and a degree of integration, rather than traditional divisiveness; and toward peaceful resolution of disputes, since over the past half century the whole West has undergone a radical change of opinion concerning the acceptability of war as an instrument of politics.[21] The new myth is strong, and it is still nationalist in that it defines what these nations are choosing for themselves. And it is still a myth.

And, as such, it leads us back to the 1918-1921 analogy, but this time as a true parallel. For at that moment, too, newly liberated Eastern Europeans looked to the West for models of liberal democracy and the free market. They felt free to do so because the great neighboring empires that had dominated them had dissolved, partly into themselves. Austria-Hungary was gone. Germany had embarked, uncertainly but hopefully, on the path to democracy. Russia was different, hostile, threatening, but also almost devoured by its own domestic preoccupations. In those days of total sovereignty, the East Europeans' image of Western Europe had no integration component. However, the East Europeans still sought forms to imitate and the closest possible cooperation with Western Europe. Cooperation at that time meant alliances, and alliances did not then require systematic homogeneity. But it was still felt that the more an East European polity resembled its stronger partner, the better the alliance would work. The linkages between external security and domestic arrangements are much stronger today, in the second decade after the signature of the Helsinki Final Act in 1975. But they were at work in 1918-21, too. And none of it helped in the end. After a decade, the East Europeans were again adrift on stormy seas, delivered to their own nationalisms and particularisms, and to foreign dependencies more excruciating than any they had yet experienced.

Most of the fault lay outside the East Europeans, with external actors and factors beyond their control. However, part of the fault was theirs. For the exploding nationalisms and particularisms of the interwar period led them in wildly diverging directions, not just in terms of solutions but also in terms of defining their problems. In fact, most major problems were common to them all. They were all heavily peasant societies with small middle classes and little capital for investment, managed by syncretic, bureaucratic elites, and bordered east and west by militarily stronger polities. But each came quickly to insist that it was unique and that its problems demanded particular solutions. This saved them from fascism and communism, for a while. It did not save them from strident competitiveness with each other, under authoritarian auspices, which led straight to a desperate search for outside sponsors and patrons. It did not save them from Nazi or Fascist or then Communist hegemony.

The great difference today is that the *new* nationalist myth, of returning to Europe, is integrally linked to domestic priorities. In the first moment of liberation after World War I, most East European nations were emerging from different systems. They were, or included, shards of the old empires. Today they are all emerging from what was to the end, despite marginal diversification within it as the years went by, a single system. Thus they all share the same basic problems of political and economic transformation and they know it. The practical underpinning for the common ideological solution they have chosen should therefore be immensely stronger than that which supported the democratic/market experiments of the 1920s.

But the solution is still a myth, and that leads us in turn back to the third characteristic feature of the area's historical experience and how it looks today.

THEIR POSTPEASANT HERITAGE

The Stalinist Vyacheslav Mikhailovich Molotov lived to the ripe old age of 96, long enough to see Gorbachev in power and long enough to regain membership in the party that had expelled him under Khrushchev. During his long decades of forced retirement he gave interviews, now published, which show that he remained both unrepentant and sharp. In one of them, from 1973, Molotov predicted that

> There'll be a fight in the party yet. Khrushchev was no accident. It's a peasant country—the right deviation is strong. Where's the guarantee they won't come to power? It's entirely possible that the anti-Stalinists—most likely the Bukharinists—will soon take power.[22]

Whether or not this is what actually happened with Gorbachev is an argument for other historians. What is of interest in our context is what it could possibly mean to say that the Soviet Union in 1973 was a "peasant country" whose peasant character was likely to produce certain kinds of political results. In 1973 the Soviet Union was no longer a very "peasant" country in demographic and sociological terms, and since then it (and its successors) has become ever less so. Nor was Molotov talking about the direct engagement of peasants in the political process. So he must have been thinking in some other terms.

Given the Stalinist attachment to "structuralist politics," I suspect Molotov was saying that a society's peasant origins mark all its structures and are likely to produce specific ideological and political results, even without peasants as agents, until all but a few have put those origins decisively behind them. "Peasant countries without peasants" brings to mind the "anti-Semitism without Jews" that was emerging in Eastern Europe at about the same time. But that too is another argument. What is clear to me at least is that Molotov's approach, understood in this way, helps explain some important things not just about the Soviet Union under late communism but also about Eastern Europe in 1993.

For if most of Eastern Europe is indeed defining its political and economic directions in terms of a great new "nationalist myth," it means that the East European intelligentsias are continuing to play an extraordinary role in shaping the area's destinies. Mythmaking has been their historic specialty, and it is their special role in the revolutions of 1989 and the transformations underway since that constitutes the area's most distinctive feature. It is a role that Western intellectuals—intellectuals in the Western world that Eastern Europe now wishes to join—no longer have (if they ever really had it). It defines, by contrast, the area's peasant heritage and (now) postpeasant character.

Intellectuals in Eastern Europe have assumed this role partly by sub-traction, partly by their own agency. Under late communism, these were still societies that had no middle classes with independent economic power to act as gearboxes for the mediation of social interests and values. They still had peasants, though fewer than before. They had more workers than ever before. They still had syncretic, bureaucratized political elites. These elites were bigger but also much less confident than at any previous time in the Communist era, and they were tending toward fragmentation, venality, and corruption. Corruption had always existed in these postpeasant societies. But as Communist ideology bled away as a cohesive force, corruption started to gallop. It seems to me that somewhere in the 1970s quantity turned to quality (to apply the old Marxist concept) and something broke in the regimes' capacity to convince anyone that their right to rule was based on anything but force.[23]

This in turn created an ideological void, and it was into this void that the intelligentsias, inside and outside the party, stepped. They were demoralized by their dalliance with communism, but they too were larger than ever before. And in the absence of middle classes, the task of societal mediation fell to them. Once again, as in pre-Communist days, all the other groups increasingly looked to them for leadership.

To a degree unknown in the West, the kind of leadership that was expected was moral leadership. This had been true in pre-Communist times, it accounted for the Communists' efforts to strap intellectuals to the chariot wheel of power, and it was still true. The churches, too, had an increasing role to play, especially in Poland. But the lead in creating and forming public opinion could be taken only by the intelligentsia. What people were looking for was not theory and analysis but moral guidance, guidance on ultimate values, on how to live rightly.

In principle, communism had tried to replace the government of men with the administration of things, to consign morality to the sphere of private life at last. But in practice the Communists had emerged from the same soil as the societies they ruled. They carried over the personalized we-versus-they view of politics from their conspiratorial origins into the way they ruled. And they felt themselves obliged to politicize every possible aspect of national and social life. The result, in practice, was not to uproot moralism from public life but to drive its roots even deeper into these societies. Politics became neither more nor less moralistic as the Communists' strategic options narrowed and they themselves became more corrupt. All that changed was that they themselves lost any moral claim to rule and put that claim—the mandate of heaven, as it is called in East Asia—up for grabs.

Slowly, in some places, and increasingly almost everywhere, some parts of the intelligentsia shook off, or worked their way out of, their flirtation with power and recovered the self-definition that had marked their origins in the area. After all, they had begun as an aspiring "governments of souls" set off from the existing power structures by their very function. Before 1944 they had seen themselves as standard-bearers and personal exemplars of truth and integrity: in a word, of morality. In the 1970s and 1980s portions of the East European intelligentsias rediscovered and reintegrated themselves into that historic tradition. The Communists had never entirely stamped it out. They had tried to co-opt the intelligentsias for their own purposes, and where they had not succeeded they had driven them into shameful internal exile, and for some countries, into external exile as well. But they had never denied the importance of intellectuals or their social role. And now intellectuals began to take up the moral torch the Communists were allowing to slip from their own hands. The intellectuals developed an ideology of rights—social, national, and especially individual—that was set against the unjust power structure and morally superior to it. As Adam Michnik put it in 1988, late in the game but at a time when no one could know how the game would end, "In our century, the struggle for freedom has been fixated on power, instead of the creation of civil society. It has therefore always ended up in the concentration camp."[24] There was even a name for it: anti-politics.

And they began to act on this ideology. "Anti-politics" was profoundly political in these societies. This was not simply because under communism *everything* was political but also because, in the East European intelligentsia tradition, personal morality was necessarily social in character. It could not be confined to a sense of personal mission. Throughout their early history, East European intellectuals had felt obliged by historical and social situations to hold out their standard of morality to others.

They thereby took over functions that are fulfilled by other groups in the Western world. Even at home, their problem had always been that there were so few others ready to follow. But that did not deter them. In the tradition, intellectuals fought for personal integrity but believed that it could not be achieved outside some larger framework, a framework of social, and above all, national integrity. Social action on behalf of higher national goals was part of the package, their true vocation.

For the intellectuals themselves, in the 1970s and 1980s recovery of their original social role was a tentative, painful, and partial process. It sometimes seemed that the impulse to recover was most urgent among those who had been most compromised by collusion with power or among their children. But recover they did. Group by small group, in country after country, harried and harassed by the authorities everywhere, they reconstructed their roots. At the time, most of them were desperately isolated. Their struggles struck responsive chords among Western intellectuals and governments. But the endless Western protests and petitions against regime repression of individuals or one or another of these groups often seemed futile throwbacks to an earlier era, rather than telltale signs that a new era was emerging.

Yet they made a virtue of their isolation, and the truth was that they were not so isolated as they thought. Even when they themselves were convinced that they were only recovering and refurbishing the best of their own past, it slowly turned out that they were also responding to new social and political needs. Paradoxically for us, their "anti-politics" led them full circle back to the politics they were fleeing. And this was not simply because their tradition made personal morality unthinkable without social action. It was also because there was a societal demand for their moral leadership.

For in the course of the 1980s, intermittently at first and then in a landslide, it became apparent that the intellectuals' purist and personalist moralism struck a responsive chord in society that was louder and stronger than ever before in their mutual history. First in Poland, with Solidarity, then in pinches elsewhere, then in the great *journées* of the revolutionary year itself, like the burial of Imre Nagy's ashes in Budapest June 16 or the Czechoslovak general strike November 27, it turned out that the workers in their factories and the remaining peasants on their farms were moralists too, ready for moral leadership, ready to fight to make politics moral again, at least for one stunning moment. Turning from connivance with state power back to their historic isolation from the masses, the intellectuals found themselves—first in one or two countries and then, in 1989, in all of them—leading those very masses in national upheavals. The revolutions of 1989 caught each country in various phases of this process. But they were all "revolutions of the soul," to use the phrase from the Solidarity Revolution of 1980-81 in Poland. They were revolutions for independence, and especially national independence, led by the intelligentsia.

Of course that stunning moment could not last. Independence was both an end and a beginning, and what it began was another painful long march, this time through Dahrendorf's "economic vale of tears." In places and at times the very moralism that ushered it in could turn that vale into a slough of despond, crying out for radical and total solutions. But the passionate desire to live in truth and freedom was not the whole story, either. There were important social and political interests involved. The new "national myth" of joining Europe also expresses the belief of some intellectuals and managers, of some workers and peasants, of all those who wish to become middle-class, that liberal democracy and the market can help them achieve better lives for themselves and their families, as well as for their society and country.

Moreover, even the ideological mixing of democracy and the market into one formula has a basis in East Europeans' own experience. Once the Soviet hand was lifted after 1987, the East European revolutionary wave was driven forward by the spreading perception that political democracy was needed if economic recovery and modernization were ever to become possible. Given the entrenched interests opposing it, economic reform was impossible without democracy. This lesson sank in later in Soviet politics. There it was not driven home until the failed putsch of August 1991, whose authors represented precisely such interests. It was also a nail in the coffin of all the "Communist federal" states, for it finally made the real centralism that these federations masked seem intolerable to economic reformers as well as nationalists. Hence the rapid sequence from the August putsch to the breakup of the Soviet Union in December. Hence also the otherwise inexplicable fact that in the endgame of Czecho-Slovak breakup in 1992, the Czechs, under economic reformer Václav Klaus, were at least as eager to get out as the Slovaks under Vladimir Mečiar.

In other words, everyone in the post-Communist world now under-stood the lesson that Solidarity had learnt in 1980-81: there can be no successful economic reform without democracy (and independence). And the travail of the transition had validated another practical basis for that lesson. In the 1980s the transition was still a thing of the future. During the 1980s it was the interlocking nature of the Communist systems they were fighting that made oppositions demand democracy as a precondition of effective reform. But even then the pain of the reform process, if it could ever be set in train, was predictable, and many of them predicted it. They foresaw that only through democracy would it be possible to secure the assent of these societies for the sacrifices that economic reform would require. Democracy could mean (as in the end it did mean) the departure of the Communists. If and when they conceived a post-Communist future, the oppositions suspected that democracy would not guarantee stable political support for economic transformation. But they also felt it would be the only vehicle through which such support could possibly be built and maintained.

The experience of the 1990s so far has validated that prediction, and on an area-wide basis. On the surface, the polities where democratic politics are newest have been those most racked and riven by political (and often national) passions, most inclined to put off hard choices for economic reform, and most tempted by the view that democracy and market reform are incompatible in post-Communist conditions. Much more conclusive has been the commonality of the problems they face and the interdependence of the political and economic solutions required to solve them.

Once the revolutionary wave had passed, it left behind fledgling democracies presiding over devastated socialist economies. All were com-mitted to economic reform in the direction of the free market, but all were saddled in the meantime with state-owned and state-run economies that had to be converted to mixed economies based on private enterprise. Conversion was sure to bring recession, which only more conversion could end. The task of mastering or even managing this quandary through democratic means was common to them all, and the effort to do so has evoked what Martin Malia has called a number of "regularities" across the area.[25]

First, as already pointed out, under late communism it came to be recognized that successful economic reform required political liberalization and democratization. Recognizing that helped show communism the door. Second, however, once party rule is gone that relationship is abruptly reversed. It then becomes evident that economic progress must kick in if democratic government is to be sustained. Third, the economic reform process starts fast, but it soon slows as it runs up against societal inertia or resistance. Governments can rather easily put in place macroeconomic measures—for which the government role is generally recognized as primary—like price liberalization, the end of subsidies, and currency reform. But the next step, microeconomic measures involving the privatization of existing state enterprises and the creation of modern private production, requires society's assent and initiative to be successful, and governments discover that such assent and initiative are extremely hard to generate.[26] Fourth, in the process, "the omnicompetent Party, . . . in dying, passe(s) on its multitudinous membership to the new order, for the simple reason that the *nomenklatura* system made Party membership and favor a condition for getting and holding almost all the skilled jobs in each society. It is with such human material that a new democratic order must be built."

At this point an even darker "regularity" appears: "the inevitability of demagogic exploitation of the people's lassitude and anxiety after years of communist decay and the disappointments of liberation."[27] Such exploitation is obviously taking place. But the real question is how widely it can succeed in capturing political support. The answer turns in part on how one views the society in which support is being sought.

Many of the new-old governments of Eastern Europe and the former Soviet Union are composed of men and women who not so many months or years ago were carried to power on a wave of moral fervor and hope that was almost beyond conception. Today they are shocked to find that they are just governments after all. They are obliged to deal with terrible problems, and they find it terrible that the baleful eye that these societies cast on all government is now turning on them, as "them," after they had convinced themselves for at least one bright moment that "us" was all there was. Pique comes naturally to such governors, and with it the temptation to see society as one heavy and inertial lump, or as a ship of fools, unwilling to be steered toward its own salvation. They were all formed under communism: "They got it into my head, they just stuffed me with it, and they've done the same to you!" Lech Wałęsa yelled at his old comrades in the Gdasńk shipyard in the spring of 1992.[28] That, of course, was also the way the communists defined their problem when they thought of the old regimes they had replaced. But on that point there is no reason to agree with either the communists or their successors. In fact, East European societies are already more differentiated than that.

This differentiation helps account for the diversification of political and economic reform processes across the area. Western commentators are describing it as fast as conference proceedings and other collections of articles can be brought to print. The "regularities" are still there and are still striking. In particular, the nexus between liberal democracy and market reform still holds. Indeed, new economic reasons are now being adduced for it in addition to the political. For instance, it may well be that individual rights secured by legal and regulatory institutions are critical to economic efficiency because their strength "in long-standing democracies is . . . a major explanation of the toleration by these democracies of large variations in short-run rates of return across firms, industries, and localities." But that does not help much in the short run that these new governments and old firms, industries and localities are facing. In that short run—on which the long run also depends—the specifics, the particularities, are becoming more important all the time.[29]

Over the long run, the differentiations within societies should help the new governments to deal with them, as long as democracy can be maintained. Eastern Europe still has peasants and workers and bureaucrats and intellectuals, and the pieces of the middle class that are emerging from each still bear the marks of their origins, including the contempt of some of those they are leaving behind in the process of adapting to market conditions. But the proportions among these groups have changed radically, almost out of recognition, toward structures that are altogether more "modern" than those of half a century ago and that are potentially capable of generating stable democracy and economic growth.

Differentiation and modernization have been masked by the resurrection of the intelligentsia on the ruins of the Marxist ideology and power structure in the 1970s and 1980s and by the role of intellectuals in 1989 and the years since. One of the best of them has suggested that the opposition movements of communism's declining years were really the dialectic antithesis of Leninism, and as such, part and parcel of the departing order rather than of the new era we now live in.[30] That appeals to my sense of what has gone and is going on. But I also suspect the intellectuals will have an important role for years to come. The question is what that role will be.

For in politics and society the intelligentsias are now hedged in on one side by a massive managerial class (ex-*nomenklatura* but also, as and if economic reform proceeds, non-*nomenklatura*) and on the other by a massive working class. These are not "classes" in the traditional Marxist sense, defined by their relation to the means of production. But they exist as self-aware, self-defined groups in society, *Klassen für Sich*. They are not doomed to clash; indeed, they are not even doomed to exist.

Ex-Communists are tempting political targets; "de-Communization" is a real political issue everywhere. It is a moral issue that evokes huge passions, which can lead straight back to the most atavistic postpeasant strains in these battered national psyches. To take a recent instance, in late 1992 the widow of the Albanian Stalinist dictator Enver Hoxha received a Western visitor in the prison cell where she was awaiting her show trial on corruption charges. She said she was not allowed a radio, but she could see her children every ten days or two weeks, and they brought her newspapers. Asked if she were also allowed visits from friends, her reply was, "Friends? What are friends?"[31] The survival of "them" and "us" and the shrinkage of the "us" down to family members only could not be more startlingly clear. Albania may be extreme, but politics and morals still remain closely intertwined in all the post-Communist countries so soon after the "revolutions of the soul."

Nevertheless, de-Communization is not *simply* a moral issue. It is also economic and social. What drives it is the success of ex-Communists in finding profitable places for themselves in the emerging democracies and market economies and the envy that success arouses among those having trouble keeping up.[32] It is the fact that these are many and now vote that makes the issue a prime candidate for demagogic exploitation.

Tarring the industrial working class with the brush of Communist origin is less frequent. Workers are more likely to suffer from economic reform than bureaucrats and managers, if only because there are more of them, and more of them are voters. They are therefore spared the sharp edge of the de-Communization impulse as individuals and courted as troops for democratic governance.[33] Where strong unions exist, as in Poland, they can help put together reform governments; where governments are wise and beholden to these unions, as in Poland, together they can negotiate the terms of further progress toward reform.

But as reform expands outward and downward from the macro-economic commanding heights to privatization of the state sector, and once trade and services and the smaller producing firms are delivered over to private entrepreneurship, and as the social safety net decays, the mastodon heavy industries remain. By modern Western standards they are heavy indeed.[34] They are the most difficult to privatize. And despite extensive shedding of the work force over the past three years, they are still home to large portions of Eastern Europe's working class. It is therefore more and more popular to recall that they were the proudest creations of communism and that the working class housed in them was not just created but favored by the old regime, in terms of wages and perquisites and ideology, as the vanguard of world socialism's inevitable systemic triumph.

Yet the tar brush of Communist origin misses the main point for all these groups. To the extent that they are products of communism, it is because Communist regimes forced on them all a degree of social homogeneity and self-consciousness already artificial in non-Communist societies. Moreover, "Communist societies" were recruited from the peasant societies that preceded them, and they carried their primary features forward, transfigured but visible to the naked eye, into the present. Today's great struggling factories are manned by the children and grandchildren of subsistence peasants. It was their children, in turn, together with smaller numbers of peasants straight from the farm and the progeny of old intelligentsia families that had made their peace with the regime, who staffed the *nomenklatura* via the regime's educational system.

It is therefore no wonder that workers in privatized factories indignantly appeal to the state to save them after their new private owners have absconded. It is no wonder that people expect to be paid according to the dignity of their group's calling, rather than their economic efficiency. It is no wonder that there is a strong strain of support among Polish workers for Employee Stock Option Plans (ESOP), as a residue of the hunger for self-sufficiency that their grandfathers brought with them from the farms and that their fathers thought they saw realized in workers' self-management in 1956. It is no wonder that all these men and women bring to the task of transformation their moralism, their right-or-wrong conceptions of politics, their us-or-them view of leadership, their hankering after total solutions, their status approach to every issue of efficiency. It is no wonder that reform is difficult.

For the groups to which they belong, the groups that were artificially preserved under Communism and in terms of which they now define themselves, are doomed to disintegrate in the post-Communist world. Economically, ideologically, and then *politically*, East European managers and workers are up for grabs. Just how they split, how their components reconfigure, and how they relate to each other and to government will largely determine the direction of political change in the area.

That in turn will depend importantly on what happens to the East European intelligentsias. The intelligentsia's tradition, its weight, and its relation to other groups vary by country. So will the results. Everywhere, however, the intelligentsia has the option of sticking to its newly recovered traditional role of expressing and representing pure and pristine moral values, classifying and labelling political and economic issues in moral terms, and using moral categories to defend and perpetuate the truth of the past against the angry and complex present. There continues to be a social demand for such a role. It is a genuine option. If they are determined, skillful, and unwise enough, intellectuals can delay the disintegration of the old social, political, and ideological blocs and preserve—for a while— their recovered privileged role in mediating among them.

There are powerful forces pushing them to pull back. One of the pre-existing intelligentsia traditions that communism reinforced was a technocratic and rationalistic approach that sought comprehensive solutions, mechanically applied, to every problem. Communism was an extreme variant of this approach, but it is implicit in the East European intelligentsia's sense of its special historic mission to speak for society and its best interests. It may well be revivified by the disappointments accompanying the piecemeal ad hoc reforms that the transition will require. To command and maintain society's support it is tempting to advertise the transition as a total reconstruction from scratch—just the kind the intelligentsia has historically felt called upon to lead. The danger is that politics will once again be seen as a preserve of experts. If so, paternalism, the psychology of dependence, the division of rulers and ruled into "them" and "us"—the whole panoply of traditional attitudes brought forward under and by communism—would survive not just unscathed but also revalidated. The kind of active participation by citizens that is now essential to legitimate the actions of democratic states and governments would be beyond reach. And in its absence, both democracy and the possibility of constructing effective market economies could well disappear together.[35]

But that is neither the inevitable nor even the most likely prospect. For East European intellectuals have another new option, which I think is equally genuine. This is the option of defining terms and programs for the breakup of the old homogeneities and for their reconfiguration into newer, more modern social and political structures.[36]

The struggle between these options is now underway. As it develops, terrible things are being done. Zviad Gamsakhurdia—Georgian dissident, then President, now guerrilla leader against the government that expelled him—did not begin as a politician: he is the son of Georgia's greatest modern novelist. Wonderful things are also being said.[37] The struggle to define and redefine the roles of the intelligentsia, of the working class, of society in politics is visible everywhere.

This struggle is at work in the emerging definitions of future options that are beginning to surface and are in competition with the new myth of Europe. Nationalism is the most familiar to us, because its explosion from the submarine world to which the regimes had tried to confine it has been the most spectacular and the bloodiest in its effects. Many in the West feel that the area's main task today is to leave behind the internecine squabbles rooted in the past, so that it can concentrate on adapting to the democratic and market structures of the larger Europe it wishes to join.[38]

That definition is certainly not unwise. Radical nationalism is of course the most traditional option for East European intellectuals, the surest in its therapy—for it solders them forever, in the mind, to the rest of their societies, and the most familiar to them as well as to us. But it also seems a bit old-fashioned these days, especially vis-a-vis its "European" competitor. And such is the strength of the latter that other options are starting to appear.

One is the pastorale, a vision of a more humane, more harmonious, more moral, and better world, which is projected for the future, at the end of Eastern Europe's current turmoil. Václav Havel has been its sweetest singer. It reached its highest pitch in his "My Dream for Czechoslovakia," published in mid-1992: "Every main street will have at least two bakeries, two sweet shops, two pubs, and many small shops, all privately owned and independent."[39] Havel's stubborn musing on the compatibility of politics and morality certainly expresses a genuine dilemma for intellectuals throughout the area. But the pastoral vision he projects to resolve it flees the nasty or awful present in which politics and morality must somehow be harmonized in practice if reform is to proceed. It points more backward than forward.

I think the same may be said of the nostalgics on the Left, who are still trying to find a place in the area's future for a vision of a better, more harmonious, more just *socialist* world amid the ruins of "real socialism." To my mind, this vision is as pastoral as Havel's, at least at this point. It has some local grounding in the memories of the East German revolution of 1989, which was led by people who shared it and who are now bitter at having been swept from the political board in the elections that followed.[40] As a kind of counterpoint it also resonates constantly in reportage on accelerating social differentiation, the rawness of the market, the tattering of the social safety net in the area.[41] Everywhere, however, it bears the terrible burden of mass memories of what "socialism" actually was and actually became in people's lives. Still, the pain of the transition could give it renewed purchase on the area's political imagination at some point in the future, especially if and where reform fails.

More palpable than either pastorale and at least for the time being more potent, is the emerging ideology of the Third Way. Like Havel's, it harks back to a barely remembered East European past. In the early postwar period, the concept of countries picking a path between failed capitalism and the threat of Soviet Stalinism had some appeal. It involved multiple forms of property, coalitions of democratic and non-democratic parties, and a great deal of national self-regard and nationalist rhetoric. Stalinism drove it underground. And although it resurfaced briefly in the longings of regime Communists contemplating the devolution of some of their power in the 1980s, by then the West had developed systems capable of providing both abundance and elementary social justice, and the Third Way was a dead option in East European political terms.[42]

Now, however, the pain of transition is resurrecting the Third Way, albeit in different forms. Only a few speak of it openly. In Poland, at least, they are politicians of the largest peasant party, who are seeking to cleanse its roots—it was a client of The Party throughout the Communist period—by harking back to agrarianism without naming its name.[43] Indeed, the political appeal of joining or rejoining democratic, market Europe is still so strong that the Third Way is an option that has no form and has not yet found its ideologist. For the same reason, radical nationalism dare not show its naked face in most places; it appears under the veil of rights, and if possible, in combination with other political forces.

The Third Way will therefore need an ideological cloak different from traditional agrarianism, traditional nationalism, and sheer nostalgia. The material for such a cloak certainly exists in the deep and widespread sense that the state is responsible for welfare and social justice. It is a heritage of the whole history of these weak societies and weak economies. It thus antecedes communist rule, which reinforced it. It was discredited with communist rule. But it remains alive under the ashes.

Speculating on what political force could mobilize it, Malia points to "an ultrapink social democracy" and looks to the powerful remnants of the nomenklatura to provide its cadres. "The principal threat to a positive exit from communism is not aggressive nationalism or saber-rattling fascism; the postcommunist world is too devastated for such exertions. The principal threat is a relapse into statist stagnation with a welfare face."[44]

I suspect that the ideological definition of the Third Way will be more diffuse, and that its appeal will extend well beyond the *nomenklatura* to elements of the working class, the peasantry, and of course the intelligentsia, whose mission it is to define ideologies. It may be all the more insidious for that reason. Even before communism the East European state was precious, to a degree that we in the West have forgotten, as an anchor for weak sovereignties. As the vehicle of party rule under communism it was pervasive, "omnicompetent," to a degree that the West has been largely spared. In the West, welfare statism is one option on a diverse political spectrum. In the European East, it constitutes the bulk of lived experience. For all its diffuseness it is therefore overwhelmingly weightier. That it is also the main alternative and threat to modernization in its "European" form I have no doubt.

THEIR OPEN FUTURE

If such is indeed the threat, how can it be met and overcome? I would argue that the peoples of Eastern Europe have more and better assets for that struggle than ever before.

For in the Eastern Europe of 1993 workers and managers and intellectuals are no longer corks bobbing on a sea of peasants. They are now large groups, by world standards very well educated, and self-conscious as well as powerful—actually and potentially—to a degree unprecedented in the area's history. In terms of social and ideological structure, and even political and economic structure, the proper parallel is no longer the Eastern Europe of 1938 but the Southwestern Europe (France, Italy, Spain) of the 1950s. Admittedly, that parallel opens up a wide range of possibilities for development. No one wishes to see versions of the French Mays of 1958 or 1968 in the European East. But the parallel opens onto a future fundamentally different from the European East of the 1930s.

Moreover, I hope to have shown that this new Eastern Europe was not only created from outside. It also helped create itself. Its dogged determination to *remain* itself had something to do with that creativity. Under Communist rule, the goal of many, even most East Europeans, was to endure: *not* to change, *not* to accept alien ways of thinking and alien rationales for acting, even when they were forced to accept alien structures and alien practices (including some that were not so alien after all). That was the part of their experience, once the rock of communism lifted, of which they were the proudest; it was the part with which the West was most familiar.

That was not new. Isaiah Berlin reminds us that in the 18th century, "Rousseau, the most spell-binding voice of this general revolt (against inauthenticity), told the Poles to resist encroachment by the Russians by obstinately clinging to their national institutions, their habits, their ways of life—not to confirm, not to assimilate; the claims of universal humanity were incarnated, for the time being, in their resistance."[45] It was also not the whole story.

For under the pressure of Communist rule, even *not* to change—to safeguard the basics—meant change. This was because it required East Europeans to identify for themselves what was essential to their personal and national experiences, like the family and the nation, and to jettison the rest. As they fought to save themselves through the decades of dark and shameful compromises they left some things behind, including some ugly ballast from their history. And over the years even those who wished to change them, or those among them who accepted the need for change only halfheartedly, regretfully, or angrily—the Stalinist rulers, their allies in the intelligentsias and working classes, and their children—had to accept this stubbornness and its consequences. They, too, were forced to adjust first their policies and then themselves if they were to hope to preserve what *they* considered essential in the strategic program (building socialism, as it was called) that they and the Soviets had embarked on in the 1940s and 1950s. Finally, in 1989, they were forced to abandon Communist power, and except in Romania, they did so without firing a shot at their compatriots, and they went on to seek new roles in freer countries, freer societies, freer economies.

The result was the emergence of a brand of social and political interaction that can scarcely be called political dialogue by any Western standard. There were frictions, agenda-setting, and compromises, day by day, year by year, over decades. These are the normal attributes of democratic politics throughout the Western world. But it was a process drenched in bitterness, bad will, and bad faith, both for governors and governed, and that too is a legacy of communism in Eastern Europe. The demands the process made were so absolute that compromise kept the bad name it had always had in these societies of moralistic politics. Political compromise meant moral compromise rather than the political management (working things out between equally legitimate groups competing for limited ends) that it means in the West.

Nevertheless, the process was real, and it produced a habit and practice of negotiation that was a tremendous asset for the future as the area ploughed through the 1990s. As a rule, the Communists struggled painfully to underpin their rule by force with a modicum of rule by assent, and as they were forced, step by step, from ideology to economic performance funded by Western credits and then back to politics, this bitter interactive process laid the basis for a politics of compromise. It was this politics of compromise that permitted the communists to depart, where they did depart, in peace, and where they did not depart, to engage peacefully in a new brand of democratic politics. And, if carried forward into the future, it is this politics of compromise that could perpetuate the new democracies; protect them with democratic political processes, the rule of law, and guarantees of individual and group freedom; and enable them to sustain the economic transformation that will be needed if they are to be stable and secure.

No future is ever entirely open. Just as the revolutions of 1989 were unmistakably East European revolutions, so too the processes they set in train have been unmistakably East European processes, recognizable to every reader of this book. Their results will be East European too.

But not for centuries has the East European future been *so* open. The open future is also a part of democratic politics. It is defined by what the area's history has made it, and it is threatened. There are alternatives to democratic politics, and the future could close down again, at least in some parts of the area. Democratic politics neither guarantees nor is guaranteed by the future. It is merely the best way the world has yet discovered to beat back the old ghosts, the demons inherited from a terrible past and the ancestral voices prophesying war, if they are to be beaten back.

The East European countries will remain small, dependent, postpeasant countries inclined to moralistic politics and drawn back toward their own historic habits of authoritarian, bureaucratic rule. And yet both they and the outside world have changed deeply over the past forty years or so. Stalinism, that modern epitome of authoritarian, bureaucratic rule, is discredited forever. The West has become liberal and democratic, and its market system can now generate prosperity without sacrificing social justice. It must work to stay that way, but I am convinced it can. The international system has become more comprehensive, more lawful, more institutionally creative, less tolerant of war as a means of resolving disputes. It must run in these directions to stay in place, but I am convinced it can. As far as Eastern Europe is concerned, it is essential that

Germany and Russia (and Italy) stay in that race, and I am convinced they can. Over the past three years, the political consensus for joining or rejoining that world, that West, and that race has remained firm in most of Eastern Europe. And more and more East Europeans have shown they know how to run too.

To lock in that capacity, and to keep and raise the pace, they are also developing the middle classes they have always lacked. For some, this is one of the main purposes of economic reform. Everywhere it is one effect of reform. For very many, depending on the specifics of tradition and experience and how reform is affecting them, it is controversial. It is hateful for some, welcome for others. In individual countries there will probably be a moment when the political view of these emerging middle-class people will crystallize one way or the other. In social reality they will cover the spectrum, but in political terms they will become either members of a legitimate social group or illegitimate parasites and bloodsuckers who deserve marginalization. But that moment has not yet come, and in the meantime they are multiplying like a force of nature all over the post-Communist world.[46]

And there is an old tradition, pre-dating and surviving communism, which says that the middle class can come of age. Having taken a hard swipe at the Polish working class during the strike summer of 1992, veteran Solidarity journalist Jan Walc admitted that

> at the same time that the myth of the miner departs into the past, together with his labor that no one any longer needs, the time is also coming for my group, the intelligentsia, which is already an anachronism in today's world, which would long since have disappeared had it not unwillingly been kept alive by the communism it had to resist for decades, and which only survived in its 19th-century forms for that reason. But that doesn't mean it can keep existing. Just like the mines, the cherry orchards must find themselves in the hands of the businessman.[47]

In Eastern Europe, therefore, the replacement of old structures by new is the stuff of both literature and hope. Moreover, the East Europeans wish to contribute to the world beyond the collapsing walls rather than merely to join it. As Václav Havel told the U.S. Congress in February 1990, they need much from us, but our relationship "doesn't have to be merely assistance from the well-educated, powerful and wealthy to someone who has nothing and therefore has nothing to offer in return. We, too, can offer something to you: our experience and the knowledge that has come from it."[48]

For once, I think Havel understates the case. For all of us are now entering an age in which economic growth depends less and less on the production of things for which the East Europeans do not have the resources (iron, coal, oil) and more and more on the production of knowledge. It is a world in which manufacturing working classes decline and political leadership depends more and more on the building of coalitions (and thus on the projection of values) among disparate groups in floating electorates to provide the only possible ideological cement and on the skill to work out pragmatic programs of governance to harmonize competing values.[49] Eastern Europe now has millions and millions of educated men and women who are just as susceptible as we are to the appeal of values that fit the modern world. And the countries of the area are now giving themselves the political and economic institutions needed to turn those men and women into citizens and make them economically competitive. They have splendid human resources in a world where human resources count more than ever.

In his book on interwar Romania, Henry Roberts ended with the question:

> For who has given to me this sweet,
> And given my brother dust to eat,
> And when will his wage come in?[50]

It is still one of the right questions to ask ourselves about Eastern Europe. And Timothy Garton Ash is also right to ask whether there is any longer any use for the adversity that the East Europeans lived through over the dark decades of communism, for them or for the rest of the world; whether they have anything to teach as they turn to us for lessons in democracy and the free market.[51]

No one can answer those questions. But I think the East Europeans are now able to give better answers than ever before in their history. We can only help; they must basically find the answers themselves. But the world's fate depends to an important degree on their capacity to do so.

This is not simply because Eastern Europe may once again be taking on its historic role as a laboratory where ideas and solutions to the problems of the modern world have been tried out.[52] The special brand of creativity this role calls for has certainly been a burden for the people of the area. At this point in their history most of them no longer wish to serve as guinea pigs to "history." Most of them want to be normal. "Can there be a more beautiful myth than normality?" Czesław Miłosz recently asked an interviewer.[53] But it is true that today's East Europeans once again stand before a choice of roles. They can continue to try to become "normal," "European." Or they can once again become a laboratory.

The post-Communist world has been there before. It has now experienced all the movements and ideologies that emerge and contend— statism, nationalism, fundamentalism, democracy, liberalism, fascism, communism—when one peasant society after another enters the coils of the "modernization" process. It straddles them all today.[54] Taken as a whole, as a community of destiny between the Elbe and the Pacific, the post-Communist world has not yet chosen the liberal-democratic, free-market option that the West now represents. But the peoples of Eastern Europe, that area of the post-Communist world described in this work, *have* made that choice. Given the area's size, their success in turning that choice into reality could determine which side of the axis the 21st century ends on. Their wage may be starting to come in at last. Eastern Europe today is a hinge of history, including ours.

NOTES

1.　Vojtech Mastny, "The Historical East Central Europe after Communism," in Andrew A. Michta and Ilya Prizel, eds., *Postcommunist Eastern Europe. Crisis and Reform* (New York: St. Martin's Press, 1992), 1-2.

2.　For a valuable review of the nationalities background to Soviet breakup, see Gail Lapidus and Victor Zaslavsky, *From Union to Commonwealth* (Cambridge: Cambridge University Press, 1992).

3. Ralf Dahrendorf, "Roads to Freedom: Democratization and Its Problems in East Central Europe," in Peter Volten, ed., *Uncertain Futures: Eastern Europe and Democracy* (New York: Institute for East-West Security Studies, 1990), 10-13.
4. 1991 commentary that focussed on elections was still relatively upbeat: Ivo Banac, "Introduction," in Banac, ed., *Eastern Europe in Revolution* (Ithaca, N.Y. and London: Cornell University Press, 1992), 7-10; and Larry Garber and Eric Bjornlund, eds., *The New Democratic Frontier. A Country-by-Country Report on Elections in Central and Eastern Europe* (Washington, D.C.: the National Democratic Institute for International Affairs, 1991). Economic reform in its first year also got passing marks: Olivier Blanchard, Rudiger Dornbusch, Paul Krugman, Richard Layard and Lawrence Summers, *Reform in Eastern Europe* (Cambridge, MA.: MIT Press, 1991). But the mood darkened as the year went on and the economic focus sharpened, until by year's end it was positively bleak: for example, see Mark Kramer, "Eastern Europe goes to Market," *Foreign Policy*, no. 86 (Spring 1992): 134-157, and Lawrence Weschler, "Deficit" (on Poland), *The New Yorker*, 11 May 1992: 41-77. It was overlaid with mixed feelings about the disappearance of Cold War certainties, e.g. "The End of the Cold War: A Symposium," *Diplomatic History*, 16, no. 2 (Spring 1992) and Michael J. Hogan, ed., *The End of the Cold War. Its Meaning and Implications* (Cambridge: Cambridge University Press, 1992). As the American presidential election ground forward the next year, this naturally surfaced as polemic over who deserved the political credit: George F. Kennan, "Who Won the Cold War? Ask Instead What was Lost," *International Herald Tribune*, 29 October 1992, and Stephen S. Rosenfeld, "The Cold War's Winners Were in Different Camps," *ibid.*, 3 November 1992.
5. Quoted in Gore Vidal, *Lincoln* (New York: Random House, 1984), 620.
6. On the Czecho-Slovak agony, see Paul Wilson, "The End of the Velvet Revolution," *New York Review of Books*, 13 August 1992: 57-63, and "Czechoslovakia: The Pain of Divorce," *ibid.*, 17 December 1992: 69-75, but also, for 1991, Mark Sommer, *Living in Freedom. The Exhilaration and Anguish of Prague's Second Spring* (New York: Mercury House, 1992). On former Yugoslavia, Misha Glenny, *The Fall of Yugoslavia. The Third Balkan War* (New York: Penguin, 1992) carries the awful story through mid-1992.
7. For a late example, see "Poland's Economic Reforms. If It Works, It's Fixed," *The Economist*, 326, no. 7795 (23-29 January 1993): 23-25, but also the previous flowers peeping through the snow in Andrew Berg and Jeffrey Sachs, "Structural Adjustment and International Trade in Eastern Europe: The Case of Poland," *Economic Policy* (April 1992): 118-173, and in the essays by Sachs, Paul Marer, Richard Portes, and Robert W. Campbell in Shafiqul Islam and Michael Mandelbaum, eds., *Making Markets. Economic Transformation in Eastern Europe and the Post-Soviet States* (New York: Council on Foreign Relations Press, 1992).
8. The West's approach was sharply criticized for its tentativeness by Zbigniew Brzezinski, "The West Adrift: Vision in Search of a Strategy," *Washington Post*, 1 March 1992, but meanwhile both constructive work and constructive thinking continued: see the essays by J.F. Brown, Robert D. Hormats and William H. Luers in Ivo J. Lederer, ed., *Western Approaches to Eastern Europe* (New York: Council on Foreign Relations Press, 1992), and by François Heisbourg and F. Stephen Larrabee in Gregory F. Treverton, ed., *The Shape of the New Europe* (New York: Council on Foreign Relations Press, 1992).

9.   Ken Jowitt, *New World Disorder. The Leninist Extinction* (Berkeley, Los Angeles, and Oxford: University of California Press, 1992), 249-283.

10. Charles Gati argues (in *The Bloc that Failed* [Bloomington, IN.: Indiana University Press, 1990], 162-164) that the gamble on Communist-led reform in Eastern Europe was lost before it began because Gorbachev deluded himself and failed to discern the depth of "the region's anticommunist, prerevolutionary condition." But it was sincerely played: reform Communists in the area really thought they could survive if only (and only if) they reformed. So did their counterparts in the Soviet Union, till very late in the game: see Stephen E. Hanson, "Gorbachev: The Last True Leninist Believer?," in Daniel Chirot, ed., *The Crisis of Leninism and the Decline of the Left. The Revolutions of 1989* (Seattle and London: University of London Press, 1991), 33-59.

11. Garber and Bjornlund, *The New Democratic Frontier*, give data for the first year's elections.

12. To take but one striking example from October 1992, despite the shadows cast over the Maastricht Treaty's future by the Danish and French elections and in a Poland laboring under its fifth post-Solidarity government with a hugely dispersed parliament, 62 percent of the Poles still wanted immediate entry into the Common Market on Maastricht terms, 29 percent had no opinion, and only 9 percent were against: *Gazeta Wyborcza* (Warsaw), 5 November 1992.

13. For examples of both, see Daniel N. Nelson, "Europe's Unstable East," *Foreign Policy*, no. 82 (Spring 1991): 137-158, which simply lists every possible ethnic/national rivalry, and Michael Dobbs, "The Eruption of Eastern Europe," *Washington Post National Weekly Edition*, 18-24 November 1991, which does the same but more briefly and with maps and also includes valuable data on the decline of the area's Soviet trade as of the time of writing.

14. Scholarly description of the region's ethnic and national woes is starting to fill bookshelves and is also provoking its own scholarly antidotes: for Eastern Europe see Judy Batt, *East Central Europe from Reform to Transformation* (New York: Council on Foreign Relations Press, 1991), 50-51; and Vojtech Mastny's magisterial review cited in note 1 above, 1-20; and for the Soviet Union see Victor Zaslavsky, "Nationalism and Democratic Transition in Postcommunist Societies," *Daedalus*, 121, no. 2 (Spring 1992): 97-121.

15. Martin Malia, "Leninist Endgame," *Daedalus*, 121, no. 2 (Spring 1992): 70.

16. There is a good capsule description of Marxism's ideological problem with nationalism in Isaiah Berlin, *The Crooked Timber of Humanity. Chapters in the History of Ideas* ([1972] New York: Vintage Books, 1992), 249ff. The Romanian attempt to wed them is noted at 253-254n.

17. Malia, in "Leninist Endgame," 66-69, is particularly good on this, but see also Lapidus and Zaslavsky, *From Union to Commonwealth* and Zaslavsky, "Nationalism and Democratic Transition."

18. The historian arguing that the persistence of memory is what is causing "the gyre of death and destruction in the Balkans" is Thomas Butler, "A 6th Century Invasion Stokes a 20th Century Calamity," *International Herald Tribune*, 2 September 1992. It is almost a relief to read Ivo Banac's careful reconstruction of how the crisis actually came (especially since 1971): "The Fearful Asymmetry of War: The Causes and Consequences of Yugoslavia's Demise," *Daedalus*, 121, no. 2 (Spring 1992): 141-174.

19. As Malia points out in "Leninist Endgame," 65.

20. Zaslavsky, "Nationalism and Democratic Transition," 110.

21. Among several changes since 1918 that give cause for optimism about Eastern Europe's chances for independence: Mastny, "The Historical East Central Europe," 19-20.
22. Cited from F. Chuyev's diary of 140 talks with Molotov, published in Moscow in 1991, in Woodford McClellan, "Molotov Speaks," *The Cold War International History Project Bulletin* (Washington, D.C.: Woodrow Wilson International Center for Scholars), no. 1 (Spring 1992), 20.
23. "The system had become thoroughly corrupt. The indigenous communist leadership in most of Eastern Europe had degenerated into a venal, arrogant oligarchy, living like oriental potentates while their own people were desperate. To be sure, Stalin's generation in Eastern Europe (Tito, Dimitrov, Ulbricht, Bierut) were his obedient puppets, but there were also the true believers portrayed by Arthur Koestler in *Darkness at Noon*. By the 1980s, the East European communists had become unprincipled cynics and hypocrites. They believed in little": William Hyland, *The Cold War Is Over* (New York: Times Books, 1990), 195. In a judicious retrospective, Daniel Chirot also focuses on moral rot as a factor forcing the regimes back onto economic performance, at which they failed: "What Happened in Eastern Europe in 1989?" in Daniel Chirot, ed., *The Crisis in Leninism*, 3-32. For insights into what it was like to live there in the 1980s, see also, despite the overwriting, John Clark and Aaron Wildavsky, *The Moral Collapse of Communism. Poland as a Cautionary Tale* (San Francisco, CA.: ICS Press, 1990) and Janine Wedel, ed., *The Unplanned Society. Poland during and after Communism* (New York: Columbia University Press, 1992). As so often, however, the spirit of the age can best be captured in literature, some of which is now translated, in particular three works by the Pole, Tadeusz Konwicki: *A Minor Apocalypse* ([1979] New York: Vintage Aventura, 1984); *Moonrise, Moonset* ([1982] New York: Farrar, Straus and Giroux, 1987), the best literary treatment of the Solidarity years, 1980-81; and, for the dry mid-decade, *Bohin Manor* ([1987] New York: Farrar, Straus and Giroux, 1990). Just as the Hungarian George Konrád was the bard of the "small stabilization" of the 1960s with *The Case Worker* ([1969] New York: Viking Penguin, 1987), for the 1980s we now have his *A Feast in the Garden* (New York: Harcourt Brace Jovanovich, 1992).
24. "Towards a New Democratic Compromise: Interview with Adam Michnik," *East European Reporter*, 3, no. 2 (March 1988), 28.
25. Malia, "Leninist Endgame," 70-73.
26. On the looming perils of the privatization process, see Mark Kramer, "Eastern Europe goes to Market"; the special edition on "Transforming Economies in East Central Europe," *East European Politics and Societies*, 6, no. 1 (Winter 1992), and Jan Winiecki, "Privatization in East-Central Europe: Avoiding Major Mistakes," in Christopher Clague and Gordon C. Rausser, eds., *The Emergence of Market Economies in Eastern Europe* (Cambridge, MA. and Oxford: Blackwell, 1992), 271-277.
27. This quotation and the one in the preceding paragraph are from Malia, "Leninist Endgame," 72-73.
28. Quoted in *Gazeta Wyborcza* (Warsaw), 16 March 1992, 3.
29. Mancur Olson, "The Hidden Path to a Successful Economy," in Clague and Rausser, eds., *The Emergence of Market Economies*, 71.
30. Dawid Warszawski (Konstanty Gebert) in *Gazeta Wyborcza* (Warsaw), 8-9 August 1992, 10.
31. Jeri Laber, "Albania: Slouching Toward Democracy," *New York Review of Books*, 14 January 1993, 26.

32. Julian Barnes has now taken Western literature's most ambitious shot so far at rendering the complexities of post-1989 Eastern Europe in *The Porcupine* (New York: Alfred A. Knopf, 1992). Built around the duel between a deposed communist leader on trial and his prosecutor, the son of an old comrade, it is haunted by the format of Koestler's *Darkness at Noon*. In Poland, Tadeusz Konwicki has continued to wrestle with the essence of post-1989 conditions in *Zorze Wieczorne* [Evening Dawns] (Warsaw: ALFA, 1991) and *Czytadło* [Reading Matter] (Warsaw: Niezalezna Oficyna Wydawnicza, 1992), both still only in Polish.

33. Nationalism can appeal to them, too: see Blaine Harden, "Serbian Leader Courts Worker Support," *Washington Post*, 18 March 1991, which recalls that Slobodan Milošević's (ex-Communist) Socialist Party got the overwhelming bulk of worker votes in the December 1990 multi-party elections.

34. Peter Murrell estimates that Eastern Europe would have to shut down half the manufacturing capacity of its large plants (and create a similar amount in small plants) to obtain a distribution of plant sizes roughly comparable to Western Europe's, and that the proportion might need to go as high as 70 percent in industries like textiles: "Evolution in Economics and in the Economic Reform of the Centrally Planned Economies," in Clague and Rausser, eds., *The Emergence of Market Economies*, 45n.

35. Batt, *East Central Europe*, 45-46.

36. S.N. Eisenstadt argues hopefully that the preconditions for doing so are already there. As he sees 1989, the late-Communist regimes represented distorted modernity rather than pre-modernity, and the revolutions against them were neither utopian nor totalistic (and violent) because they were already imbedded in modernity and caused by its internal contradictions: "The Breakdown of Communist Regimes," *Daedalus*, 121, no. 2 (Spring 1992), 37.

37. Let us listen again to Wałęsa, speaking to his old Gdańsk comrades: "The only class which has passed the test is the one I come from. . . . Where are all these wiseacres who used to talk so beautifully and pose as a legal and economic elite? They've been giving you a hard time. The ordinary guys were working, the top dogs weren't." (Quoted in *Gazeta Wyborcza* [Warsaw], 16 March 1992). And later, asked why Premier Jan Olszewski, a prominent lawyer with solid credentials defending dissidents against the regime, had failed so badly in 1992, Wałęsa said he thought it was because Olszewski had never gone to work at 6:00 a.m.:

> That man has a biological clock that is set differently. He used to sleep late, went to bed when he wanted to, and then suddenly one day he had to change his whole biological clock, had to get up very early and could almost never go to bed when he wanted to. Added to that were big problems, big tasks; and his biological clock simply couldn't take it.

Wałęsa added that as a worker he had gotten up every day for 25 years at 5:00 a.m., and even though his life had changed over the last decade, he still did. Later in the same interview, he was asked why he never talked about culture. "What do we have the intelligentsia for? To solve problems. Already in 1983 I asked: gentlemen, we will certainly win, but get some plan ready right now, corrections for science, for the economy. Nothing came of it. We were prepared only for 'wartime'; we have nothing ready for 'peacetime'" (Quoted in *Zycie Warszawy* [Warsaw], 5-6 September 1992).

Still smarting from their long march through communism, Polish intellectuals are supersensitive to such remarks from Wałęsa, and make them a political issue, charging him with "divisiveness." Most Poles still prize unity, and find divisions disturbing. But there is also some sentiment for counter-mobilization under the old banner of group unity. In January 1993 the Rector of Warsaw University keynoted a conference on "the Polish intelligentsia today" with a statement that, "The intelligentsia is living through (its) worst period in Poland's postwar history. We now have our government, (but it) treats us worse than the previous authorities." The root of the problem, he argued, was the lingering Communist view that only material production counts, which defines intellectuals as parasites. A prominent novelist urged foundation of a Polish Intellectuals' Party, since only the intellectuals could lead a "Philistine society submerged in the Polish Podunk" out of its "God-forsaken provincialism, away from the sacristy door." Still another participant thought the intelligentsia should not just pressure government, but "work out a long-term program for various sectors of social life," i.e. Wałęsa's failed 1983 idea as a future objective. Only one theoretical physicist spoke up to say that he knew of many highly developed countries where there is no talk either of an ethos or a historic mission for the intelligentsia. He felt that the most important problem was to educate highly qualified people. He himself had no historic mission except to teach physics well. (But he is known as something of a maverick.) (*Gazeta Wyborcza* [Warsaw], 11 January 1993, and *Zycie Warszawy* [Warsaw], 12 January 1993.)

38. Michta and Prizel, "Conclusion: Beyond Communism: Eastern Europe or Europe?" in Michta and Prizel, eds., *Postcommunist Eastern Europe*, 197-198.

39. Václav Havel, "My Dream for Czechoslovakia," *New York Review of Books*, 25 June 1992, 8.

40. See Dirk Philipsen, *We Were The People. Voices from East Germany's Revolutionary Autumn 1989* (Durham, N.C.: Duke University Press, 1992).

41. For examples of such reportage, see Daniel Singer, "Poland's New Men of Property," *The Nation*, 11 November 1991: 574, 590-593, and at greater length, John Feffer, *Shock Waves. Eastern Europe after the Revolution* (Boston, MA.: South End Press, 1992).

42. Mastny, "The Historical East Central Europe," 19-20.

43. A Warsaw daily reported in January 1993 that when asked what kind of Polish economy they wanted, 6 percent of farmers said "socialist," 20 percent "capitalist," 51 percent "medium" or "in-between" (pośredni), and 23 percent found it "hard to say": "Chłopska 'trzecia droga'" [The Peasant "Third Road"], *Zycie Warszawy* (Warsaw), 25 May 1992, 3.

44. Malia, "Leninist Endgame," 73-75. See also the Polish economist Jan Winiecki's bitter charge that big-factory workers find statism so appealing that they can turn Poland into a "socialist outdoor museum (*Skansen*) in a changing central Europe": "Ideały 'Solidarności' cyli o antykomunistycznych bolszewikach" ["Solidarity's Ideals or On Anti-Communist Bolsheviks"], *Zycie Warszawy* (Warsaw), 25 May 1992, 3.

45. Isaiah Berlin, *The Crooked Timber of Humanity*, 260.

46. Let us pause to watch, before he disappears into offices with potted plants: "The average candidate for a Polish capitalist stands ankle-deep in mud, freezes in chilly weather and takes a pee in a staircase nearby. He buys during the night and sells during the day. He has a folding table, a camp bed, a suitcase, then a tent, and later a wooden hut. Then maybe a small shop or wholesale operation based in his aunt's apartment. He started trading because others did the same, because the time was right or simply because he had to survive. If possible, he still draws unemployment benefits. Only one in ten, or even one in a hundred, will ever move up the social ladder, open a real shop or set up a company. Not everybody can become a businessman. . . . Therefore businessmen may

respect Mazowiecki (the Catholic journalist who was post-Communist Poland's first premier), but they voted for Wałęsa. The latter is a man of success, he is dynamic and determined. They hope that their time is yet to come": Danuta Zagrodzka, "Nowa Klasa" ["A New Class"], *Gazeta Wyborcza* (Warsaw), 29 December 1990.

47.   Jan Walc, "Tąpnęło (Cave-in)," *Życie Warszawy* (Warsaw), 24 July 1992. Jan Walc died after a short and surprising illness in February 1993, at the age of 45. He was very much a member of the generation of 1968 that helped make the revolutions of 1980-1981 and 1989. He was buried in the Lutheran cemetery in Warsaw, capital of a nation 95 percent Roman Catholic. I never met him, but I also hear the thud of the axe at the base of the cherry trees, and I also hope that enraged intellectuals will not seize it once again.

48.   Quoted in *The Washington Post*, 22 February 1990.

49.   As I suggested at greater length in remarks made in June 1987 at Helsinki and reprinted as "Technology and Public Policy in East-West Relations," in F. Stephen Larrabee, ed., *Technology and Change in East-West Relations* (New York: Institute for East-West Security Studies, 1988), 199-206.

50.   Henry Roberts, *Rumania. Political Problems of an Agrarian State* (New Haven, CT.: Yale University Press, 1951), 351.

51.   Timothy Garton Ash, *The Magic Lantern* (New York: Random House, 1990), 154-156.

52.   Jowitt, *New World Disorder*, 284-285.

53.   "The Most Beautiful Myth: Normality (Czesław Miłosz Talks with Elzbieta Sawicka," *Rzeczpospolita* (Warsaw), 13-14 February 1993.

54.   "Separatist nationalisms are one expression of the politicization of the world's peasantries. But other ideologues compete for peasant and ex-peasant support. Indeed, religious fundamentalism and communism are almost as attractive as nationalism, and in ex-peasant societies the future probably belongs to various blendings and combinations of the three. How much local regimes will fit with the emergent cosmopolitanisms of Europe and North America remains to be seen. That may well become the principal axis of 21st century politics." William H. McNeill, "The Peasantry's Awakening All Over the World," *Washington Post National Weekly Edition*, 7-13 January 1991, 24-25.

APPENDIX

LEADERS OF EASTERN EUROPE SINCE 1945

BULGARIA

King Simeon II   August 1943 - September 1946

Prime Minister:
Kimon Gheorghiev   September 1944 - October 1946

General Secretary:
Vulko Chervenkov   October 1946 - March 1954

First Secretary of the Central Committee:
Todor Zhivkov   March 1954 - November 1989

Chairmen of the Presidium of the National Assembly
Vasil Kolarov   September 1946 - December 1947
Mintso Neychev   December 1947 - May 1950
Georgi Damianov   May 1950 - November 1958
Dimitar Ganev   November 1958 - April 1964

Chairman of the Presidium of the Council of Ministers:
Georgi Traikov   April 1964 - April 1971

Chairman of the Council of State:
Todor Zhivkov   April 1971 - November 1989

Prime Ministers:

Georgi Dimitrov	October 1946 - July 1949
Vasil Kolarov	July 1949 - January 1950
Vulko Chervenkov	January 1950 - April 1956
Anton Yugov	April 1956 - November 1962
Todor Zhivkov	November 1962 - April 1971
Stanko Todorov	April 1971 - June 1981
Grisha Filipov	June 1981 - March 1986
Georgi Atanasov	March 1986 - February 1990

Presidents:

Petur Mladenov	April 1990 - July 1990
Zhelyu Zhelev	August 1990 -

Prime Ministers:

Andrei Lukanov	February 1990 - November 1990
Dimitur Popov	December 1990 - November 1991
Filip Dimitrov	November 1991 - December 1992
Lyuben Berov	December 1992 -

CZECHOSLOVAKIA

President:

Edvard Beneš (*in exile*)	July 1940 - March 1945
Edvard Beneš	March 1945 - June 1948

Prime Ministers:

Jan Sramek	March - April 1945
Zdeněk Fierlinger	April 1945 - June 1946
Klement Gottwald	July 1946 - June 1948

First Secretaries:

Klement Gottwald	February 1948 - March 1953
Antonín Novotný	March 1953 - January 1968
Alexander Dubček	January 1968 - April 1969
Gustáv Husák	April 1969 - December 1987
(*General Secretary from 1971*)	

General Secretary:
Miloš Jakeš   December 1987 - November 1989

Prime Ministers:
Antonin Zapotocky   June 1948 - March 1953
Vilem Siroky   March 1953 - September 1963
Jozef Lenart   September 1963 - April 1968
Oldrich Cernik   April 1968 - January 1970
Lubomir Strougal   January 1970 - October 1988
Ladislav Adamec   October 1988 - December 1989

President:
Václav Havel   December 1989 - July 1992

Prime Ministers:
Marián Čalfa   December 1989 - June 1990
Marián Čalfa   June 1990 - July 1992
Jan Straský   July 1992 - December 1992

THE CZECH REPUBLIC

President:
Václav Havel   January 1993 -

Prime Minister:
Václav Klaus   January 1993 -

SLOVAKIA

President:
Michal Kovac   January 1993 -

Prime Minister:
Vladimir Meciar   January 1993 -

GERMAN DEMOCRATIC REPUBLIC

President:
Wilhelm Pieck   October 1949 - September 1960

Chairmen of the State Council:

Walter Ulbricht	September 1960 - August 1973

(*Secretary General/First Secretary of Communist Party*, July 1950 - May 1971)

Willi Stoph	October 1973 - October 1976
Erich Honecker	October 1976 - October 1989

(*General Secretary of the Communist Party*, May 1971 - October 1989)

Egon Krenz	October - December 1989

(*General Secretary of the Communist Party*, October - December 1989)

Prime Ministers:

Otto Grotewohl	October 1949 - September 1964
Willi Stoph	September 1964 - October 1973
Horst Sindermann	October 1973 - October 1976
Willi Stoph	October 1976 - November 1989
Hans Modrow	November 1989 - April 1990
Lothar de Maiziere	April 1990 - October 1990

HUNGARY

Regent Ferenc Szálasi	October 1944 - April 1945
(*and Prime Minister*)	
Regent Béla Zsedenyi (*acting*)	November 1945 - February 1946

Prime Ministers:

Ferenc Szálasi	October 1944 - April 1945
Béla Dálnoki-Miklós	April 1945 - November 1945
Zoltán Tildy	November 1945 - February 1946

Ferenc Nagy	February 1946 - May 1947
Lajos Dinnyés	May 1947 - December 1948
István Dobi	December 1948 - August 1952
Mátyás Rákosi	August 1952 - July 1953

Secretary General of the Communist Party:

Mátyás Rákosi	August 1949 - July 1953

"Triumvirate":

Mátyás Rákosi/Lajos Acz/Béla Vég	July - November 1953

Prime Ministers:

Imre Nagy	July 1953 - April 1955
András Hegedüs	April 1955 - October 1956
Imre Nagy	October - November 1956

First Secretaries:

Mátyás Rákosi	November 1953 - July 1956
Ernó Geró	July - November 1956
János Kádár	November 1956 - May 1988
Károly Grósz	May 1988 - October 1989

Prime Ministers:

János Kádár	November 1956 - January 1958
Ferenc Münnich	January 1958 - September 1961
János Kádár	September 1961 - June 1965
Gyula Kállai	June 1965 - April 1967
Jenó Fock	April 1967 - May 1975
Gyórgy Lázár	May 1975 - June 1987
Károly Grósz	June 1987 - November 1988
Miklós Németh	November 1988 - May 1990

President:

Arpad Göncz	May 1990 -

Prime Minister:

Jozsef Antall	May 1990 -

POLAND

President:

Władysław Raczkiewicz (*in exile*)	September 1939 - June 1945

Prime Ministers:

Tomasz Arciszewski (*in exile*)	November 1944 - June 1945

President:

Bolesław Bierut	January 1945 - November 1952

First Secretaries:

Władysław Gomułka	January 1945 - September 1948
Bolesław Bierut	September 1948 - March 1956
Edward Ochab	March 1956 - October 1956
Wladyslaw Gomulka	October 1956 - December 1970
Edward Gierek	December 1970 - September 1980
Stanisław Kania	September 1980 - October 1981
Wojciech Jaruzelski	October 1981 - July 1989

Prime Ministers:

Edward Osóbka-Morawski	January 1945 - February 1947
Józef Cyrankiewicz	February 1947 - November 1952
Bolesław Bierut	November 1952 - March 1954
Józef Cyrankiewicz	March 1954 - December 1970
Piotr Jaroszewicz	December 1970 - February 1980
Edward Babiuch	February - August 1980
Józef Pinkowski	August 1980 - February 1981
Wojciech Jaruzelski	February 1981 - November 1985
Zbigniew Messner	November 1985 - September 1988
Mieczysław Rakowski	October 1988 - July 1989

Presidents:

Wojciech Jaruzelski	July 1989 - December 1990
Lech Wałęsa	December 1990 -

Prime Ministers:

Tadeusz Mazowiecki	August 1989 - January 1991
Jan Krzystztof Bielecki	January - December 1991
Jan Olszewski	December 1991 - May 1992
Waldemar Pawlak (*caretaker*)	May - June 1992
Hanna Suchocka	June 1992 -

ROMANIA

King Mihai	October 1940 - December 1947

Prime Minister:

Nicolae Radescu	December 1944 - February 1945

First Secretaries:

Gheorghe Gheorghiu-Dej	December 1947 - April 1954
Gheorghe Apostol	April 1954 - October 1955
Gheorghe Gheorghiu-Dej	October 1955 - March 1965

General Secretary:

Nicolae Ceauşescu	March 1965 - December 1989

President:

Mihai Sadoveanu	December 1947 - April 1948

Presidents of the State Council:

Constantine Parhon	April 1948 - June 1952
Petru Groza	June 1952 - January 1958
Ion Maurer	January 1958 - March 1961
Gheorghe Gheorghiu-Dej	March 1961 - March 1965
Chivu Stoica	March 1965 - December 1967
Nicolae Ceauşescu	December 1967 - December 1989
(just President from 1974)	

Prime Ministers:

Petru Groza	March 1945 - June 1952
Gheorghe Gheorgiu-Dej	June 1952 - October 1955
Chivu Stoica	October 1955 - March 1961
Ion Maurer	March 1961 - March 1974
Manea Manescu	March 1974 - March 1979
Ilie Verdet	March 1979 - May 1982
Constantine Dascalescu	May 1982 - December 1989

Presidents:

Ion Iliescu (*interim*)	December 1989 - May 1990
Ion Iliescu	May 1990 -

Prime Ministers:

Petre Roman (*interim*)	December 1989 - May 1990
Petre Roman	May 1990 - September 1991
Theodor Stolojan	October 1991 - November 1992
Nicolae Vacaroiu	November 1992 -

Eastern Europe in 1914

Eastern Europe in 1923

Eastern Europe in 1941

Eastern Europe 1945-90

Eastern Europe in 1993

INDEX

CPSIA information can be obtained at www.ICGtesting.com
Printed in the USA
LVOW11*1452110114

369049LV00001B/1/A